Deleuze and Theology

Christopher Ben Simpson

BLOOMSBURY
LONDON · NEW DELHI · NEW YORK · SYDNEY

Bloomsbury T&T Clark
An imprint of Bloomsbury Publishing Plc

50 Bedford Square   175 Fifth Avenue
London   New York
WC1B 3DP   NY 10010
UK   USA

www.bloomsbury.com

First published 2012

© Christopher Ben Simpson, 2012

All rights reserved. No part of this publication may be reproduced or transmitted in any form or by any means, electronic or mechanical, including photocopying, recording, or any information storage or retrieval system, without prior permission in writing from the publishers.

Christopher Ben Simpson has asserted his right under the Copyright, Designs and Patents Act, 1988, to be identified as Author of this work.

No responsibility for loss caused to any individual or organization acting on or refraining from action as a result of the material in this publication can be accepted by Bloomsbury Academic or the author.

British Library Cataloguing-in-Publication Data
A catalogue record for this books is available from the British Library.

ISBN: HB: 978-0-5673-6335-0
PB: 978-0-5674-4575-9

Typeset by Deanta Global Publishing Services, Chennai, India
Printed and bound in India

Deleuze and Theology

CONTENTS

Introduction 1

PART ONE: DELEUZE IN BRIEF 3

1 Gilles Deleuze (1925–95):
  Biography and bibliography 5

2 Deleuze's philosophical system 11
  2.1 Saying 'Yes' to the ocean: Affirmation
      and the Dionysian world 12
  2.2 Speculative materialism: The virtual and the actual 20
  2.3 Schizoid ethics: Escape and affirm 40

PART TWO: DELEUZE AND THEOLOGY 47

3 Approaching Deleuze's theology and
  theological appropriations 49
  3.1 Deleuze and theology? 49
  3.2 Deleuzian theologies: The secular trajectory 51
  3.3 Theological critique of Deleuze:
      The confessional trajectory I 54
  3.4 Theological appropriation of Deleuze:
      The confessional trajectory II 59

4 The Divine Life I: Difference, becoming and the Trinity 63
- 4.1 Deleuze's divine difference engine 63
- 4.2 Deleuzian theologies of life 65
- 4.3 Virtual life and the dark pleroma 67
- 4.4 The Trinity and eternal dynamism 70

5 Creation, transcendence, immanence 74
- 5.1 Deleuze being done with the judgement of God: Immanence over transcendence 74
- 5.2 Deleuzian theologies of immanence 77
- 5.3 Degenerative pantheism and the moral lobster 78
- 5.4 Creation theology: St Thomas saying 'Yes' to the ocean 82

6 The human and the inhuman 89

7 The Christ of philosophers 94

8 The Divine Life II: Salvation, affirmation and becoming-God 98
- 8.1 Deleuze's salvation from/in the world 98
- 8.2 Worldly spirituality and immanent liberation 100
- 8.3 Stuck in the desert, saying 'Yes' to the ocean 102
- 8.4 Agapeic communion, becoming-God and ecclesial assemblage 105

Notes 111
Bibliography 164
   Works by Gilles Deleuze 164
   Works by Gilles Deleuze and Félix Guattari 166
   Other works 166
Index 173

Introduction

Gilles Deleuze (1925–95) has emerged in the decade (and now almost two) after his death as a powerful voice in continental philosophy that would seem to make some return to a positive metaphysics after the insistent and ground-clearing negativity of deconstructive 'post's and 'anti's of the late twentieth century. After the funeral of God, the human and being, Deleuze's work proposes an affirmative vision of difference, becoming and life.

What can a theologian do with Deleuze? While using philosophy as a resource for theology is nothing new, Deleuze presents a kind of limit-case for such a theological appropriation of philosophy: a thoroughly 'modern' philosophy that would seem to be fundamentally hostile to Christian theology – a philosophy of atheistic immanence with an essentially chaotic vision of the world. Nonetheless, Deleuze's philosophy can generate many potential intersections with theology opening onto a field of configurations: a fractious middle between radical Deleuzian theologies that would think through theology and reinterpret it from the perspective of some version of Deleuzian philosophy, and other theologies that would seek to learn from and respond to Deleuze from the perspective of confessional theology – to take from the encounter with Deleuze an opportunity to clarify and reform an orthodox Christian self-understanding.

This book falls into two parts. The first part is a brief presentation of Deleuze's life (in Chapter 1) and thought (in Chapter 2); the second part is an examination of the relation between Deleuze's thought and Christian theology. Chapter 3 introduces the second part and addresses the relation between philosophy and theology more generally. The remaining five chapters lay out (hopefully fruitful) pairings between several central doctrines of Christian theology and several key *topoi* of Deleuze's philosophy: Trinity and difference (in Chapter 4), creation and immanence (in Chapter 5), the *imago Dei* and the fractured self (in Chapter 6), Christ and

Spinoza (in Chapter 7) and salvation/theosis and believing in the world (in Chapter 8). Some parts of Chapter 2 are quite dense, especially the technical presentation in 2.2; one can move past these parts to 2.3 and still grasp the general vision in Deleuze's thought.

A note on notes: This book is saturated with citations of Deleuze's works and of the works of other philosophers and Christian theologians – making explicit the way in which this book is a node of intertwining lines of thought that can be followed to other such nodes. The hope is that these references may be a helpful way into Deleuze's writings and into the question of Deleuze and theology . . . a hall with a thousand doors, a rhizome.

The following deserve my acknowledgement and thanks for their part in this project. Provost Clay Ham at Lincoln Christian University enabled and encouraged my work on this book in numerous ways. My colleague Steven D. Cone provided me with an enlightening soundboard with many helpful conversations about this book throughout its development. William Desmond, Gregory Voiles and Ian DiOrio read early drafts and offered helpful comments on some of the more difficult parts of the manuscript. Michael Robinson, my research assistant, put hours of work into this labour-intensive project and provided helpful comments on drafts. Jim and Karen Estep regularly extended their hospitality to me throughout the process of writing. Neil Turnbull, editor of *Radical Orthodoxy: Theology, Philosophy, and Politics*, provided the permission to use some elements of my essay on William Desmond in its inaugural issue in a few places throughout this book. The programmers and designers at Literature and Latte have developed and support a truly fantastic writing program called 'Scrivener', which I used to construct this complex project from the very beginning. Thomas Kraft at T&T Clark has been an available and invaluable help in shepherding this project through the editorial process. Finally, I am deeply grateful to and for my wife Kaysha, our son David, and our daughter Lydia, with whom I share my life.

PART ONE

Deleuze in Brief

1

Gilles Deleuze (1925–95): Biography and bibliography

Gilles Deleuze was born in Paris on 18 January 1925 to Odette Caumaüer and Louis Deleuze, an engineer. He grew up in the shadow of his heroic older brother Georges, who died in a concentration camp for being part of the French Resistance. Gilles Deleuze's passion for philosophy was present from the time he first began studying it in his last year at the Carnot High School. His time here was to be followed by two years of university preparatory courses at the Louis Le Grande High Schools and Henry IV before going on to study philosophy at the Sorbonne from 1944 to 1948. He was in poor health from the time he was a young man.[1]

In 1946, while studying at the Sorbonne for his *agrégation* (the examination for teaching in the public education system of France), Deleuze wrote (under a pseudonym) an introduction to a new edition of Johann Malfatti's *Mathesis: or Studies on the Anarchy and Hierarchy of Knowledge*.[2] This, his first publication was on Johann Malfatti de Montereggio (1775–1859), an odd figure who combined esoteric mathematics with theosophical thought and who, along with Hoëne Wronski (1776–1853) and Francis Warrain (1867–1940), played a key role in the revival of the modern European esoteric, occult tradition.[3]

High school (*lycée*) students in France commonly take a philosophy course in their last year requiring many (some 8,000) trained high school philosophy teachers – commonly teaching high school while preparing doctoral theses.[4] Deleuze taught philosophy in several Paris *lycées* from 1948 to 1957.[5] Superficially known for his hat, his long fingernails and his chain-smoking during class, he is broadly remembered by his former students as an engaging, humorous and inspiring teacher (making regular reference to literature and film). He would give an impression of presence and ease in his lectures, as if he were speaking extemporaneously, though he would spend many hours in meticulous preparation.[6]

He published his first book in 1952 with André Cresson, a short introduction to Hume,[7] which he then followed up with his own monograph on Hume (*Empiricism and Subjectivity*) in 1953.[8] These begin a series of studies in the history of philosophy that would wind its way through his authorship. During the long and formative 'period of latency' between the publication of *Empiricism and Subjectivity* (1953) and *Nietzsche and Philosophy* (1962), Deleuze did a considerable amount of teaching on the history of philosophy.[9] Significantly, and more specifically, Deleuze was working on Henri Bergson (he wrote two essays on Bergson, published in 1956), Spinoza (he largely completed what would be published as *Expressionism in Philosophy: Spinoza* in the late 1950s) and Nietzsche (the next book he would publish was *Nietzsche and Philosophy* in 1962). In 1956 he met and later married Denise Paul 'Fanny' Grandjouan, to whom he remained married until his death some thirty-nine years later.[10]

After 1957, Deleuze took some assistant teaching positions in universities: at the Sorbonne from 1957 to 1960, a sabbatical from 1960 to 1964, at Lyon from 1964 to 1969. During this formative period, Deleuze would develop a long-standing friendship with Michel Foucault. As a part of the philosophical generation of the 1960s (including Foucault and Derrida), and unlike Sartre and Merleau-Ponty before them, Deleuze could be seen as following a common rejection of humanism and a basic view of the world as 'unredeemable' while yet seeking to give some guidance and meaning to fundamentally decentered and adrift humans.[11] Yet, Deleuze was also breaking with other contemporary trends and philosophical fashions in France, particularly the philosophical canon of the 3 'H's: Hegel, Husserl and Heidegger.[12] Deleuze is arguably the least Hegelian, least Heideggerian and least Husserlian of the eminent figures of his generation. Be this as it may, he still developed his own thought through ongoing interaction with other thinkers, with the problems they were trying to solve, and his publications in this period reflect this collaborative thinking-with and thinking-through. Reflecting back on his work in a letter to Arnaud Villani in 1986, Deleuze proposed the three functions of a useful philosophical book: (1) to correct an error regarding a given topic (the polemical function); (2) to repair an oversight or retrieve a lost insight (the inventive function); and (3) to create a new concept (the creative function).[13] Such a book is not simply a continuation of a traditional, received philosophy, but a revolutionary retrieval, an intentionally different and creative repetition of past ideas (that have been ignored and misunderstood). He published *Nietzsche and Philosophy* in 1962,[14] *Kant's Critical Philosophy* in 1963,[15] and *Proust and Signs* in 1964.[16] After taking a position at the University of Lyon 'to teach a course on morality' (about which he was less than enthusiastic),[17] he published a brief introduction to Nietzsche in 1965,[18] his *Bergsonism* in 1966[19] and a book on Sacher-Masoch, *Masochism: Coldness and Cruelty*, in 1967.[20]

Over against a Hegelian understanding of difference as subservient to a dialectical unity, Deleuze looked to Nietzsche for the beginnings of a non-Hegelian understanding of difference, a difference that is not contradiction.[21] An active member of the French Society for Nietzsche Studies, Deleuze was instrumental in organizing a colloquium on Nietzsche in 1964 and in supervising the publication of Nietzsche's complete works in French (to which Deleuze and Foucault wrote the introduction) in 1967.[22] His influential *Nietzsche and Philosophy*[23] – his first book since *Empiricism and Subjectivity* in 1953 – was published in 1962 in the midst of the resurgence of interest in Nietzsche that Deleuze was actively fostering – to be followed by a brief introduction to Nietzsche in 1965 in a series of introductory volumes to major philosophers.[24] Deleuze found in Nietzsche's affirmation of life and of the world of becoming and difference a critique of any metaphysics that would 'judge and depreciate life in the name of a *supra-sensible* world'.[25]

Likewise, Deleuze found in Bergson's understanding of the world as a living, evolving whole an alternative to a dualism that would place consciousness over against the world. Even though Bergson, unlike Nietzsche, was out of fashion after the War in France,

Deleuze had a consistently high regard for and loyalty to him, making him a regular part of his teaching throughout his career.[26] In 1956, Deleuze published an article on Bergson's conception of difference[27] and was asked by Maurice Merleau-Ponty to write a chapter on Bergson in a collection on famous philosophers.[28] He published his *Bergsonism* in 1966[29] and would return to Bergson in his later works on cinema.

To Heidegger and his declaration of the end of philosophy and metaphysics, Deleuze preferred Spinoza, the 'absolute philosopher', the 'prince of philosophers', even the 'Christ of philosophers'.[30] Indeed, Spinoza occupied a special place of interest for Deleuze as the figure he worked and taught on more than any other.[31] Deleuze published his minor/complementary thesis *Expressionism in Philosophy: Spinoza* in 1968 (though much of it had been written long before then).[32] He would edit a Spinoza anthology in 1970[33] and produce an accessible handbook/introduction to Spinoza (based on some previous writings) entitled *Spinoza: Practical Philosophy* in 1981.[34] Spinoza, for Deleuze, was the most faithful and consistent philosopher of the affirmation of immanence, perhaps 'the only philosopher never to have compromised with transcendence and to have hunted it down everywhere' – 'denouncing all that separates us from life, all these transcendent values that are turned against life'.[35]

When the May 1968 student protests erupted in France, Deleuze was teaching at the University of Lyon. Deleuze was sympathetic, and was the only professor at Lyon to publicly declare his support for the movement. At this time he was intent on completing his doctoral thesis and contending with being hospitalized for tuberculosis. His major thesis, *Difference and Repetition*,[36] published in 1968, was the fruit of his more 'historical' works – a new ontology, another metaphysics bringing together and presenting the corrected, retrieved and newly created concepts contracted from Nietzsche, Bergson, Spinoza and others.[37] Also, looking back on *Difference and Repetition*, Deleuze wrote in the preface to the English edition in 1994 (the year before he died): 'All that I have done since is connected to this book'.[38] In the same year as the original publication (1968), he published his minor thesis, *Expressionism in Philosophy: Spinoza*.[39] After his doctoral defence at the Sorbonne in early 1969 (one of the first defences after the protests) he underwent surgery removing a lung and some ribs – a procedure requiring an entire year to recover from (during which he first met Guattari) and leaving him plagued with pulmonary problems for the rest of his life.[40]

In 1969, the same year he published *The Logic of Sense*,[41] Deleuze accepted a teaching position at the new (opening only a year earlier) experimental University of Paris-VIII, Vincennes. Vincennes was founded, at least in part, to be an educational institution attentive to the concerns of the students behind the May 1968 student protests – a radical enclave with courses focused on discussions in small classrooms, encouraging interdisciplinarity. His friend Michel Foucault, the head of the new philosophy department, invited Deleuze to the position (in a department with other figures such as Jean-François Lyotard and Alain Badiou). Though Deleuze delayed his appointment until the autumn of 1970 when he had recovered sufficiently from his surgery to teach, he quickly secured a reputation as a 'fantastic teacher' – regularly packing to overflowing his classrooms and engaging students (often from around the world) with power and drama – preparing for a good part of the week for each Tuesday seminar.[42] He continued to teach there until his retirement in 1987.

Around the time of the student protests, Deleuze met Félix Guattari, a militant philosopher and psychoanalyst working at the experimental psychiatric clinic of La Borde. Sharing a break with reigning Lacanian psychoanalysis and Marxism, Deleuze and Guattari co-authored (largely over correspondence) the two volumes of *Capitalism and Schizophrenia: Anti-Oedipus* (1972)[43] and *A Thousand Plateaus* (1980).[44] These texts came about as an expression of the political environment in France during May 1968. *Anti-Oedipus* appeared to wide acclaim. They continued their partnership with a book on Kafka in 1975[45] and the massive *A Thousand Plateaus*, which continued, though differently, Deleuze's positive project of an ontology of difference, a metaphysics of immanence. Unlike *Anti-Oedipus*, *A Thousand Plateaus* was largely received with confusion and indifference.[46]

In 1981 Deleuze published his more popular level introduction to Spinoza, *Spinoza: Practical Philosophy*, and a study of the art of the twentieth-century artist Francis Bacon.[47] Following the great collaboration with Guattari, Deleuze poured himself into a philosophical examination of film – of how the nature of the cinema can transform the horizons of philosophical reflections, revealing new ways to conceive of thought and the world. Arising from three years of seminars on cinema between 1981 and 1985,[48] Deleuze published two volumes on film: *Cinema 1: The Movement-Image* in 1983,[49] and *Cinema 2: The Time-Image* in 1985.[50] Leading up to and following his retirement from Vincennes in 1987, Deleuze could be seen as returning to his friends (and his friends' memory) and to more traditional philosophical topics. After Foucault's death from AIDS in 1984, Deleuze penned a book on the thought of his friend to be published in 1986.[51] In 1988 he published the last books by him alone: *The Fold*, a book on Leibniz,[52] and a book on François Châtelet, his friend and one of the founders of the philosophy department at Vincennes who died in 1985.[53] Deleuze and Guattari's long-standing collaboration concluded with their *What is Philosophy?* in 1991.[54] Guattari would die of a heart attack less than a year later at the age of sixty-two.[55]

Deleuze was unable to attend Guattari's funeral – he was unable to leave his home, being confined and hooked up to oxygen tanks in his apartment, 'like a dog', as he said. Even with the constant use of the oxygen, Deleuze breathed with greater and greater difficulty – progressively unable to work on his writing or to talk with anyone. He had seen his friend François Châtelet endure the extended suffering of 'increasingly violent bouts of suffocation' before he had died.[56] His last unfinished project was to bear the title *Ensembles and Multiplicities*.[57] He had written the first two chapters: 'Immanence, A Life'[58] and 'The Actual and the Virtual'.[59] Three years after his friend Guattari's death, Deleuze took his own life – throwing himself from the window of his third-floor apartment in Paris on 4 November 1995.

2

Deleuze's philosophical system

Deleuze's thought can be properly described as a kind philosophical system. This 'philosophical system', for Deleuze, presents various 'descriptive notions' and structures them as functioning in relation to each other and constituting the 'conditions of real experience'.[1] This system, indeed, unfolds towards an interrelated 'totality' of philosophical categories and processes and, indeed, 'the categories of every system in general'.[2] Yet this 'totality' is a strange one. While endeavouring to describe things fully, Deleuze's system, as arising from the particulars of this description, is an 'excessive' and 'open system'[3] – an 'acentered' and 'uncertain system'.[4] Unlike a 'closed system',[5] this kind of organization 'has no need whatsoever of unity in order to form a system'.[6] On the way to mapping the odd territories and trajectories of such 'an antisystematic system', I will approach Deleuze's broad corpus (including his work with Guattari) with an eye towards the more systematic presentation in *Difference and Repetition*, a book that Eric Alliez in *The Signature of the World* contends, 'should be conceived as the matrix of Deleuzism'.[7]

Some may object that Deleuze's understanding of philosophy is more a way of thinking as an immanent creation of concepts than a system of concepts, a metaphysics (following Deleuze and Guattari's *What is Philosophy?*). I grant that this is an element in Deleuze. But, there is another element that dominates. Even in Plato, Deleuze and Guattari maintain, Plato's concepts are his (his own creations, perhaps to his chagrin) – with the 'made by Plato' tag. The bulk of Deleuze's work is the production of his own original concepts – a set of created metaphysical concepts 'made by Deleuze'. This set of concepts is what I mean by 'Deleuze's philosophical system', and to proceed in these terms is to do no violence to Deleuze's own self-understanding as following the model of a classical philosopher.[8]

This chapter, as an introduction to Deleuze's thought, his philosophical system, is written with the understanding that Deleuze's metaphysics is an experimental one[9] before whose strangeness and complexity the imagination reels – such that the attempt to capture it in a neat system may be an exercise in futility.[10] Mindful of this, I present such an introduction as a progression through three unequal parts: first, a presentation of Deleuze's central philosophical concerns and his broad metaphysical vision (Saying 'Yes' to the Ocean: Affirmation and the Dionysian World); second, a more particular presentation of the complex processes that constitute the given world for Deleuze (Speculative Materialism: The Virtual and the Actual); and third, a presentation of Deleuze's prescriptive ethics and politics in light of the preceding descriptions (Schizoid Ethics: Escape and Affirm). Along the way I make pervasive (perhaps perverse) citation of Deleuze's works with the hope that this brief introduction may serve as a useful way into the authorship.

2.1 Saying 'Yes' to the ocean: Affirmation and the Dionysian world

> A single and same voice for the whole thousand-voiced multiple, a single and same Ocean for all the drops, a single clamour of Being for all beings.[11]

2.1.1 Affirmation

Deleuze, who considered himself 'a pure metaphysician',[12] worked towards a 'new metaphysics' adequate to an orientation towards life and difference – 'an entirely positive, affirmative ontology'[13] that he intended to be a thoroughgoing materialism.[14] Deleuze intended his work to be a philosophy of affirmation. Following Nietzsche, he seeks to make difference an object of 'pure affirmation', of 'enjoyment' – to take difference as primary and positive[15] – to affirm multiplicity as the most fundamental unity[16] and becoming as constitutive of being,[17] to affirm chance as the highest necessity.[18] At 'the pinnacle, the heroic moment of a pure, speculative philosophy', being is affirmed as full and absolutely positive – such that 'the negative expires at the gates of being'[19] – affirmed as univocal and immanent, not lacking and subordinate relative to another 'true' world – such that 'with immanence all is affirmation'.[20] This affirmation of 'a concept of difference without negation' as positive and primary, puts negation in its place – reversing, overturning a situation where difference is the by-product of negation or opposition,[21] dethroning negation as the primordial equal of affirmation and the positive and installing instead a secondary, corollary, derived, 'nondialectical negation' guarding, in service of the primary, original affirmation of difference.[22]

Deleuze proposes a philosophy that truly affirms life.[23] One has such confidence in life – 'unknown, resilient, obscure, stubborn life'[24] – so as to deny, to denounce (along with Spinoza and Nietzsche) any authoritative, transcendent values superior to life (and in opposition to life) that would disparage, depreciate, poison, suffocate or mutilate life – that would kill life, that would make it unreal.[25] Life does not need to be judged, justified, measured or redeemed.[26] Instead of such a 'nihilistic' thought that judges, denies and betrays life subjecting it to 'the great death'[27] – instead of this morbid kind of thought, Deleuze seeks to see the manner in which life activates thought and thought affirms life.[28] This is an affirmation of life as active expression over and against the reactive.[29] This active affirmation of life operates in terms of creativity – thought's task in this context is that of invention, of presenting new possibilities of life,[30] and the task of philosophy is the creation of concepts towards this end.[31] Thought thus takes part in life's constant renewal and transformation, in its immanent organization through the process of the generation and actualization of the virtual (to be explained below).[32]

To truly embrace difference, becoming, life and creation necessitates, for Deleuze, liberation from the classic, illusory 'image of thought'. Much of philosophy, for Deleuze, operates from a presupposed,[33] classical[34] and orthodox (regarding right *doxa* or received opinion)[35] image of thinking framed by thought's good nature, good will and common sense; and by thought's task of representation 'in terms of the identical, the similar, the equal or the opposed'.[36] Deleuze sees this classical image of thought as founded in Platonism;[37] as subordinating difference to the one through analogy, similarity and opposition;[38] as fixating on the question of identity, of what something is;[39] as judging between rival claimants or copies (which is the true X?)[40] relative to a ground (in terms of relative degrees of participation);[41] as beginning (as an idealism and a rationalism) with abstractions and then looking for what measures up to these abstractions.[42]

Deleuze (and Guattari), instead of accepting this image, propose a 'noology' – a thinking about alternative images of thought.[43] 'Shaking off' the received model, Deleuze proposes a new image of the world and of thought – 'a thinking', Claire Colebrook, suggests, 'that is not that of representation so much as production, mutation and creation',[44] an image of thought less grounded in the orthodox than the paradox as the 'passion of philosophy' beyond good and common sense.[45] This, for Deleuze, would be a truly modern ('a *finally contemporary*') image of thought.[46] As such, this new image of thought would be a *renversement* (an overcoming, overturning or reversing) of Platonism[47] – an overcoming that not only overturns ('denying the primacy of original over copy, of model over image'),[48] but indeed reverses, making what was primary, identical stable essences second, and a product of what was secondary, multiple changing differences, but is now installed as primary: 'glorifying the reign of simulacra and reflections', 'to make the simulacra rise and to affirm their rights among icons and copies'.[49]

2.1.2 Life, becoming, difference

What is this life that is affirmed? Following Bergson, Deleuze presented a monist vision of 'life' as an immanent power from early in his career until his last writings where he says 'of pure immanence that it is A LIFE, and nothing else'.[50] As a kind of vitalist,[51] Deleuze sees the world as constituted by an all-embracing life in the sense of a dynamic animating process of becoming,[52] of genuinely creative differentiation and actualization.[53] This life as protean power of becoming – of an evolving and creative production and generation of difference[54] – develops through 'problems', through the conjunctions and relations between forces and differential velocities,[55] such that one needs to use care when presenting Deleuze as a 'vitalist' in that the organic is but one expression of a more fundamental 'nonorganic' or 'anorganic' life in an 'impersonal, hylozoic' (seeing matter as having an immanent vital power or energy) cosmos.[56] For Deleuze, 'the world before man', is an ongoing process of 'universal variation',[57] 'of universal undulation, universal rippling', a ceaseless becoming, 'a generalized drift'.[58] Only becoming, 'the dynamic order', is ultimately real, and all relatively stable beings are temporary coagulations of a permanent becoming, of pure variation.[59] This immanent becoming is the positive movement of being, the internal living force or causality, the internal dynamism and spontaneity that is the ontological grounding of becoming's universal production, its immanent generation of difference.[60] The becoming of 'the fluid world of Dionysus'[61] is one that is many, an ongoing process of plural processes,[62] a multiplicity of forces and processes in relation[63] – of molecular becomings[64] that constitutes the mad element(s) beneath things.[65] Such a world is non-hierarchical, an 'in between'[66] without a center or an end, without progress[67] and without imitation of a prior original.[68]

Time, for Deleuze, (or 'duration', following Bergson) is coextensive with this cosmic becoming as the whole of relations 'filled by change' that 'changes – is constantly changing in nature – each moment'.[69] Time or duration is the becoming, the vital force behind movement.[70] This 'non-chronological' time as 'the powerful, non-organic Life which grips the world' is 'a flow of differing difference' that serves as the 'unconditioned' foundation, the 'hidden ground' of movement.[71] This movement as the continual, indivisible, irreducible 'fugitive being' of 'pure relations of speed and slowness ... below and above the threshold of perception'[72] prior to being arrested, restricted by the impositions of a transcendent eternity[73] – this movement reveals the living world as the whole that changes, that creates itself, as 'the Open': 'the opening of the world'.[74]

The fluid world of becoming and time and movement is thinkable on the other side of Deleuze's affirmation of difference as primary, as rescued 'from its maledictory state' and not subordinated to prior identity (for where would such a founding identity lay in the universal undulation of becoming?) – after the Copernican revolution in which identity is made to 'revolve around the Different'.[75] Deleuze's work, perhaps primarily, is a metaphysics of pure and absolute difference.[76] Instead of being the product of some more fundamental being, difference, for Deleuze, is itself the founding dynamic of being (of becoming, of time)[77] – the *'causa sui'*, 'something powerful in itself'[78] inasmuch as 'being differs with itself immediately, internally'.[79] 'Difference', Deleuze writes, 'is behind everything', as the disparate 'living depths', 'but behind difference there is nothing'[80] yielding, as Daniel Smith observes, 'a kind of Spinozism *minus* substance, a purely modal or differential universe'.[81]

It is precisely this world of becoming and difference that is obscured and bound by the classical image of thought. Generally, Deleuze presents representation's quadripartite 'yoke' – the four 'fetters' or 'iron collars': the 'four principal aspects to "reason" insofar as it is representation' – as functioning to negate genuine difference by mediating it and subordinating it to something else.[82] These four aspects of representation are identity, analogy, opposition and resemblance. More specifically, difference is subordinated to identity or the Same; namely, the identity of a concept (the 'same' 'thing' that is re-presented in representation).[83] The identity of the concept, in turn, is ultimately guaranteed, founded upon the unity of the thinking subject.[84] But this identity (of self and concept), for Deleuze, is a produced effect, an illusion, a false depth.[85]

The process of difference and becoming are at work in what Deleuze calls multiplicities.[86] The world is 'plural',[87] a 'pluralism' of unnamed differences in which any individual is, in turn, a multiplicity – of individuals that are multiplicities – such that 'each individual is an infinite multiplicity, and the whole of Nature is a multiplicity of perfectly individuated multiplicities'.[88] Multiplicity is 'in between'[89] and irreducibly multiple – not binary – against both the one and the many (as the opposite of and still subordinate to the one).[90] The 'one' that is *is* the 'plural' – thus Deleuze and Guattari 'arrive at the magic formula . . . PLURALISM = MONISM.'[91]

Regarding Deleuze's idea of multiplicity, the corresponding 'fetter' or aspect of representation is opposition. Multiplicity, the 'deeper "disparateness"' is cancelled, reduced or tamed when it is re-presented as the many in contradiction, in opposition to the One, to an organizing central point.[92] Multiplicity is then structured in an oversimplified binary or 'biunivocal' system, reducing to two in order to order to the one.[93] However, as Deleuze writes, 'it is not difference which presupposes opposition but opposition which presupposes difference'.[94]

2.1.3 Immanence, univocity, anarchy

Deleuze's vision of the world is one of pure immanence in place of any transcendent or hierarchical structuring of being. Whereas a hierarchy would represent the whole from a privileged point of view,[95] in place of such a regal hierarchy, Deleuze envisions 'crowned anarchies' (Antonin Artaud's phrase) – an overturning, reversing and un-founding of hierarchy.[96] This escape from hierarchy is enabled, for Deleuze, paradoxically, through his understanding of the univocity of being (as presented by Duns Scotus and Spinoza[97]) – 'a single voice', he writes, 'raises the clamour of being'.[98] Being, what is, is said in 'a single voice', 'in a single same sense' such that 'Being [then] is the same for everything about which it is said'.[99] However, the 'same way' in which being is said of all things should be understood in terms of pure differences; the 'being' of 'the univocity of being' is difference such that the univocity of being is a 'subterranean affirmation' of difference.[100] To repeat: being is said 'in a single and same sense, of all its individuating differences' which 'do not have the same essence'; 'being is said in a single and same sense of everything of which it is said, but that of which it is said differs: it is said of difference *itself*'; 'being itself is univocal, while that of which it is said is equivocal'.[101] The univocity of being should be seen as 'the equality of being' which undercuts hierarchy by putting everything on the same plane, a plane of crowned anarchies[102] such that, in *A Thousand Plateaus*, univocity is replaced by the logic of 'and'.[103]

Being is laid out, for Deleuze, in a plane of immanence[104]: a 'flat ontology' in which everything is included on one 'common' plane, not immanent 'to' something else, to some 'supplementary dimension'.[105] The one plane is the monism that denies dualism (of higher and lower) in order to yield pluralism.[106]

The plane of immanence, the 'plane of Nature'[107] as coextensive with 'the material universe',[108] has a fundamentally fluid composition (a plane of infinitely fine undulations) of becoming, of 'speeds and slowness . . . relations of velocity between infinitesimal particles', of shifting intensities, of unfolding processes and multiplicities.[109] With the plane of immanence, Deleuze intends to present a 'materialism' that functions as a corrective to or rejection of any idealism that would give priority to any transcendent mind, ideas or psyche, seeing instead minds, ideas and psyches as constituents of the plane as well.[110] For Deleuze, there is nothing transcendent beyond immanent processes. Transcendence (a particularly Western and European disease), then, is illusory, a product of immanence resulting from a failure to think immanence.[111] This false 'missing' transcendence then functions to arrest and order the movement of immanence.[112] In the pre-modern world, this transcendence was God; in the modern world this transcendence is the Self (whether it is in philosophy, politics or psychoanalysis). From this transcendence, the universe is structured in emanating, descending and diminishing order from an eminent height in which 'the difference of beings is in general conceived as a hierarchical difference . . . and is defined by the degree of distance that separates it from the first cause or first principle'.[113] It is in relation to such a transcendent eminent hierarchy (over and against the plane of immanence) that analogy as part of the quadripartite yoke of representation would lay upon and so distort immanence. With analogy, the judgement of identity or relative identity subordinates difference, judging it in terms of its proximity to a higher identity or authority.[114] This judgement is a work of distribution (in terms of 'common sense') and hierarchization (in terms of 'good sense')[115] yielding a hierarchy based on relative proximity to ultimate determinate identity (be it concept, self or God).[116]

2.1.4 Repetition and chaos

In his examination of the immanent process that underlies all identities, Deleuze revivifies the concept of repetition. There are two types of repetition: repetition as we would commonly understand it as extrinsic, physical repetition – as the same thing again[117] – and a more fundamental (if 'secret') dynamic, generative or productive repetition arising from internal difference.[118] This latter repetition is at once the being of all differences[119] and is inclusive of difference 'at its heart, as the essential variant of which it is composed, the displacement and disguise which constitute it as a difference that is itself divergent and displaced'.[120] Deleuze describes repetition as difference without a concept[121] – for in it 'there is no first term which is repeated'.[122] Difference itself (without any unifying identity) repeats – difference through repetition of itself generates difference.

This transgressive and differing repetition is not rooted in sameness or resemblance and differs in kind from generality and law.[123] Rather, the repetition of the same is a product of, is constituted by, this 'other', 'second' repetition.[124] Against the 'false movement of the abstract', this repetition consists of 'essentially mobile individuating differences'.[125] Thus within this immanent differential process of repetition is the production of the new.[126]

It is with this understanding of repetition in mind that Deleuze appropriates Nietzsche's concept of the eternal return. What returns eternally, for Deleuze, is difference as the one constant; what returns or persists is the different; the eternally returning, sameness is said only of difference.[127] Deleuze writes: 'The repetition in the eternal return is the same, but the same in so far as it is said uniquely of difference and the different.'[128] This eternal return is 'the being of becoming', the formlessness of becoming itself as all that truly has being.[129] With the eternal return as a 'universal ungrounding', said 'of a world without identity',[130] one enters the realm of simulacra – 'copies' of 'copies' without an original that are always different from one another.[131] Its return is not so much the circle of a cycle[132] as it is a centrifugal force[133] functioning as a test or a 'selection' such that the reactive and seemingly stable is expelled, thrown away and only the different returns.[134] In the eternal return, what remains is the ever-new.[135] Thus, the eternal return is 'the secret coherence which establishes itself only by excluding my own coherence, my own identity, the identity of the self, the world and God'.[136] With the eternal return, Deleuze also introduces the affirmation of chance. As what returns, what stays the same, is difference, so the only necessity is chance.[137] The eternal return is a 'divine game' in which 'there is no pre-existing rule.'[138] This affirmation of repetition, eternal return, simulacra and chance breaks with the yoke of resemblance and the order of generality that would subordinate difference.[139]

Finally, as intimated above, Deleuze sees the world as including an irreducibly chaotic, oceanic, Dionysian depth.[140] The world, then, is no longer a world as an ordered unity or whole, but a 'world that has lost its pivot', a monstrous whole – 'a formless ungrounded chaos which has no law other than is own repetition, its own reproduction in the development of that which diverges and decentres'.[141] The plane of immanence is an acentered world without hierarchy and transcendence.[142] However, the 'world' in which chaos is the original, primary milieu[143] is not, for Deleuze, an utter chaos. There is temporary, provisional order – the chaos is structured, 'composed'.[144] Chaos – 'the chaos that creates' – creates order from chaos, as from chaos come milieus and rhythms that give rise to actual 'territories'.[145] But these provisional orders and consistencies are also eventually undone by chaotic eternal return rumbling and turning beneath them.[146] The world of becoming and difference that Deleuze affirms is a 'properly chaotic world without identity' – a 'chaos = cosmos' that yields (following James Joyce) a 'Chaosmos'.[147]

2.2 Speculative materialism: The virtual and the actual

2.2.1 Transcendental empiricism: From the actual to the virtual

How does becoming proceed? How does one give an intelligible account adequate to the unfolding of the world?[148] In the previous section, we laid out Deleuze's philosophical system along the lines of the order of being, the order of the world as an *ordo doctrina*, a teaching, a presentation of what is not necessarily accessible to us. In the present section, we will follow another route of explication – that of the order of knowledge, of discovery – an *ordo inventionis*, moving from manifest effect to cause. Against a Kantian view that sees various 'domains' of reason's legislation, Deleuze sees 'only a single *terrain* (*terrain*), that of experience'.[149] Deleuze proposes an empiricism that begins with the given of experience as a plurality, as a collection of this AND this and so on.[150] Beginning with the mixed phenomena – the processes and provisional stabilities, the 'composed chaos', of what is given (in Claire Colebrook's description, 'a radicalization of phenomenology'[151]) – beginning with this experience, one then asks the transcendental question of how it came to be, its genesis, how it is produced.[152] This is a stepping back from consciousness of the everyday world to think, to speculate about the conditions of real experience, about what something is an expression 'of'.[153] Deleuze described this process as a transcendental empiricism, a 'science of the sensible' that sees in the given (empirical, sensible) the difference that is the (transcendental) 'reason behind' it, even if it is a 'strange reason' – looking from the sensible to 'the very being of the sensible: difference, potential difference and difference in intensity as the reason behind qualitative diversity'.[154] This reason is 'strange', for transcendental empiricism finds or construes an alien unconscious foundation for everyday experience – a ground not 'model[ed] . . . on that which it grounds'.[155] In this search for transcendental conditions, Deleuze presents 'an empiricism of the Idea' in which thought ascends from actual states of affairs towards 'the virtual'.[156]

This transcendental empiricism, meditating upon what is given, forms the basis for Deleuze's speculative distinction between the virtual and the actual.[157] The real, for Deleuze, following Bergson, consists of both the virtual and the actual – it is, as James Williams writes, 'a structure of relations that hold between the virtual and actual'.[158] These two, the virtual and the actual, are the two asymmetrical 'unequal odd sides' or 'dissimilar halves' of reality[159] – forming a 'circuit' moving back or up (transcendentally) from the actual to the virtual and forward or down in the actualization of the virtual.[160] Transcendental empiricism, then, beginning with the actual, sees the actual extensive depth of bodies as pointing to a 'deeper' depth – as he writes in *Difference and Repetition*: 'The ground [*fond*] as it appears in a homogeneous extensity is notably a projection of something "deeper" [*profond*]: only the latter may be called *Ungrund* or groundless.'[161] Alternately, Deleuze (echoing the Stoics) in *The Logic of Sense* presents the depth of 'the primary order' of actual corporeal bodies, causes and states of affairs as producing a 'secondary order' of 'sense' upon an incorporeal virtual surface.[162]

Deleuze describes the access to the virtual in various ways: as *ascending* – a climbing to the surface in which the nature of that which ascends changes (from actual to virtual);[163] as *deduction* – in which something actual is understood through deducing its virtual conditions;[164] as *implication* – in which the intensities of the virtual '"deeper" depth' are implicated 'in the perception of extensity';[165] as *extraction* or *counter-actualization* (*contre-effectuation*, also translated as 'counter-effectuation') – where virtual multiplicities, 'poses', events or concepts are extracted/counter-actualized, abstracted, from 'the state of affairs', 'the series of reals', the actual movement of 'the world of forces'.[166]

2.2.2 The virtual plane

The virtual plane, for Deleuze, echoing a Scholastic understanding of the virtual as a real and not abstract 'transcendental',[167] is, however, not a 'preformed order' but a 'chaotic virtuality', a realm of pure becomings and variations.[168] The virtual provides a 'leaner ontology' of virtual processes, relations and structures – 'the totality of Ideas and intensities' – at once effecting and disguised in the actual, replacing laws and essences.[169] The virtual, then, is a way of accounting for the apparent finite stabilities in the world in a manner consonant with Deleuze's understanding of the priority of difference and becoming. Regarding the status or being of the virtual, virtual objects 'have the property of being *and* not being where they are' – in 'a paradoxical place between existence and non-existence'.[170] For Deleuze, the virtual is fully objectively real, if opposed to the actual – (quoting Proust) 'real without being actual, ideal without being abstract' – to be actualized, not realized.[171] It is not the possible which Deleuze sees as a double or resemblance that is the same as the real but opposed to the real, lacking reality; the virtual is real but not actual and unlike the actual.[172] While virtual 'objects' are always fragmentary, displaced simulacra,[173] the virtual is 'completely determined', constituted by differential relations and singularities characterizing and determining the content of its virtual multiplicities, problems and ideas.[174] The virtual plane is a continuum – 'one and simple', a whole[175] – that is the being-together, coexistence, conjunction of elements[176] – a 'system' of intensive relations.[177] Deleuze, following Bergson, often describes the virtual in terms of pure recollection, retrieved from an unconscious pure past – 'a gigantic memory, a universal cone in which everything coexists with itself', the 'virtual sheets of the past' contracted into the present.[178] Noumenal and ideal, the virtual is a sub-representative and unconscious domain that is not psychological or mental – an 'ontological unconscious'.[179]

In *The Logic of Sense*, the incorporeal surface,[180] the domain of sense[181] is occupied and composed by incorporeal surface effects and events that do not so much exist as 'subsist or inhere', constituted on and constituting the surface.[182] Over the depth of bodies,[183] this 'metaphysical' surface or frontier between propositions and bodies or things – at once separating and connecting them[184] – is the locus of sense as 'that which happens to bodies and that which insists in propositions'.[185] He also refers to sense as 'sense-event' and makes the distinction between sense as inhering in propositions and events as happening in states of affairs.[186] Thus both series (things and propositions) are 'articulated at the surface' in the 'expressed' of propositions and the 'attributes' of things.[187]

In their collaborative work, Deleuze and Guattari present the virtual plane in terms of what they call (in Antonin Artaud's phrase) the body without organs (or BwO).[188] The body without organs as an immanent zero-intensity ('intensity = 0') is populated by flows, by relative intensities and degrees of intensity,[189] as 'the zero degree of intensity that all modes of being share'.[190] As populated by circulating intensities and 'operat[ing] entirely by insufflation, respiration, evaporation, and fluid transmission'[191] – with 'various zones and intensities, with gradients of passage'[192] – Deleuze and Guattari observe that (in one of their odder statements) 'the body without organs is an egg' defined 'by axes and vectors, gradients and thresholds', by 'becomings, rises and falls, migrations and displacements'.[193] The BwO in its broadest sense (as 'the' BwO) is also called 'the plane of consistency', a plane of 'continuous variation'.[194] This plane of consistency (also described as the plane or field of immanence[195]) is the virtual continuum, the smooth space, 'fluid and slippery', composed and filled by haecceities, by 'modes of individuation proceeding neither by form nor by the subject' – 'relations of speed and slowness between unformed elements'.[196] This plane, the BwO, is occupied by a multiplicity of these degrees of intensity that constitute the organs or partial objects that are the 'working parts' that cling to and emanate from the BwO.[197] The 'without organs' of the body without organs, then, is not an absence of 'organs' as such; it is not 'an empty body stripped of organs', but a priority over and a continual dismantling of 'organism' in the sense of the organization of the organs.[198] This organization is described in terms of the 'stratification' of the BwO, capturing and organizing its constituents into more fixed aggregates.[199] Various 'mechanic assemblages' mark and effect the transitions between the BwO/plane of consistency and the strata.[200]

The agent or 'operator' that effects the drawing of the virtual is given several exotic-sounding names in Deleuze's work in *Difference and Repetition* and *The Logic of Sense*: the quasi-cause, nonsense, the paradoxical instance or entity or element, the dark or obscure precursor,[201] the aleatory point and the Event (with a capital 'e').[202] As that which draws the virtual domain of thought, as 'the reality of thought itself', this 'operator' is unconscious and 'can only be thought as nonsense' – 'always Other' to thought, unthinkable.[203] This paradoxical element/instance/instant is the aleatory point ('aleatory' meaning contingent, uncertain, a function of chance – an *aleator* being Latin for a gambler) as an ungrounding ground, the active energy or 'force of the unconscious' that escapes consciousness and is unthinkable, unlocatable.[204] The aleatory point as a point of nonsense, the paradoxical and supremely strange entity/element/instant has two aspects, is a 'double-headed thing', having two sides – two 'unequal or uneven "halves"': one side is an empty place without an occupant, the instant as 'always missing from its own place' ('the empty square'); the other side is an unknown and displaced occupant without a place (*atopon*), the instant as 'endlessly displaced' ('the mobile element') – 'at once excess and lack'.[205] As such, this point is a fugitive *'perpetuum mobile'* that circulates, endlessly displaced.[206] This two-sided paradoxical entity is also described as the imperceptible and 'perfectly indeterminate' 'dark precursor' which enables/ensures/ causes communication/resonance between difference as such – as the 'differentiator' between the different and the different, between the series without the series losing their difference – 'difference in the second degree, the self-different which relates different to different by itself'.[207] That this is the connecting agent functions to loosen the grid of any linguistic or cultural structuralism. If a structure is minimally the relation between 'two heterogeneous series of terms', the paradoxical element, as relating the two series, enables one to think difference without thinking identity first, with the paradoxical element between (as the between of) the different series.[208] Finally, this paradoxical instance is the one unique 'Event [with a capital 'e'] in which all events communicate and are distributed'.[209] This one aleatory point of nonsense 'the eternally decentered ex-centric center' that 'functions as the zero point of thought' traces the line of sense and draws and establishes the surface of the virtual, the plane of sense – 'the point which traces the line; the line which forms the frontier; and the surface which is developed and unfolded from both sides'.[210] If this seems almost hopelessly obscure it is for good reason – we cannot think what makes thought possible.[211] (How does one draw a plane? With a mobile point?)

In *A Thousand Plateaus*, Deleuze and Guattari describe analogous processes in terms of lines of flight, abstract machines and deterritorialization.[212] One movement of abstract machines – as deterritorialized 'unformed' and 'nonformal functions'[213] – is that of 'constantly setting things loose', multiplying connections and so drawing the 'plane of consistency' or 'body without organs' (rough synonyms for the virtual plane, as we will see).[214] Furthermore, the virtual plane of consistency is drawn, we are told, by abstract lines of flight or deterritorialization[215] – by processes of deterritorialization and destratification.[216] Deleuze and Guattari describe this kind of deterritorialization that draws the virtual plane of consistency as an 'absolute deterritorialization', an 'absolute line of flight' that escapes the actual and rises to the virtual surface.[217] In sum, deterritorialization can extend a line of flight and become an abstract machine drawing the plane of consistency.[218] (We will return to many of these ideas below.)

When it comes to the relation between the virtual and the actual, there is something of a tension in understandings of Deleuze (if not in Deleuze himself) between an account that sees, as does Williams and others, a more robust 'reciprocal determination' between the actual and the virtual (seeing 'differentiation' as the process of moving from the actual to the virtual),[219] and an account that sees the virtual (more like Bergsonian memory) as primary, as self-generating, whereas the actual is generated by the virtual through a complex process (Alliez, DeLanda and Hardt seem to follow this reading). At the very least, there is a strong asymmetry with the virtual being presented in terms of the excessive difference itself and the actual being presented in terms of a relatively impoverished fixation in more static forms and with there being a focus on the complex process of actualization (described below in 2.2.4. and 2.2.5.) and nothing like a parallel emphasis on 'virtualization'. The movement is not totally one-way, but it does seem that if all there is for Deleuze is the material, the virtual is the generative, dynamic depth or surface of matter that can be returned to (though differently) in a sense from the actual in terms of counter-actualization, deterritorialization and lines of flight.

2.2.3 Multiplicity, intensity, contraction, time

What occupies or constitutes the virtual plane? What is 'the Matter of the Plane' that occurs 'in the body or plane'?[220] Deleuze (and Guattari) see the virtual plane of consistency as filled with *multiplicities*.[221] Ideas, 'problems' and differential relations (as we will see later) are virtual multiplicities.[222] Deleuze distinguishes such virtual multiplicities – as continuous, qualitative, internal, non-numerical multiplicities with regard to difference in kind[223] – from actual multiplicities – as discontinuous, quantitative, exterior, numerical with regard to difference in degree.[224] In *A Thousand Plateaus*, Deleuze and Guattari distinguish between 'striated', 'arborescent', binary, segmentary multiplicities on the one hand, and smooth, 'nomadic', 'rhizomatic' multiplicities on the other.[225] The virtual realm in particular is an order of 'intensive multiplicities' – an intensive order.[226] The virtual is a realm of pure becomings, of intensities, of changes that cannot be 'captured in terms of a final identity'.[227] The body without organs, then, is a 'matrix of intensity' (an intensive depth, 'the depth of difference'[228]), an intensive spatium, a smooth space populated by distributions of, varying degrees of, or bands of intensity – relations of speed and slowness.[229] (This would seem to imply that the actual is the domain of striated, segmented, sedentary binary multiplicities and the virtual as that of smooth, nomadic, 'intensive multiplicities'.[230]) For Deleuze, intensity is difference, 'difference in itself', 'the unequal in itself'[231] expressing differential relations.[232] Intensive difference as a difference 'in' intensity[233] or 'of' intensity is an inequality or disparity[234] between differences in tension with one another.[235] Difference in itself is the 'living depths' – the intensive depth or intensive field – as populated by 'the disparate', by 'bundles and networks' of 'differences without negation'.[236] This 'intense world of differences' as 'the reason behind qualitative diversity'[237] yields on the virtual plane differences of intensive quantity or energy[238]

Difference in intensity arises from an encounter with the actual in sensible excitation, from the 'becoming of forces' and the contracted vibration that is *sensibility*.[239] Sensation is the contemplation or contraction of intensive difference, and is as such a 'passive creation'.[240] Difference in intensity is 'the being of the sensible',[241] that by which the diverse given (the 'flux of the sensible') is given.[242]

Intensive difference lies behind the paradoxical functioning and the 'peculiar limit' of sensibility – in that such difference is 'a "something" which simultaneously cannot be sensed (from the point of view of the empirical exercise) and can only be sensed (from the point of view of the transcendent exercise)'.[243] Sensibility's 'essential encounter' of intensive difference forces thought, such that 'the path which leads to that which is to be thought, all begins with sensibility'.[244] This 'transcendent exercise' of the sensibility – the manner in which the faculty of the sensibility is transcended – awakens 'memory', understood by Deleuze (reading Bergson) as the broader domain of the virtual plane.[245]

As on the virtual plane, new contractions of intensity are in relation to prior contractions, prior contemplations. Indeed, time or duration, if it is to have content, is not mere succession of discontinuous points but is a matter of contraction, of synthesis, of bringing together. In *Difference and Repetition*, Deleuze describes several different 'passive syntheses of time'. Key to this understanding of virtual contraction or *contemplation* for Deleuze is the work of habit as the first passive synthesis of time – as 'the state of successive instants contracted in a present present of a certain duration'.[246] *Habit* is a contraction – a drawing together of elements – and a contemplation – a bringing together (con-) in time (temp) of the past into the present, preserving 'the before in the after'.[247] Habit arises from repetition as binding or a production of continuity such that 'there is no continuity apart from that of habit'.[248] Following Bergson, Deleuze writes that while 'all habits are arbitrary . . . the habit of taking on habits is natural'.[249] Habitual continuities are products of what Deleuze calls *passive synthesis* – passive in that they are unconscious, 'sub-representative', 'not carried out by the mind, but [occur] in the mind which contemplates, prior to all memory and all reflection'.[250] The living present is constituted by a contraction of 'independent instants into one another' – a passive synthesis in which the past is contracted into the present.[251] Deleuze describes habit as the 'originary synthesis' or 'foundation' of time, 'the moving soil occupied by the passing present' (as different from memory as the 'fundamental synthesis' or 'ground' of time).[252]

The second synthesis of time, for Deleuze, arises from what he calls 'the paradox of present'; that is, that habit works 'to constitute time while passing in the time constituted. We cannot avoid the necessary conclusion – *that there must be another time in which the first synthesis of time can occur.*'[253] This second synthesis is that of *memory* as 'the fundamental synthesis of time which constitutes the being of the past', of 'time as a pure past' – the 'Bergsonian/ Proustian virtual past'.[254] This memory is 'a substantial temporal element' that is the ground, the transcendental ground of habit.[255] Behind the passing present there is the 'more profound' structure that causes the present to pass – 'the passing of one present and the arrival of another'.[256]

Following this understanding of memory, Deleuze sees the virtual in terms of a 'pure past' or of 'pure recollection'. This *pure recollection* as not that which is remembered – as the actualized 'recollection-image' in consciousness – but always remains 'pure' in its virtuality.[257] Such a pure recollection 'exists outside of consciousness, in time, and we should have no more difficulty in admitting the virtual insistence of pure recollections in time than we do for the actual existence of non-perceived objects in space'.[258] The virtual here is a 'pure past' – 'a pure memory identical to the totality of the past' that 'IS, in the full sense of the word: It is identical with being in itself.'[259] This pure recollection is unconscious – not in the sense of 'a psychological reality outside consciousness', but as a 'pure ontology'.[260] These 'vaster circuits' of memory, the 'sheets of past' (the sections of the Bergsonian cone), coexist with the contracted point of actual present – surrounding it 'with a cloud of virtual images'.[261] For Deleuze, following Bergson, 'duration' is the (vital) virtual whole of relations that is continually changing, continually differing with itself and generating the new.[262] This pure duration is the virtual plane, is the virtual multiplicity.[263]

From *The Logic of Sense* on, Deleuze (and Guattari) make a distinction between two understandings of time: *Chronos* and *Aion*.[264] Chronos – in which only the present exists, the 'actual is defined by this passing of the present' – is the living present, the corporeal time 'of bodies and states of affairs is the present'.[265] Aion (or 'Aeon' in *A Thousand Plateaus* or 'Cronos' in *Cinema 2*), however, is the virtual, unthinkable[266] 'nonchronological' time that coincides with Bergson's 'past'[267] – as the other temporal dimension to the material 'present' – the strange virtual time that founds actual, everyday time.[268] Deleuze envisions this reading of time as an unlimited elongated line, infinitely divisible and subdivided, extending in both directions of past and future,[269] eluding, 'sidestepping', the limited present[270] – occupied not by living presents, but by infinitives,[271] neutral and impassive.[272] Deleuze describes the line of the Aion as the 'Event for all events',[273] the place or 'locus' of incorporeal events (to be explained below) in which events 'communicate'.[274] Like events, sense 'rests with', is 'gathered over the line of the Aion'.[275] The line of the Aion, then, is the virtual surface, border or frontier between propositions and things – articulating, organizing and relating propositions and things through the sense and events 'upon' it.[276]

2.2.4 Events, sense, differentiation, problems, ideas, unconscious, desiring-machines

Virtual *events* are ideal[277] and incorporeal entities or surface effects[278] that occur or happen – that are realized or embodied or actualized – in actual things, in the physical qualities and relations of bodies and states of affairs.[279] Deleuze describes such events as singularities, 'ideational singularities',[280] and (in his work with Guattari) as 'haecceities' – as things that happen, 'incorporeal transformations', as 'nonpersonal individualit[ies]'.[281] Events/haecceities are pure becomings – they are less names that name identity than verbs that name becomings consisting of 'relations of movement and rest' and 'forces in their various relationships'.[282] Deleuze sees events as 'problematic' (in the sense described below), as determining the conditions of problems, as 'problematizing'[283] and so constituting or providing the conditions for sense.[284] Events are not living presents; they are virtual happenings expressed by verbs and particularly by infinitives as expressing 'becomings or events that transcend mood and tense'.[285] As such they operate 'upon the line of the Aion'[286] in a 'pure *reserve*'.[287] In presenting the paradoxical instance (that draws the virtual plane) as the unique event, 'the Event' in which all events 'communicate and are distributed', Deleuze also presents the Event in terms of 'univocal Being', as the 'univocal Being [that] is the pure form of the Aion', as the one and same saying of Being attributable to all events.[288] Finally, Deleuze finds in these events 'the power of nonorganic life' – an immanent and indefinite life of virtual events and singularities that are actualized in states of things, in subjects and objects.[289] This realm of events is that of simulacra or of phantasms as surface phenomena[290] in which there is no original or prior constituted identity,[291] but identity and resemblance are produced effects of simulacra[292] as an 'always becoming other'.[293] Sense is the companion, the other side of the event. As the product of surface energy or surface formations,[294] the effect produced by (the point of) nonsense,[295] sense is on (the line of) the Aion,[296] the incorporeal surface – forming 'letters of dust'[297] – the border, the frontier between things and propositions.[298] Sense corresponds to the 'problematic' distribution of points in tension.[299] As constituted by nonsense, sense is paradoxical – 'para-sense' (contrary to good sense or common sense)[300] – in that one can 'always take the sense of what [one says] as the object of another proposition', leading to an infinite regress.[301] Sense, as Deleuze writes in *The Logic of Sense*, is not 'a predicate or a property but' an event[302] – it is what happens or occurs to or in bodies/things/states of affairs.[303] Deleuze sometimes makes a further distinction, seeing sense and event as 'the same thing', as two sides of the paradoxical element in which 'events' designate more of what happens in things, bodies or states of affairs and 'sense' designates that which 'insists' in propositions,[304] what is expressed by or expressible in propositions.[305]

On the virtual plane of sense and events, there begins the process of what Deleuze calls 'the order of reasons' – of the four interrelated processes of 'differentiation-individuation-dramatisation-differenciation' or awkwardly combined in the 'complex notion' of 'indi-different/ciation (indi-drama-different/ciation)'. This total process – the 'totality of the system which brings into play the Idea, its incarnation and its actualisation' – is one of moving from the virtual to the actual.[306] The first of the order of reasons is differentiation (with two 't's) in the virtual. This is, as Eric Alliez in *The Signature of the World* describes it, the virtual's 'own movement of internal difference (differentiation)' – in which 'what differentiates itself is first and foremost what differs from itself, to wit the virtual'.[307] Differentiation is the determination of the content of an Idea as a 'virtual multiplicity'[308] through the two 'aspects' of differentiation, the two 'principal characteristics' of an Idea: differential relations and the distribution of singular points.[309] The virtual-ideal field is made up of a group of differential relations 'which exist and are determined only in respect to one another' – 'existing only through their reciprocal determination' as a kind of 'mathematical function'.[310] Deleuze sees the process of virtual repetition as the 'emission' of 'non-exchangeable and non-substitutable singularities' that have 'no equal or equivalent'.[311] These singular points (that with differential relations determine the content of 'problems' and Ideas) are the displaced and divergent product of a virtual hidden repetition – 'the repetition of an internal difference', an immanent, internal variation and differentiating – in which 'there is no first term which is repeated' – a surface disguise in which there is nothing under the 'mask'.[312] In *Difference and Repetition*, Deleuze associates differentiation with the process of 'complication' and the 'question'.[313] Complication is a centripetal 'folding' or gathering-in containing differential relations.[314] Such gatherings together in contemplations of pure difference are 'questions'.[315] Deleuze writes: 'We regard as fundamental this "correspondence" between difference and questioning, between ontological difference and the being of the question.'[316] The *question* has its origin in the internal differentiation of repetition with which it (the question) is 'consubstantial' and is determined by the aleatory point, the paradoxical instance as drawing the virtual plane of differential relations between intensities.[317] These questions determine, ground and develop into problems[318] or the virtual content of the Idea as a problem – the Idea 'responds' to the 'call of certain questions'.[319] The question, determined by an aleatory point, determines the multiple singular points that constitute the problem.[320]

Problems, in the special sense that Deleuze means them, are problems without solutions (like Kantian ideas).[321] The being of the problematic is that of an ideal virtual multiplicity[322] – a series of tensions, of differential intensity[323] – in a state of 'perplication'.[324] These virtual problems are 'of the order of events'[325] and are the locus of sense (relative to which propositions are particular solutions)[326] – the result of a 'differential and iterative' sub-representative unconscious.[327] They are the drawing together of divergent series – 'multiplicities made up of differential relations and variations of relations, distinctive points and transformations of points'.[328] As part of his larger project of overturning Platonism, Deleuze writes that 'Being (what Plato calls the Idea) "corresponds" to the essence of the problem'; that is, to difference itself.[329] Indeed, Deleuze describes Ideas as problems, sees that problems 'objectively characterize the nature of Ideas as such'[330] such that there are 'problematic Ideas', 'ideal problems'[331] consisting in 'a system of ideal liaisons or differential relations'.[332] Differentiation, then, (the 'question') determines the differential relations of problems which are the content of Ideas.[333]

Ideas ('problems-Ideas') are not 'contained in the mind', for Deleuze, but are necessarily unconscious – regarding an 'unconscious of pure thought' that lives 'on problems and differences', 'a theatre of problems'.[334] Ideas are virtual and inessential surface effects, 'existing in an obscure zone which they themselves preserve and maintain'.[335] Deleuze describes Ideas as structures of events and sense[336] that are positive multiplicities[337] – with Ideas, 'the reality of the virtual is structure'.[338] 'An Idea', Deleuze writes, 'is neither one nor multiple, but a multiplicity constituted of differential elements, differential relations between those elements, and singularities corresponding to those relations.'[339] There are three (inseparable) aspects of the structure of virtual Ideas: elements, relations and singularities. As the first two aspects are so closely related (elements as only determined in relations), one can see how Deleuze elsewhere only includes two aspects: the differential relations and distributions of singularities – this coheres with the 'two aspects of differentiation' above.[340] First are the differential elements[341] – the virtual and ideal elements 'without figure or function' as pure differences, 'differential glimmers'.[342] Second are differential relations and ideal connections between the elements in which the elements are determined reciprocally.[343] Third are the singularities – the distribution of singular 'points' – that 'correspond' to the differential relations (more on these singularities later).[344] As such, Ideas are 'fluent' syntheses of difference – 'complexes of coexistence' giving determinacy and consistency.[345] In his overturned Platonism, Deleuze's Ideas, the only universals, are not simple essences but problems[346] as 'multiplicities made up of differential relations and variations of relations, distinctive points and transformations of points'[347] – matters of differential intensity whose virtual content is determined by differentiation and responds to the 'questions' of pure difference.[348] For Deleuze and Guattari, the concepts created by philosophy[349] apprehend, designate or express[350] – even bring forth[351] – virtual events. Such a concept is a fragmentary whole[352] that corresponds to problems[353] and 'confer[s] consistency' to the virtual[354] and so thinking the virtual behind the actual.[355]

In their *Anti-Oedipus* and *A Thousand Plateaus*, Deleuze and Guattari present a set of ideas that would seem to complement Deleuze's earlier understanding of the virtual plane. The unconscious – or 'social unconscious'[356] – of schizoanalysis (Deleuze and Guattari's alternative to psychoanalysis) is an unconscious composed of plural (schizoid) multiplicities, 'a crowd' that is less a 'theater' than a 'factory' that works, produces – an auto-production that reproduces itself.[357] This unconscious is constituted by many 'desiring-machines'.[358] Deleuze and Guattari present a vision of the world in which 'everything is a machine' – functioning and operating[359] through the producing, connecting and interrupting of flows[360] of energy[361] or intensities or singularities[362] traversing the plane of the Body without Organs.[363] Life is mechanic – with the organic and the mechanic as but two states of the immanent production of the living/machine.[364] This conjoining of the vital and the mechanical is supremely evident in the desiring-machines of the system of the unconscious.[365] Desiring-machines, functioning on[366] and organizing the BwO,[367] make up the schizophrenic[368] population of the (social) unconscious.[369] Upon this plane they work producing and forming connections[370] – connecting and coupling to other machines[371] – producing, directing and breaking the flow of the energy of desire.[372]

2.2.5 From the virtual to the actual

On the way from the virtual towards actualization, towards the actual, there is a kind of middle ground, a place of transition from one to the other. The virtual surface is a *transcendental field* that provides an alien ground of consciousness – such that consciousness is grounded in something unlike itself – not made in the image of consciousness.[373] This transcendental field of 'virtuals', 'a pure plane of immanence', the virtual plane of Ideas gives rise to surface organization of singularities and is 'incarnated in' *fields of individuation*, intensive fields of pre-individual ideal singularities.[374] These 'intensive fields of individuation' are what 'determines the Idea to actualize itself, to incarnate itself in a particular way'.[375] The virtual passing towards the actual is 'an immanent life carrying with it the events or singularities that are merely actualized in subjects and objects'.[376] Against a modern conception of the identical self as the ground of knowledge,[377] Deleuze sees that – in 'the world before man'[378] – that from which individual thoughts and things arise is not of the order of general or universal forms but rather (arising from virtual multiplicities) the play of 'pre-individual singularities' that are truly singular – 'non-exchangeable and non-substitutable singularities'.[379] If there are any subjects operative in this domain they are 'larval subjects', 'passive selves', or 'contemplative souls' – emergent agencies of 'syntheses and habituses capable of contracting the cases or the elements into one another' – 'contemplations not yet organized into a self'.[380] The pre-individual 'virtual-ideal' transcendental or problematic[381] field is determined by distributions of nomadic singularities[382] and these corresponding to the differential relations (these together constituting Ideas).[383] These singularities are then differential determinations relative to differential relations.[384] Such singularities, on the way to actualities, are not things but intensities, energies,[385] haecceities, 'depending on their degree of speed or the relation of movement and rest into which they enter'[386] and funding the process of (or 'serv[ing] as principles for the constitution of'[387]) individualization and actualization.[388] 'Actualization', Deleuze writes, 'belongs to the virtual. The actualization of the virtual is singularity whereas the actual itself is individuality constituted'.[389] Ideas are expressed in 'individuating factors' through 'implication' – expressed as implicated intensive quantities. This 'implication' is a process that determines (with regard to intensities) the enveloping and the enveloped, (with regard to questions) the solving and the solved.[390] Ideas are implicated in that which explicates them.[391] Before the extensive and qualitative order of explication, however, there is the intensive order of implications, of implicated difference – 'the implicated world of intensive quantities'.[392] These intensities as 'implicated multiplicities' that 'direct the course of the actualization of Ideas and determine the cases of solution for problems'.[393]

Deleuze's speculative materialism, beyond narrating the transcendental ascent to the virtual and describing the constitution of the virtual plane, presents the process of the *actualization* of the virtual – the way that the transcendental virtual plane is incarnated in the actual world of thoughts and things.[394] 'There is a big difference', Deleuze writes, 'between the virtuals that define the immanence of the transcendental field and the possible forms that actualize them and transform them into something transcendent'.[395] How does this process of actualization then proceed? Actualization proceeds immanently by difference and creation – the actual is not a copy or an image of the virtual, it is a (different) product of it.[396] 'Chaotic virtuality' is actualized in the relative stabilities of actual thoughts and things.[397] Deleuze, following Bergson, sees actualization as 'differentiation' in a general sense (not the sense of differentiation as regarding differential relations on the virtual plane). 'It is difference', he writes, 'that is primary in the process of actualization – the difference between the virtual from which we begin and the actuals at which we arrive.'[398] Deleuze describes a virtual event as 'happening', as being actualized in 'the living present' – in 'the present of bodies',[399] in a 'state of affairs'.[400] This process is one of static genesis (or passive synthesis), a 'genesis without dynamism' going 'from the structure to its incarnation', from problem to cases of solution, from virtual sense (and nonsense) to individuals[401] – as sense on the virtual surface is the product of static genesis from actual bodies.[402] Actual thoughts and things, then, are expressions[403] and incarnations[404] of virtual Ideas.

More particularly, returning to Deleuze's 'order of reasons', following from virtual differentiation are the processes (or perhaps sub-processes) of 'individuation-dramatisation-differenciation' through which actualization happens.[405] Between differentiation (with two 't's) within the virtual and differenciation (with a 'c') into actuality, individuation and dramatization act as mediators. *Individuation* is an intermediary 'series of processes' (a 'cascade of actualizations') relating virtual Ideas and pure intensities to actual things[406] and so governing actualization and ensuring the 'embedding' of the 'two dissimilar halves' – the virtual and the actual.[407] Between differentiation and dramatization, individuation – as 'the act by which intensity determines differential relations to become actualized' – functions to determine 'the relations that it expresses . . . be incarnated in spatio-temporal dynamisms (dramatisation)'.[408] This process is 'essentially intensive'[409] with intensive individuations as replacing general classes of things.[410] In the process of individuation, intensive 'individuating factors'[411] and 'fields of individuation' express prior virtual differential relations and singularities[412] and are formed through the 'implication' and enveloping of these prior differential relations and pre-individual singularities.[413] In *A Thousand Plateaus*, Deleuze and Guattari describe individuations or 'modes of individuation' in terms of haecceities – as a node or rhizome of intersecting lines.[414] Intensive individuation determines and gives rise to differenciation – developing species and parts, qualities and extensities.[415] Individual beings are the outcome of such processes, becomings, individuations.[416] These individuals are multiplicities that then consist of 'populations of smaller scale individuals' and also populate larger scale individuals – 'and so on to infinity'.[417] Intensity, then, as 'a dimension of the idea, that which, within the idea, causes the virtual to pass into the actual',[418] determines actualization through individuation. Intensity develops and effects the passage, 'directs the course' from the virtual to the actual and this as an energy that explicates itself in qualities and extensive quantities; thus it 'determines the movement of actualisation' such that difference in intensity is 'the reason behind qualitative diversity'.[419] Intensity is implicated difference, implicating and enveloping multiplicities[420] and the relations of envelopment between intensities – with enveloped intensities within, filling the enveloping, and enveloping intensities expressing differential relations within.[421] This intensive process of individuation, then, is the 'first level' of actualization.[422]

Next in the 'order of reasons' in the process of actualization is *dramatization*. Intensity dramatizes the unconscious Idea – 'incarnating the differential relations and singularities of an Idea' – before it is expressed in thoughts and things.[423] Deleuze defines dramatization as the 'dynamisms, dynamic spatio-temporal determinations, that are pre-qualitative and pre-extensive, taking "place" in intensive systems'.[424] These spatio-temporal dynamisms are the actualizing, differenciating agencies, the 'dramas of Ideas'[425] operative within fields of individuation – presupposing and determined by a prior intensive field (distributed differences of intensity) – 'expressing simultaneously the resonance of the coupled series and the amplitude of the forced movement which exceeds them'.[426] Deleuze describes these spatio-temporal dynamisms as 'agitations of space, holes of time, pure syntheses of space, direction, and rhythms'.[427] These idea-dramatizing dynamisms then determine the arena of differenciation.[428]

Finally, *differenciation* is 'the production of finite engendered affirmations which bear upon the actual terms which occupy these places and positions, and upon the real relations which incubate these relations and these functions'.[429] Frequently used as synonymous with actualization,[430] the term differenciation (as opposed to the virtual differential relations of differentiation) is used to accentuate that actualization produces something (actual) that is not the same as and does not resemble that which it comes from, that which actualizes it (the virtual) – it is less copying

DELEUZE'S PHILOSOPHICAL SYSTEM 37

than creation.[431] Differenciation, a determinate actualization conditioned by the problematic field, has to do with the cases of solution to differentiated (two 't's) problems.[432] In this creative process of differenciation, intensity is explicated and explicates itself in qualities and extensities (which are differenciated)[433] – in actual or extensive forms or identities that mask, disguise or cancel difference in the form of intensities – such that the virtual is concealed in the actual.[434] In differenciation, the intensive order of implications, of individuation is actualized and passes into the extensive and qualitative order of explication.[435] Furthermore, differenciation happens through the agency of (dramatic) spatio-temporal dynamisms – dramatization, 'the differenciation of differenciation', 'differenciates the differenciation of the actual in its correspondence with the differentiation of the Idea'.[436] Regarding those determinations which constitute actual existence, Deleuze presents 'two correlative aspects of differentiation' – a 'double differenciation'.[437] First is the qualitative (or 'specific') differenciation in which the differential relations of the virtual Idea (through intensive individuation and dramatization) determine the qualities and form of the actual thought or thing. Second is the extensive (or 'organic') differenciation in which the singularities of the virtual Idea (again, through intensive individuation and dramatization) determine the parts, partition, matter and organization of the actual thought or thing.[438] Thus, differentiated virtual Ideas (through individuation and dramatization) are actualized, incarnated or differenciated[439] in(to) the extensities and qualities of actual thoughts and things.

2.2.6 The actual

The actual is made up of 'actual-individuals', of 'individual' entities – composed of smaller scale entities and composing larger scale entities[440] – the 'bodies, things, or objects that enter physical systems, organisms, and organizations'.[441] The virtual is actualized in *states of affairs*[442] that 'correspond' to but 'do not resemble' the virtual.[443] Transcendent actual things – qualitative, exterior and discontinuous multiplicities[444] with qualified and limited identities[445] – incarnate virtual Ideas.[446] Deleuze describes the present of bodies and states of affairs, the time of actualization, as 'the vast and deep present of Chronos'[447] that measures and situates things and persons in the present[448] (relative to a system of judgement[449]). Virtual surface events are actualized in states of affairs as the mixture and depth of bodies.[450] Virtual sense, at once, is the attribute of (occurring in) things or states of affairs[451] and is designated by (inhering/insisting in) propositions.[452] As Deleuze writes: 'On the side of the thing, there are physical qualities and real relations which constitute the state of affairs; there are also ideational logical attributes which indicate incorporeal events. And on the side of the proposition, there are names and adjectives which *denote* the state of affairs; and also there are verbs which *express* events or logical attributes.'[453]

On the way to describing the actual, Deleuze and Guattari (in *Anti-Oedipus* and *A Thousand Plateaus*) make a distinction between two broad kinds of multiplicities (rhizomatic or arborescent), exhibiting two different kinds of distribution (nomadic or sedentary) and yielding two different kinds of space (smooth or striated).[454] *Arborescent* multiplicities follow a tree or root structure – 'the most classical and well reflected, oldest, and weariest kind of thought'[455] – organized by the law of the One that sets the world on a pivot or axis, that divides from the One into a seeming multiplicity in submission to a center, as a circle around a 'central Point'.[456] In relation to this one point, there is a logic of opposition trading on binaries, dualisms and dichotomies.[457] This 'arborification of multiplicities'[458] then entails the 'tracing' and reproduction of a hierarchy[459] resulting in a closed and 'rigid segmentarity' – a 'network gridding the possible'.[460] The multiplicities of the *rhizome* type, however, are true heterogeneous multiplicities that are not subordinated to the One.[461] Such as multiplicity is a becoming,[462] a system of lines[463] in the middle (*intermezzi*)[464] connecting and decentering[465] and so forming open, 'uncertain' systems[466] of swarm, packs, bands.[467] So as to not set up yet another dualism, Deleuze and Guattari see how both kinds of multiplicities can both be operative, shifting into one another – with trees becoming rhizomes (escape) and rhizomes becoming trees (capture).[468]

Likewise, there are different kinds of distributions of space. A *sedentary* distribution marks, divides and closes off a distributed, fixed and rule-governed space.[469] Such a sedentary space is homogeneous, centered, *striated*[470] – walled off by limiting boundaries[471] – metric, counted, methodically pre-measured.[472] Deleuze and Guattari describe such sedentary space as biunivocalizing and thus 'reactionary' or even 'fascist'.[473] By contrast, nomadic multiplicities distribute themselves, filling an open space.[474] *Nomadic* space is a *smooth* space of rhizomatic multiplicities[475] – errant,[476] intermediate,[477] nomadic.[478] Like the rhizomatic and the arborescent, smooth space can become striated while striated space can become smoothed.[479] Deleuze (and Guattari) tend to see nomadic distributions and smooth space in terms of the virtual. Ideas, events, pre-individual singularities, problems and questions are all described as nomadic and/or occupying a smooth space.[480] The body without organs is envisioned as a smooth space filled with events, haecceities and intensities[481] – 'a field without conduits or channels' that is the site of becoming.[482]

Deleuze and Guattari present a parallel to Deleuze's virtual and actual in the distinction between what happens on 'the Body without Organs or the destratified Plane of Consistency' (and its absolute deterritorialization) on one hand, and 'the system of the strata' with its 'territorialities, relative deterritorializations and complementary reterritorializations' on the other – the virtual plane of consistency and the actual 'plane of organization'.[483] This actual system of the strata, the plane of the organization of territories is made by movements of *territorialization*, (relative) *deterritorialization* and *reterritorialization*. Territories or territorialities refer (as DeLanda, in his *Intensive Science and Virtual Philosophy*, writes) to 'the different extensities and qualities which characterize the actual world'.[484] In territories as the 'first assemblage' the vibration of intensities becomes a refrain, a rhythm that coagulates from a movement into a state[485] – 'There is a territory precisely when milieu components cease to be directional, becoming dimensional instead, when they cease to be functional to become expressive. There is a territory when the rhythm has expressiveness.'[486] In this territorialization, matter is captured, coded, segmented and organized[487] – stratified into strata, into 'forms and subjects, organs and functions'.[488] These territories are the product of sedentary distribution and division – marking distances and separating flows.[489] However, in any assemblage, any territory, there is a 'point of deterritorialization',[490] a line of flight, a 'movement by which "one" leaves the territory'.[491] Such a deterritorialization is a decoding, a breaking-down of subsisting codes,[492] and these deterritorialized or decoded flows[493] move as a positive molecular power[494] against molar organization.[495] These deterritorialized flows are then accompanied by reterritorialization 'as its flipside or complement' such 'that there is no deterritorialization without a special reterritorialization'.[496] These sedentary reterritorializations overcode the decoded flows.[497]

These 'territorialities, relative deterritorializations and complementary reterritorializations' form the 'system of the strata'.[498] Territorialization gives rise to the *strata*,[499] to the 'sedimentations, coagulations, foldings' that compose 'the plane of organization'.[500] This stratification is actualization with the strata being 'the different spheres which make up the actual world'.[501] These strata as 'phenomena of centering, unification, totalization, integration, hierarchization, and finalization' form what Deleuze and Guattari call the 'system of the judgement of God'.[502]

The three 'great' or 'principal' strata that concern human beings are *organization* or organism, *signification* and *subjectification*.[503] Beyond the actualization of simple things, biological organism organizes the body without organs with 'a pre-linguistic layer of meaning at the level of bodies'.[504] Signification concerns 'the production of chains of signifiers' that make up the structure of language[505] that grounds the 'determination of propositions and their assigned relations'.[506] Here the active syntheses of conscious thought, of memory and understanding, of representation are founded upon the virtual passive syntheses.[507] Finally, the strata of subjectivity, of our understanding of ourselves, is constructed through the process of subjectification or 'subjection'.[508]

2.3 Schizoid ethics: Escape and affirm

2.3.1 Escape

In the face of these majority territorializations and stratifications, of 'the system of the judgement of God', Deleuze and Guattari's revolutionary prescription, in part, is one of *escape*. We should work at discovering the transversals, the crossings of destratification as the other side of stratification, of deterritorialization as the other side of the territorial assemblage[509] – at 'discovering the immanent processes of decoding and deterritorialization at work in the production of strata, and intensifying their effects'.[510] As they write in *Anti-Oedipus*, 'a true politics of psychiatry, or antipsychiatry' is one of undoing all the reterritorializations and liberating the schizoid deterritorialization – deterritorialization with regard to which one can never go too far.[511] The schiz of the valorized schizoid here is the splitting, the pluralizing, of the multiple, of immanent difference. In this one instantiates, in the midst of, but escaping from, the majoritarian strata, a 'becoming-minoritarian' where 'there is no medium of becoming except as a deterritorialized variable of a minority'.[512] In this deterritorialization, one should run lines, 'extend the line of flight to the point where it becomes an abstract machine covering the entire plane of consistency' and so ascend or return to the virtual plane.[513] 'We're tired of trees', Deleuze and Guattari write, 'they've made us suffer too much.'[514] Instead, one should seek out and form rhizomes and their nonconformist 'adventitious growths'.[515] 'Make rhizomes, not roots, never plant! Don't sow, grow offshoots! Don't be one or multiple, be multiplicities! Run lines, never plot a point!'[516]

For Deleuze and Guattari, one should seek to escape the major strata. First (and foremost) this entails escaping *subjectification* – becoming 'inhuman'. In such a 'non-humanist philosophy' we are not, as Williams, in *Gilles Deleuze's* Difference and Repetition, writes, 'fixed selves or subjects. Underlying those identities are mobile individuals, set in motion by unidentifiable intensities'.[517] Beneath is a nomadic 'space of play' in which 'nothing pertains or belongs to any person, but all persons are arrayed here and there in such a manner as to cover the largest possible space' where 'the proper name is the instantaneous apprehension of a multiplicity'.[518] Modern autonomy's seeing the self as giving order and law – 'as the form and guarantee of identity'[519] – makes the subject an instance of transcendence,[520] and this humanism and 'subjectivism' for Deleuze, as Colebrook writes, is '*the* obstacle to thinking becoming'.[521] The self, for Deleuze, is grounded on something else;[522] subjectivity is a constituted effect, is 'subjected'.[523] The subject is made up of pre-individual singularities[524] such that everyone is a little group (*un groupuscule*) – as Deleuze and Guattari write, 'neither men nor women are clearly defined personalities, but rather vibrations, flows, schizzes, and "knots". The ego refers to personological co-ordinates'[525] These impersonal individuations – 'modes of individuation beyond those of things, persons, or subjects'[526] – are the multiplicities of the unconscious, impersonal and pre-individual transcendental field.[527] Self, then, is rooted in a process of 'universal primary production' (of desiring-machines)[528] such that 'the only subject', Deleuze and Guattari write, 'is desire itself on the body without organs, inasmuch as it machines partial objects and flows, selecting and cutting the one with the other, passing from one body to another, following connections and appropriations that each time destroy the factitious unity of a possessive or proprietary ego.'[529] The *subject*, as commonly understood, is rather a produced residuum,[530] on the periphery, decentered,[531] a dissolved self,[532] a fragmented, fractured, cracked I.[533] Deleuze and Guattari ('Why have we kept our own names? Out of habit, purely out of habit.'[534]) then take up the task of destroying or undoing the illusion of the ego, of 'tirelessly taking apart egos'[535] – to find the nomadic beneath the sedentary.[536] This entails a devaluation of consciousness as a reactive illusion,[537] as purely transitive, as a passage,[538] and seeing the image of thought as founded upon such an illusory unified self.[539] The self rather is a contemplation ('we exist only in contemplating'[540]), a habit ('the habit of saying I')[541] composed of many 'contemplative' and 'passive' selves, intensive souls,[542] larval subjects and passive syntheses.[543] Man is not, then, 'the king of creation, but rather ... the being who is in intimate contact with the profound life of all forms or all types of beings'.[544]

The reality of the subject is that of a kind of *schizophrenia*, and the task of Deleuze and Guattari's schizoanalysis is that of taking apart egos and liberating the prepersonal singularities,[545] the schizzes, the impersonal parts – 'of very different natures and speeds'[546]—the multiplicity, the crowd, the pack, the legion that is the self.[547] In this way, schizophrenia 'as a process' (not a 'clinical entity')[548] is the highest power of thought (opening onto difference),[549] revealing and putting us in contact with 'the beating heart of reality', with nature as a process of production.[550] This 'schizophrenia' is a process of desiring-production[551] – seeing the schizoid subject as a wandering[552] function of the decoded and deterritorialized flows on the body without organs.[553]

To escape subjectification is to become *inhuman*. Deleuze's anti-humanism[554] advocates a 'becoming-inhuman'[555] – in that 'humans are made exclusively of inhumanities'.[556] In bringing to the fore the pre-human dimensions of subjectivity,[557] desubjectification – the deterritorialization of subjectivity[558] – enables the discovery of 'other modes of consciousness beyond the confines of normalization'.[559] Such an 'a-subjective consciousness' opens our awareness to a non-individual life – 'the singular life immanent to a man who no longer has a name'.[560] This desubjectification is to become 'a becoming [that] lacks a subject distinct from itself', a becoming a part of the world that escapes from what keeps us from being in the midst of things.[561]

To escape the strata of *signification* is to think differently.[562] It is to escape thought purely in terms of identity[563] and to take on a new image of thought, to think difference, to think in terms of problems.[564] The '(asubjective) impersonal' is linked to the '(asignifying) indiscernible'.[565] Such an escape from signification engenders a nomad or minor science that thinks about things in terms of becoming, flows and heterogeneity, instead of a static system of reference.[566]

To escape the strata of subjectification, signification and organization entails a way of being politically, being a corporate body, being a multiplicity. Instead of a becoming-one, this escape from *organization* is a becoming-multiple – packs or multiplicities that 'continually transform themselves into each other, cross over into each other'[567] – rhizomatic, acentered, nomadic, anarchic multiplicities.[568] This is to free and follow rhizomatic (vs. arborescent) lines of flight[569] from within territorialities[570] – a deterritorialization 'by which "one" leaves the territory'[571] and escapes from segmentarity.[572] This escape is a becoming-minoritarian – from the majority's 'state of domination' and determination of identity.[573] This is a human destiny beyond the face – a life of 'strange true becomings' – a becoming-anorganic, a *becoming-imperceptible* – a returning to the plane of consistency, to the virtual.[574]

Before this seemingly radical escape from the strata, however, Deleuze and Guattari (following Spinoza[575]) advise *caution*. There can be the danger of a too-violent or too-sudden destratification that leads to empty Body without Organs, a suicidal state of 'chaos, the void and destruction'.[576] The 'art' of caution is needed to 'keep small rations' or 'supplies' of organism, significance and subjectivity, to enable one to 'respond to the dominant reality', to 'mimic the strata' and so stave off a 'demented or suicidal collapse'.[577]

2.3.2 Affirm

For Deleuze, to escape is relative, but to affirm is absolute. *Affirmation* is the broader positive frame. He writes: 'There is no

Good or Evil, but there is good and bad.'[578] Morality represents, for Deleuze, precisely the kind of thing that we need to escape from. Morality is our being dominated by, subjugated, subjected to moral ideals as transcendent values that stand over and against life – 'Morality is the judgment of God, the *system of Judgment*'.[579] Morality imposes obligation to a moral law – to 'the negative law, the extrinsic rule, and the transcendent ideal' – 'judging life in the name of a higher authority'.[580] Deleuze's ethics of affirmation, however, is not a morality, but 'a thought beyond good and evil'.[581] Such an ethics 'is a matter, on the contrary, of evaluating every being, every action and passion, even every value, in relation to the life which they involve'.[582] Endeavouring to think and act without hierarchy, it evaluates the good and the bad on the basis of the qualitative difference of immanent modes of existence.[583]

Seeking 'an entirely positive and creative mode of existence',[584] Deleuze presents *active* evaluation and affirmation of life as against all resentment and hatred of life – against the nihilistic judging and belittling of life.[585] This would be an active and affirmative way of being that is in accord with being's positivity – being's positive movement and differentiation where 'the negative expires at the gates of being'.[586]

The affirmation of difference, multiplicity and becoming (see 2.1.1.) in Deleuze's philosophy issues in an impulse to *affirm life* – to advocate 'the affirmation of life (its extreme valuation)'.[587] Taking our cue from Dionysus, the god who affirms life (as just),[588] we should at once affirm the goodness of life and have confidence in life, in 'the exigency of life'.[589] This affirmation and confidence in life issues in our own participation in life as constantly unfolding and creating through our own generous creation.[590]

Deleuze's ethics of affirmation affirms *chance* – 'the *all* of chance'.[591] Chance is affirmed as the innocent 'divine game', where there is no pre-existing rule – where it is 'a question of a throw of the dice, of the whole sky as open space and of throwing as the only rule' – and one wins necessarily by affirming the game.[592] To affirm chance is to will the event – to will to be worthy of what happens.[593] This is an orientation towards the future – the third and most fundamental synthesis of time – as the always-different unfolding of time.[594] One affirms the circle, the centrifugal wheel of the eternal return – the repetition of difference alone.[595] One affirms the eternal return – as the highest, the most intense thought[596] – as an affirmation of the multiple, different – so making repetition the very object of willing.[597] Deleuze's ethics of affirmation is also an ethics of positive *desire*. The logic of desire, for Deleuze and Guattari, is productive, creative, positive.[598] Desire does not arise out of lack but out of its own fullness – as they write: 'Desire is agape.'[599] This immanent desire that 'lacks nothing' is intrinsic, a spontaneous and revolutionary emergence issuing from itself 'without reference to any exterior agency'.[600] It is, Deleuze and Guattari write, 'as though desire were filled by itself and its contemplations'.[601] Desire is a rhizomatic moving and producing that makes connections with other desires, making a social field such that, here, *'there is only desire and the social, and nothing else'*.[602] Deleuze and Guattari's schizoanalysis then functions to help keep desire from desiring its own repression[603] and to liberate desire's own schizoid, multiplying productivity.[604] This, then, will unleash desire's revolutionary essence to cut against extrinsic, transcendent, hierarchical organization.[605]

The good life, for Deleuze, is that which entails the *creation* of new values, new possibilities of life.[606] Artistic becoming, coalescing with Deleuze's understanding of the will to power as essentially creative, is an operation of what he provocatively calls 'the power of the false' as the creation of truth[607] – such that 'there is no other truth than the creation of the New: creativity, emergence'.[608] Deleuze, in fact, presents the goodness of life in terms of such active, creative metamorphosis.[609] The *noble*, then, for Deleuze, is that which is able to transform itself – the generous good of the 'outpouring, ascending life' that 'allows itself to be exhausted by life' in creation.[610]

What is affirmed, what one strives to affirm, in Deleuze's ethics is the world. 'The modern fact is that we no longer believe in this world' – 'the link between man and the world is broken.'[611] In the face of this disconnection, of the alienating organization and stratification of our modern way of thinking, we must restore, have restored, our belief in the world.[612] We do not need to believe in another world; we need to come to believe in this world, in this life, in this body.[613] What must be restored to us, what needs to be saved, is not our eternal souls, but the 'flesh' of our bodies – we must believe in the body as 'the germ of life'.[614]

Finally, Deleuze's ethics is an ethics of joy. Following Spinoza, Deleuze sees joy as that the only worthwhile ethical practice open for human beings.[615] Speculative affirmation of the Dionysian world issues in a correlative ethics of joy – the critique of anything that would mortify life serves a 'cult of affirmation and joy' in and in the midst of the difference and becoming of life.[616] Joy as 'the affirmation of being in the moment of its practical constitution'[617] is immanent to desire – 'as though desire were filled by itself and its contemplations, a joy that implies no lack or impossibility and is not measured by pleasure since it is what distributes intensities of pleasure and prevents them from being suffused by anxiety, shame, and guilt'.[618] The immanent life that constitutes us and of which we partake is not lacking (there is nothing relative to which it falls short) – it is 'complete power, complete bliss';[619] the immanent joy of active creative power.[620]

PART TWO

Deleuze and Theology

3

Approaching Deleuze's theology and theological appropriations

3.1 Deleuze and theology?

'Deleuze', Philip Goodchild writes, 'would appear to be among those least concerned with religion in his own generation'.[1] Deleuze, as we saw in our introduction to his thought, has relatively little to say about theology or religion – so little that one can present a fairly complete depiction of the main lineaments of his philosophy without any substantial discussion of God. He is largely indifferent to religion – not as much anti-clerical as aclerical.[2] Deleuze's indifference to theological discourse as something simply irrelevant to his metaphysics[3] (as evident in Deleuze's summary dismissal of Ricoeur in an interview: 'Yes, but he is a Christian.'[4]) arose from a confident horizon of atheism, 'so confident', Barber writes, 'that it need not defend, much less name, itself'.[5] Our task of thinking of the 'and' of Deleuze and theology would seem prima facie to be either quite easy (they have nothing to do with each other) or more of a puzzle: how does one think about theology in relation to a thinker that would seem to not care less about God and religion?

When Deleuze does, on occasion, have something to say about God or religion or theology, he is usually quite negative. Sometimes he sees religion and God as standing in the way of the genuine practice of philosophy – such that god must be forgotten for philosophy to begin.[6] Deleuze can be seen as having, indeed, an 'anti-theology', seeing God as a kind of dam that needs to be burst, a fetter to be loosed in order for the 'nonorganic vitality' to emerge, to flow forth and for philosophy to play its part in the flow. Here Deleuze can be seen to be taking over Nietzsche's diagnosis of the stultifying disease of theism (as traditionally understood, anyway).[7] However, one feels little of the urgency of Nietzsche's condemnation of God and religion in Deleuze – it would seem that he sees the death of God and the need for liberation from the dead God to not be news. (Deleuze need not trouble himself to light a lantern in the bright morning hours and run to the marketplace.)

This said, Deleuze, is not necessarily dead-set against God or religion or theology in any form. As one would expect from someone with such high regard for thinkers such as Leibniz and Spinoza, Deleuze does not claim that philosophy is necessarily atheistic.[8] Indeed, the idea of God can function as 'a transcendental ideal which incites us to take thought beyond the limits of possible experience'[9] – the thought of God can make the world strange, as something like the opposite of God as the Archimedean point to make the world rationally tamed to the terms of human representation. As Deleuze writes in *The Logic of Sense*, one can remain an atheist and recover 'theology' as 'the science of nonexisting entities' as a 'structure' that 'animate[s] language'.[10]

In the chapters to follow, we will mine and present Deleuze's perspectives on topics related to theology. However, if we were to simply re-present 'Deleuze on Theology', we would be left with thin soup indeed. To think through the possible conjunction of Deleuze and theology more robustly, we will also examine the ways that theologians have appropriated Deleuze's thought. Deleuze's philosophy opens many potential positive or negative intersections (provocations, interventions, insurrections) with theology. Between philosophy and theology, one can imagine a continuum between a 'pure' secular philosophy (free of the contagion of theology) and a 'pure' confessional theology (free of the contagion of philosophy, one thinks of Tertullian). Between these two extremes are intermediate positions tending more towards one side or the other. More on the philosophy side, we could have the kind of philosophy of religion or philosophical theology or 'secular theology' that endeavours to think about God or religion or theology from a perspective outside of confessional theology, in some sense, and perhaps reconfiguring God or religion or theology in a more 'secular' mode. More on the theology side, we would have the kind of confessional theology and philosophical theology that uses the resources of philosophy within theology and develops a perspective on philosophy from a confessional perspective. Of the many intersections between Deleuze's philosophy and theology observed or enacted by recent theologians, I will present sets of some such insights that can be organized around two broad trajectories: a secular trajectory and a confessional trajectory. To approach things from a slightly different perspective, if Deleuze's philosophy is in a kind of fundamental opposition to confessional theology, the options for one trying to think between these two poles would seem to be: (1) a trajectory that would mediate between them by thinking through and reinterpreting the latter from the perspective of the former – Deleuzian theologies, perhaps – or (2) a trajectory that seeks to appropriate, respond to and critique the former from the perspective of the latter – to learn from and respond to Deleuze from the perspective of confessional theology. These two trajectories, it must be said, are something of a fractious middle such that I suspect that partisans of either trajectory may well find little palatable in the rival trajectory – each is likely to see the other as not being true either to Deleuze or to theology or to neither.

3.2 Deleuzian theologies: The secular trajectory

The secular trajectory of understanding the relation between theology and Deleuze's philosophy distinguishes itself from a confessional understanding of theology. A secular theology seeks to rattle 'inherently conservative' theologies beholden to confessional authorities.[11] Clayton Crockett presents the prospect of such a theology that 'is no longer restricted to apologetics in the service of dogmatics'[12] and can thus 'only appropriate . . . philosophical insights and critiques for the purposes of a pre-established Christian agenda'.[13] The violent and triumphalist stance of 'a more conventional theological discourse' demands 'the humiliation and debasement of philosophy before the Queen of the sciences, theology'[14] and then 'simply declares victory and believes that it can thereby dispense with any considerations of the secular' so stifling and restricting 'any authentic theologizing to the churches'.[15] Instead, in defiant opposition to such 'reactionary' discourses,[16] theologians such as Crockett advocate a radical and 'relentlessly honest' and open questioning that is liberated from the dogmatic assumption of immediate answers[17] and is 'detached from ecclesiastical or pastoral commitments and concerns. Radical theology'[18] follows something like Tillich's 'Protestant principle', 'which protests "against the identification of our ultimate concern with any creation of the church, including the biblical writings"'.[19]

This secular alternative presents a radical recasting of theology as a thinking of transcendence within immanence – a theology within, of and for the world, the saeculum – of and on the plane of immanence. Secular theology is an immanent theology.[20] Such a theology is also a constructive, creative, affirmative theology.[21] On the model of Deleuze and Guattari's creation of concepts, a secular theology takes its task as the creation of theological concepts that help us believe in this world and is otherwise free from any extrinsic justification[22] – such that 'what is justified, if anything, is the creation itself . . . beyond good and evil' – an experimenting on and with theological and religious materials.[23]

Secular theology presents itself as a radical theology, drawing inspiration from and continuing along the line of the American Radical Theology or Death of God Theology of the 1960s, reacting to and attacking a preceding (confessional) neo-orthodoxy.[24] Finding common cause in the work of 'restor[ing] our belief in the world, this world',[25] 'radical' theology, old and new, seeks the depth (*radix*, root) dimension that gives the religious meaning and makes all of life religious (secular). For Thomas J. J. Altizer, for example, we find religious meaning or the 'sacred' in the midst of the profane; in fact, it is by rejecting the sacred and passionately affirming the profane that one comes to receive the sacred.[26]

Such a secular or radical theology is 'a formal theology' (as opposed to 'a content-driven theology') that would 'free theological discourse to investigate other terms, other powers, other expressions';[27] indeed, even seeing, as does Barber, religion or God as naming in some sense creativity itself – as fictive and immanent names for 'the capacity of immanence to produce beyond all limits of propriety'.[28] A formal theology sees religion as a structure that refers to the best, most profound and most inclusive plane of the real, of human experience,[29] and so echoing, as Crockett notes, Tillich's theology of ultimate concern, his 'understanding of religion as the depth aspect of human spiritual life' – making theological discourse something 'that would not be recognized as anything other than philosophy for much of what passes for theology in current intellectual circles'.[30]

Along these lines, recent secular theologians have found Deleuze to be particularly useful for such a theological project – occupying something like the place Nietzsche held for the radical theologians of the 1960s (though it is hard to imagine 'God is a lobster' on the cover of *Time* magazine). This posture would be to situate oneself (variously) within Deleuze's thought and to think what God or theology could mean there – to find one's home in Deleuze's philosophy (to some degree) and to entertain theology on occasion, perhaps regularly, perhaps even inviting theology to move in. So, if the secular trajectory rejects confessional theology, it then re-appropriates 'theology' in terms meaningful for a secular context – here, Deleuze's world. One tack (of several) taken, is to argue that, contrary to the way things initially appear, Deleuze's philosophy is already theological or religious, just in a different sense[31] – a strange, unorthodox religiosity more in proximity to 'H. P. Lovecraft's Outsider abominations, via witchcraft, trickery, and all things unholy'[32] – and to then unpack, elaborate and advocate this Deleuzian way of being religious and/or thinking about God. It is taken as an 'axiom' that Deleuze's philosophy is 'a spiritual philosophy of a certain sort', 'at once a spiritual and political exercise, an exercise in the emancipation of life: it is a spiritual politics'[33] – seeing in Deleuze something akin to Pierre Hadot's understanding of philosophy as a spiritual exercise, a spiritual way or style of life.[34]

Beyond finding a religiousness within Deleuze, thinkers in what I am calling the secular trajectory have also worked to produce theologies informed by or based on Deleuze's philosophy.[35] This can be framed in terms of assisting a project, such as Philip Goodchild advocates, of a theology that coheres with an intrinsic relation between thought and life, a thought thrown into life[36] – a theology grounded entirely in the life of faith, as reconstituted in relation to certain modes of existence.[37] Such a theology is often framed in a more political mode, seeing the political potential of 'a theological materialism',[38] or examining (as in Kristien Justaert's thoughtful work) the possibility of using Deleuze's thought as a new alternative ('holistic and immanent') philosophical 'mediation for a postmodern liberation theology'.[39] This 'liberating' and 'mutating' of theological practice – a 'proliferation of heresies and experiments'[40] – looks to bring about a different conception of God that will yield another way of being in the world, another politics.[41]

3.3 Theological critique of Deleuze: The confessional trajectory I

3.3.1 Deleuze, theology, Gnosticism

Another trajectory would be to think about Deleuzian philosophy from the side of theology, more specifically from the perspective of confessional Christian theology. This trajectory would more of an Augustinian model than a Tertullianian model (that pagan philosophy only inspires heresy) – taking a critical but appreciative and, indeed, appropriative stance, open to learning from the rich insights that Deleuze has to offer. Generally my version of such a confessional appropriation of Deleuze draws from the work of figures such as Irenaeus, Thomas Aquinas, Søren Kierkegaard, Teilhard de Chardin, William Desmond, David Bentley Hart and John Milbank. On the critical side, I will argue that often the version of confessional theology that Deleuze (along with many of those following a secular trajectory) rejects is overly simplistic at best and cartoonish at worst. Put another way, the God and the Christianity that Deleuze (along with many of those following a secular trajectory) rejects are often pale shades, caricatures, counterfeit doubles that are worthy of rejection. As Jacob Sherman notes, what Deleuze rejects and is reacting against is poor, anemic theology, 'an already censured theology':[42]

> Part of this failure is no doubt due to the dismal state of so much theology in late modernity, not least in France during the middle of the last century. Exciting developments were afoot, but during Deleuze's formative period immediately after World

War II, bold new theological voices such M. D. Chenu, Maurice Blondel, Teilhard de Chardin, and Henri de Lubac were regularly under official censure and more or less unavailable to non-specialists. Inasmuch as Deleuze's encounter with theology was shaped by either the neo-Kantianism of the theological left, or the manual Thomism of the right, his rejection of transcendence is understandable.

It would seem that Deleuze, confessional theology and secular theology all have a common enemy in Gnosticism – at least as thought generally as privileging an alien transcendence over and against the immanent, the material and the bodily. While confessional theology has often (and often rightly) been tarred with the label of Gnosticism, Christianity is to be seen as, in David Bentley Hart's words, 'an evangel promising newness of life, and that in all abundance, preaching creation, divine incarnation, resurrection of the flesh, and the ultimate restoration of heavens and earth'.[43] We hope to show, however, that the opposite case has more traction; that is, the otherworldly paganism that Christianity developed in relation to (surely suffering from but also able to resist from its contagion) has strong echoes in Deleuze's thought. My strange intuition is that such a would-be world-affirming materialism as Deleuze's is in odd proximity to Gnosticism. Part of what is counter-intuitive about this critique is that what is most objectionable in Deleuze's work for the confessional theologian is not his atheistic materialism but the presence in his thought of elements of a Gnostic religious narrative that functions as a parody and an inversion of Christianity. While there are many definite resonances with my reading of Deleuze and that of Peter Hallward in his brilliant and controversial *Out of the this World: Deleuze and the Philosophy of Creation*, I see Deleuze's thought as more equivocal, plurivocal, even at odds with itself.[44] My conclusion regarding the persistent and pervasive gnostic themes in Deleuze comes in part (a smaller part) from a recognition of a plausible genealogical account of how this strain of thought could have come down to Deleuze (depending largely on the work of Christian Kerslake) and in (a larger) part from seeing the consistent structural similarities between Deleuze and Gnosticism (depending largely on the work of Cyril O'Regan).

3.3.2 Wronski, Warrain, Malfatti, Boehme

Thinking in terms of 'a somewhat speculative genealogy',[45] Deleuze stands in a certain relation to minor authors[46] such as Johann Malfatti de Montereggio (1775–1859), Hoëne Wronski (1776–1853) and Francis Warrain (1867–1940) who were key in the revival of the modern European esoteric, occult, 'heretical' tradition with ties to the Gnostic return in modernity.[47] Malfatti and Wronski were especially influential, indeed providing the 'theoretical foundations' for the French esoteric movement of Martinism, 'one of the main currents of occultism in the nineteenth-century'.[48] Today (as in Deleuze's time) Malfatti and Wronski 'remain almost unknown, and', Kerslake notes, 'Deleuze was unusual for referring to them at all'.[49]

Deleuze mentions Wronski in the context of his discussion of the 'esoteric' use of calculus in *Difference and Repetition*.[50] Beyond specific mention, it is evident that Deleuze 'ended up appealing to [Wronksi's] ideas to ground his philosophy of differentiation'[51] and his formulation of the distinction between the virtual and the actual echoes the manner in which, for Wronski, 'knowledge and Being are opposed as creation to inertia, as spontaneous calculation versus preservation and petrifaction. Given this context, we can imagine the creative principle and the preservative principle combining in a principle of transformation.'[52]

Francis Warrain – who 'published several major studies of Wronski, as well as editing the collection of papers by Wronski to which Deleuze refers in *Difference and Repetition*'[53] – expanded Wronski's thought towards a metaphysical vitalism that focused on the idea of a 'non-organic life' as having to do with the 'pulse of differentiation', of intense 'vibrations' (repeated differences).[54] Such a mathematical vitalism was also connected by Warrain to cabbalist mysticism, working towards a 'rational' (not revealed) religion in an esoteric mode.[55]

One of Deleuze's first publications (when he was twenty-one) was an introduction to a new edition of Johann Malfatti's *Mathesis: or Studies on the Anarchy and Hierarchy of Knowledge*, published 'by a small publishing house, "Griffon d'Or", which published books mostly on occult themes in the immediate aftermath of the war, including a number of books on Martinism'.[56] Malfatti's *Mathesis* combined esoteric mathematics with theosophical thought. Seeing theosophy as having its origins in Hindu mysticism, Malfatti (a heterodox physician) found an 'occult anatomy, in which the vital forces that rule the body were ordered hierarchically in polarities, potencies and planes'.[57] Malfatti and Wronski stand as central figures in nineteenth-century esoteric, occult, theosophical Martinism, which stands in a line of descent (focusing on an esoteric, secret tradition of 'initiates') originating with the ancients, passing through Jakob Boehme in modernity and revived in their own day.[58]

Mark Bonta observes the 'rather startling resonance' between Deleuze and Jakob Boehme. Boehme's vision of the divine as highly complex and radically anti-hierarchical, and of the world as a 'manifestation of a drama taking place in God himself' represent the kind of 'subterranean mystical currents' subject to the nineteenth-century occult revival to which Deleuze was indebted.[59] With Boehme – 'a highly plausible candidate for designating the alpha point of the genealogy of Gnostic return in modernity'[60] – we can see the revivification of a 'hidden, or heretical, tradition'[61] that mutated in the European occult tradition fostered by Malfatti, Wronski and Warrain. It is of this strange, esoteric teaching that one may hear something of 'the last, dying and frenzied echoes' in the equally strange work of Deleuze.[62]

3.3.3 Deleuze and Valentinian narrative grammar

David Bentley Hart characterizes the postmodern ethos as entailing an irreconcilable tension between 'pagan exuberance tempered by gnostic detachment', as represented by the (in Hart's words) 'outrageous juxtaposition of Deleuze and Levinas'[63] – a LeviNietzscheanism such as one finds in the later Jacques Derrida and John D. Caputo.[64] My suggestion is that Deleuze does not just stand at one pole of this (equivocal? schizoid?) tension – the 'two extremes constitut[ing] a difficult choice or a mad oscillation; between the pagan and the gnostic'[65] – but the tension is present in Deleuze's work as a whole. The strange part of this tension is the 'gnostic detachment'. Nonetheless, I will argue that Deleuze fits within the movement of a broader Gnostic return – a haunting, a return of a 'putatively dead discourse'[66] – in modernity.

For an understanding of this Gnostic return, I depend upon Cyril O'Regan's seminal work, *Gnostic Return in Modernity*[67] from which I trace an uncanny systematic coherence or isomorphism between Deleuze's thought and Gnosticism as presented by O'Regan.[68] O'Regan defines Gnosticism in terms of a Valentinian narrative grammar and the rule-governed deformation of classical Valentinian narrative genres. The Valentinian narrative grammar is 'an invariant sequence of episodes' in the story of 'the becoming of the perfection of the divine', of the loss and recovery of divine perfection.[69] This 'invariant sequence of episodes' mimics, doubles, 'transgressively interprets' the central episodes of the biblical narrative,[70] such that in this counterfeit doubling of Christianity counter-positions are held regarding 'the nature of the divine, the value of creation, the interpretation of the fall of human being, Christ and his redemptive mission, and finally the nature of salvation'.[71] The six narrative episodes of the Valentinian narrative grammar are:[72]

1 A realm of pure and undisturbed divine perfection, presumptively immune from change and narrative adventure.

2 The introduction of fault into the realm of divine perfection and the fall from the divine that is the fall *of* the divine and the emergence of the creative capacity that parodies the creator God of Genesis.

3 The positing of a source in and from the divine that reveals itself as non-divine and the emergence of evil as associated with the creation of the material and psychic world.

4 The fall of human 'pneumatic being' through a kind of forgetfulness.

5 The appearance of 'a redeemer figure who is associated with Jesus' and who delivers liberating knowledge apart from any saving activity of an atonement.

6 Salvation as 'the realization of a human perfection, associated with knowledge, and the full-scale reconstitution of divine perfection'.

The 'systematic deformations' of the classical Valentinian genre are the 'theogonic [regarding the origin of God/gods], pathetic, and world-affirming figuration[s]'.[73] Deleuze, we will suggest, echoes all six narrative episodes and two of the three common modern 'systematic deformations' of the Valentinian narrative grammar (the theogonic and the world-affirming). Deleuze's reversed Platonism ends up entailing something like a strange Gnosticism – without an arche, without a One – an orthodox heterodoxy in which, as Hart observes, the 'mirror preserves the image it inverts'.[74]

3.4 Theological appropriation of Deleuze: The confessional trajectory II

To think the 'and' of 'Deleuze and theology' from the side of theology, is (for us) to think from the perspective of the Christian confession or narrative as situated outside Deleuze's thought from within the concepts associated with the names and the historical particularities of the Christian tradition. The Christian confession or narrative is rooted in revelation, biblical revelation in particular,[75] such that a confessional philosophical theology is, as David Burrell argues, 'more properly a subdiscipline of theology, since it cannot hope to make any progress without attending to the religious traditions which animate its inquiry'[76] – because revelation opens new horizons such that philosophical concepts and categories must be taught new moves, stretched to fit 'a revelation whose affirmations exceed its proper reach'.[77] Whereas pagan philosophies saw the divine as representing persistent necessities, as 'part, the best and governing part, of nature',[78] the Christian understanding of the divine and of creation is something different, and is based on a more fundamental distinction that 'cannot be understood in terms of any action or any relationship that exists in the world'.[79]

Such faith in Christian revelation is axiomatic – as presenting something genuinely new it cannot be truly established by any prior premises.[80] Faith brings one into another world, another frame of what is possible.[81] Faith, as Thomas Aquinas sees it, gives us an access to things unseen, to things that are not believable to those who do not believe.[82] Reason in theology then follows after faith in the unseen and yet foundational truth of revelation.[83]

From such a confessional perspective, appropriating Deleuze's work (thinking of a conjunctive and not merely disjunctive 'and') is to take Deleuze's thought as a provocation to think through things again, to take up 'what belongs to another' without simply accepting or rejecting it.[84] Such appropriation seeks, as Merold Westphal observes, 'a middle way between the total rejection of the refusenik and the equally uncritical jumping on the bandwagon of this month's politically correct fad'.[85] How can Deleuze help us do theology better? In what helpful ways can the discourse of theology change as a result of what theology takes away from its dialogue with Deleuze?

Christianity has a long history of being constructively informed by pagan philosophical metaphysical visions – commonly from Greek philosophy in the West, but even including, on the margins of Christianity, Buddhist and Taoist philosophy in the East.[86] From the beginning, theology has worked with the help of philosophy – such that without philosophy as an 'astute' handmaid 'the fare which theology serves can be ill-chosen and underdone'.[87] Even the '*theos*' of 'theology' (like 'God' or 'Deus') is a name borrowed from pagan thought.[88] But this appropriating of philosophy is always transforming, reformulating, subverting – 'a doubly violent act' of rejection (distinguishing 'the wheat from the chaff' – discarding) and recontextualization.[89] This appropriation can be conceived as guided by a two-fold impulse to be true to the tradition and to be open to new ways of thinking that may help us think through our confession in a manner that makes sense in the context of the way we actually experience the world – in David Tracy's terms, to seek conceptions *adequate* to our experience of the world and *appropriate* to the tradition.[90] In this two-fold way, a theological appropriation of philosophy would function 'to extend philosophical patterns of analysis to allow the ensuing tradition its proper voice'.[91] Theology is served, often well-served, by philosophical concepts, but it also transforms these philosophical concepts relative to the new horizons opened by revelation.

Such a theological appropriation of Deleuze would lead us to think in a way that is not Deleuzian (as Deleuze and Christian theology have different axiomatic beginnings), but it is also not what Deleuze is wanting to avoid – that there is community that is not simply reducible to difference or unity, that the pilgrim that is not simply reducible to the nomadic or the sedentary, that the true one is one and many, that the true transcendent is transcendent and immanent, that the true eternity is eternal and becoming, that the true human is human and inhuman. There is something here of a Christian logic – as, in Hart's words, 'another grammar, an alternative rhetoric, a fuller vision, whose own inner rationality can argue for itself'.[92] This Christian logic (often distorted or recessed in the Christian tradition), as rooted in revealed doctrines of Trinity, Incarnation and Creation, is a fundamental structure of otherness in relation, of paradox and between-ness, of community (not simple unity or dispersal, but a 'unity' that always entails a togetherness of difference) over and against dualism or monism or nihilism – the false two, the false one, the false zero – or the false three of dialectic which reduces to the false two of dualism which reduces to the false one of monism which reduces to the false zero of nihilism. This logic (in the sense of Hegel's 'logic' as the deep structure of things) draws on the work of William Desmond who presents the metaxological sense of being as a 'three' other than the dialectical 'three' (as returning to 'one' after the 'two' of difference) which privileges the whole, the one over the infinite, transcendence, otherness.[93] Desmond proposes the metaxological as a 'transdialectical logos of the metaxu' (the between), where community, pluralized intermediation and 'being in relation' are held up to be the more universal and ultimate categories.[94] Against the dialectical return to the univocal, Desmond presents the metaxological as an affirmative equivocity.[95]

As we related in Chapter 1, Deleuze laid out what he considers tests for a useful philosophical work: 'I believe that a worthwhile book can be represented in three quick ways. A worthy book is written only if (1) you think that the books on the same or a related subject fall into a sort of general error (polemical function of a book); (2) you think that something essential about the subject has been forgotten (inventive function); (3) you consider that you are capable of creating a new concept (creative function).'[96] The encounter between a Christian theology – which too easily succumbs to sundry dualisms and onto-theologies – and Deleuze's philosophy may be worthwhile as at once spurring the retrieval of forgotten insights of the tradition (such as the 'logic' mentioned above in doctrines of God, Creation, Trinity, Incarnation, etc.) and holding forth the possibility of a new, or perhaps renewed vision, a different return, a non-identical repetition.

The remaining five chapters of Part Two move in something of a chiastic structure: from the divine life in terms of the immanence differential life of the divine (in Chapter 4) to the relation between transcendence, immanence and creation (in Chapter 5) to the understanding of the desiring nature and disorientation of human beings (in Chapter 6) to the relation between the divine and the human in the activity of a savior of sorts (in Chapter 7) to the nature of a human being's participation in the divine life (in Chapter 8). Each chapter follows the four parts of this chapter: (1) an exposition of Deleuze's own position on the topics under consideration; (2) a survey of theological appropriations of Deleuze's thought following the secular trajectory; (3) the critique of Deleuze's thought from a confessional theological perspective; and (4) a presentation of confessional theological appropriations of Deleuze's thought.

4

The Divine Life I: Difference, becoming and the Trinity

4.1 Deleuze's divine difference engine

There is no room for God, as traditionally understood, in the Deleuzian chaosmos.[1] There is in Deleuze's thought, however, another divine, a different absolute, an atheistic sense of the absolute.[2] Deleuze's absolute is absolute difference; difference is unknowable, inexplicable, 'transcendent', the sole transcendental.[3] In his pluralist monism there is only 'one' 'thing': difference – a 'many' that dissolves (and constructs) all 'things' – as Daniel Smith describes it: 'a kind of Spinozism minus substance, a purely modal or differential universe'.[4] This 'ontology of difference' as a continuous revolution against any static structures is an axiomatic fundamental ontology 'which fixes its gaze on difference as the condition of possibility for thought and action'.[5] With being itself (which is never itself) as difference, as a 'continuously differentiating force',[6] the univocity of being, what it is, is difference, equivocity.[7] What is primordial is the 'pure heterogeneity' of difference.[8] This is why Deleuze so naturally replaced univocity with the logic of 'and' in *A Thousand Plateaus*.[9] This absolute difference is not Hegelian negativity 'which', as Baugh writes, 'makes "difference" into a passing "moment" of Being "contradicting itself" via its multiple determinations in the "Absolute Idea"', but a logic of affirmative difference.[10] Difference itself as absolute is not subordinate to any unity, dialectical or otherwise. This difference, however, is not a mere abstraction; it is a life. Difference and life are fundamentally connected.[11] In Deleuze's 'peculiar theology of absolute immanence'[12] a kind of 'life' takes the place of "God" – the life of the immanent divine game/power/creativity. Instead of the fictional divine or 'God' as standing in opposition to life, as 'the means of depreciating life'[13] – against 'the transcendentalism of God's judgment', against God as a dominating will[14] – Deleuze's absolute or divine is an 'auto-generating' and 'totally unpredictable auto-creative force' or 'nonorganic vitality'.[15] Like Nietzsche's Dionysius as the 'god of indestructible life, ecstasy, joy, and power',[16] this 'indomitable will to live'[17] is the virtual non-psychological, nonorganic life of 'spirit' that 'grips the world'.[18] The virtual as 'the (non-)Being of difference', as 'the becoming of Being', is the life of the world, that from which the world lives – 'a kind of cosmic unconscious'.[19] Central to this virtual life is the dark precursor: a 'primitive' power that is unconscious, invisible, 'impenetrably dark'.[20] The dark (invisible) precursor is the virtual 'in itself' of difference that is 'at the origin of things'.[21]

The virtual, for Deleuze, is a creative power – the constant is the continual creation of the new, the different.[22] It is not entirely unlike process philosophy: being as creativity produces difference.[23] There is a power or energy immanent in matter,[24] a Dionysian 'will to power, a free and unbound energy'.[25] This divine difference engine – a deified or simply divine impersonal process of becoming[26] – presents 'the order of the Antichrist' in which 'the disjunction (difference, divergence, decentering) becomes as such an affirmative and affirmed power'.[27] The ultimate is a process of becoming without purpose, without end.[28] 'God, as the Being of beings', Deleuze writes, 'is replaced by the Baphomet, the "prince of all modifications", and himself modification of all modifications'.[29] Instead of God as lord, judge, tyrant, ruler – imposing rational order – the absolute is a divine game of chance with no pre-existing rule – 'a pure Idea of play'.[30]

4.2 Deleuzian theologies of life

Various theologies grouped around a secular trajectory present ways of thinking of divinity in terms of a vitalism, a force of creativity inherent in life itself. Taking the late 'Immanence: a Life' essay as a touchstone, Philip Goodchild sees in Deleuze a presentation of a fundamental, immanent life as transcendental field,[31] as the unconscious forces which shape what we think and do.[32] This immanent power of life[33] is not a 'One' as much as a complex underlying cosmic network[34] – as Catherine Keller writes, 'the ecosocial web of all life', the 'self-organizing complexities by which life comes forth'.[35] Anthony Paul Smith sees in Deleuze the possibility of conceiving of divinity in terms of 'the creative energies of the universe', echoing Bergson's understanding of the 'very process that is living, immanent and indefinite within life' and of the dynamic religion that 'opens itself up to the flow of nature and flows with it'.[36] Such a Deleuzian divinity is a generative power of affirmation and creativity immanent to life itself naming 'the capacity of immanence to produce beyond all limits of propriety'[37] – 'an infinite creativity', as Anthony Paul Smith writes, such that 'our creativity is thus like a divinity within us'.[38]

This more fundamental life is the collection of unconscious forces, the sources of life, which shape what we are think and do.[39] Clayton Crockett presents the possibility of seeing 'God' as being this sublime unconscious.[40] The more fundamental Deleuzian unconscious divine life from which we live, as Clark observes, is 'profoundly schizoid',[41] such that the divine is understood as 'the Divine Schizophrenic',[42] the One that is many, and to think of the divine in this mode is 'a distinctly postmodern avatar of polytheism: a vision of multiple "little divinities" effecting random syntheses of differential elements within an immanent space of possibilities'.[43] The plural 'dark' 'divine elements' that make up 'the Divine Schizophrenic' present us with a God that is 'impenetrably dark'[44] – unrecognizable, 'as one of H. P. Lovecraft's Outsider abominations'.[45]

Against a reductionistic 'dominological Christianity' that would 'evict us from the world', Catherine Keller in her *Face of the Deep: A Theology of Becoming* presents the divine of a 'tehomic theology' as the depth of the world – the deep, the tehom, chaos, a 'tehomic infinite', an open infinity.[46] This tehom is echoed in Deleuze's *Ungrund* as 'the place of all relations, all virtualities', which Deleuze 'freely translates this bottomless place of places as "chaos"'.[47] Such a deep chaos is 'not an undifferentiated chaos, but a chaos from which difference unfolds a cosmos'.[48] It is 'an alternative order', an 'originary indeterminacy' that generates the organization of the world, from which order emerges.[49] Such a divine, chaotic depth is not other to the world but the world's 'radically anti-hierarchical' self-origination.[50]

As an 'explicitly anti-theological' philosophy of nature (where the 'theological' is here understood in terms of a transcendent God),[51] Deleuze's immanent God/divinity names the 'surplus of immanence', its capacity 'to produce beyond all limits of propriety',[52] Spinoza's God,[53] 'nature naturing', nature itself (*Deus sive natura*) as 'a site of production, metamorphosis, creation'.[54] Deleuze thus funds 'a poststructuralist process theology' where, as Keller writes, 'relationality as a beginningless process . . . an unoriginated and endless process of becoming'[55] is 'a becoming God' – the tehom as process – that makes 'God' 'possible for the anti-theist Deleuze'.[56] Such a 'becoming God' as the becoming depth of nature is not a fundamentally singular 'God', but rather an 'elohimic multiple', an originating beginning as difference, 'a multiplicity of differences-in-relation, a multiplicity that as such is the relational, might even thaw open the logic of the Christian trinity'.[57] This kind of understanding of God as multiple and becoming also has potential for a postmodern liberation theology, as Kristien Justaert observes, with liberation theology's emphasis on constructed, plural, fluid identities.[58]

Finally, a Deleuzian divine is presented as an immanent power of life[59] – 'a power', Justaert writes, 'that runs through every being' such that our life is an expression of a Life, of Being, that can be understood as God.[60] Thus Crockett proposes thinking of God in terms of *'potentia'* (as enabling, creative power) instead of *postestas* (as dominating, coercive power)[61] such that 'God' names 'the virtual *potentia*', the virtual power that exceeds all actual power 'even as it gives rise to it'.[62] Here Deleuze's 'pure implex' – his potentiality, 'the virtual' – is the matrix of 'difference itself', 'a heterogeneous and thus differential depth'.[63] As Daniel Barber writes, 'God here names an unconditioned power', the world's own 'infinite power of existing' 'that exceeds its given expression' – the virtual expressed in and yet exceeding the actual.[64] That which is 'simply the immeasurable itself', as Anthony Paul Smith writes, is 'the [virtual] constitutive power underneath the [actual] organization of power'.[65] The divine life, the divine energy, the pure dynamism that is the affirmative force or power of repetition and differentiation[66] is the life that expresses itself in individuals,[67] the unthinkable underlying modes of existence,[68] the deep source of the events that happen to us.[69]

4.3 Virtual life and the dark pleroma

The notion of the virtual as a power of which the actual world of our experience is an expression displays the connection between the virtual and 'virtue' in the sense of power – as Hallward notes, 'the older, now archaic meaning of the word, which relates it to the possession of inherent virtues or powers'.[70] This can be seen against the background of a genealogy tracing from late medieval voluntarism (focusing on Divine will and power as 'the only explanation for the way things are'[71]) to the modern focus on the autonomous power and will of the human person to the late modern focus on a thoroughly inhuman impersonal power beneath the human person – such that we, as William Desmond writes, 'participate in living in an organic nature alive with a darker, sublimer energy'.[72] One thinks of Schopenhauer, but also of Spinoza, Bergson and Nietzsche. (I imagine the descent of mad power from the heavens to the proud mortals to the darkly rumbling earth itself beneath them.) As with Wronski's 'creative virtuality' proper to the Absolute as a 'continuous self-differentiation of creative becoming', Deleuze's virtual is a fundamental autogenic power,[73] such that, as Hallward writes, 'existent individuals are simply so many divergent facets of one and the same creative force' or power.[74] This fundamental movement of power is the divine game; 'that is, the game of unqualified creation as such, behind which there lies only the pure potential of absolute constituent power or play'.[75]

Deleuze's thought can be presented as a kind of pantheism, emphasizing the becoming of the divine as, in Desmond's terms, an erotic origin, a divine self-origination, 'self-determining eternity that determines itself in its own temporal productions'.[76] Such a 'dialectical monism', as Desmond tells the story, is a version of human self-determining self-transcendence.[77] Reflecting, as

Hallward observes, 'the notion that the universe and all it contains is a facet of a singular and absolute creative power', Deleuze 'annuls the difference between God and world . . . in favour of God, not world';[78] that is, instead of installing a dualism between God and the world, Deleuze sees the world as a function of God, or the divine power or game: 'dualism is therefore only a moment, which must lead to the re-formation of a monism'.[79] Here Deleuze's philosophy generally parallels Boehme's theosophy in which 'the course of the world', Kerslake writes, is 'understood as the manifestation of a drama taking place in God himself'.[80] In this Deleuze follows the general thrust of the Gnostic narrative of 'the becoming of the perfection of the divine'.[81]

Seeing difference in itself as the divine, unknowable, 'transcendent', inexplicable – a difference that 'withdraws from thinkability'[82] – Deleuze represents, for David Bentley Hart, a postmodern 'narrative of the sublime' for which the unrepresentable (here difference itself) *is* and is more true than the representable.[83] The visible world is the effect of an invisible potential.[84] Here, as Milbank writes, the 'ungrounded "mythical" content of difference', Deleuze's positive difference as the sole transcendental, is 'the "original" and continuous variation of a primordial "unity"' as 'always, endlessly, "other" to itself'.[85] Reflecting modern Gnosticism's different understanding of difference in the absolute as a change 'in the meaning and function of the Trinity',[86] Deleuze's fundamental reality is a deified 'non-relational difference' – a self-differing power, 'a differing [that] differs itself by itself'.[87] With such an absolute, Hallward observes, 'there can be no "substantial" difference between a purely self-differing unity and a purely self-scattering multiplicity, since in either case there is no place for any relational conception of "self"'.[88]

The Deleuzian divine is a God rendered unrecognizable,[89] in Desmond's terms, a dark origin. Behind Nietzsche's Dionysius, 'the system behind Nietzsche's anti-system',[90] is Schopenhauer's Will – a 'dark self-expressing energy', a dark origin, 'out of which all comes to be and into which all things pass, as into an ultimately inarticulate night' – with which 'there is no point to its striving beyond itself', the apotheosis of the autonomous self into a blind Will at the root of the world.[91] Likewise, Deleuze's axiomatic decision to think difference is a decision for that which 'overreaches thought', which is invisible, imperceptible, immeasurable, which is not thinkable.[92] The will to power in Deleuze as the power of difference itself is indeed a reversed Platonism, with the absolute not as the sun in the sky above, but as that under the ground of the cave – for, Desmond writes, 'Will is no sun, is no good, but a dark original, darker even than the shadow land of representation'.[93] Such a dark divine, 'a dark origin more primordial than the half-light half-darkness of the Cave', is more like Lovecraft's Cthulhu – a madness underneath our shadowy sanities – for in this reversal 'the good God has flipped into its opposite and shows a face more like the evil genius disporting with itself'.[94] The Deleuzian 'One', then, is a chaotic 'One' – a fecund Chaos that 'stands in the place of the One', an eternal becoming that stands in the place of an eternal unity.[95] Instead of a transcendent divine will violently imposing order upon the world, Deleuze's is an essentially chaotic, problematic, agonistic, 'violent' will or power.[96] This, in Desmond's terms, accords with Gnosticism's own 'immanent divine agonistics' as 'an equivocal agon both within the divine as such'.[97]

The first narrative episode of O'Regan's Valentinian narrative grammar presents 'the fullness of the divine as both the alpha and the omega of a drama in which the aboriginal integrity of the divine is lost and regained'.[98] Deleuzian life as virtual difference follows the pattern of this becoming divinity. Life in the Gnostic Valentinian narrative grammar 'is ascribable to the pleroma and is a property of any being who participates in it', such that the 'extrapleromic realm is the realm of death'.[99] The divine life in Deleuze, likewise, is not as much one being as a domain of being, difference itself, a dark pleroma.

For Deleuze, after Wronski and Warrain, life itself is internally plural, dynamic, problematic, differential – such that life itself as difference itself is the 'vibration', the 'ultimately non-organic pulse of differentiation' of a virtual 'transcendental calculus'.[100] 'The endless, goalless, production of Difference', for Deleuze, is a fundamental plurality of 'innumerable forces at play' – 'multiple "little divinities" effecting random syntheses of differential elements'.[101] The divine life, for Deleuze, is a virtual movement of being in itself as an 'infinitely powerful' creativity.[102] The internally multiple 'One', the Deleuzian dark pleroma, is virtual difference itself becoming itself in its own creative generation.[103]

4.4 The Trinity and eternal dynamism

In the Christian doctrine of God, in particular, of God as Trinity, one can find an alternative axiomatic mythos regarding the fundamental place of difference – a different ontology, to be sure, but one with the potential to resonate with and attend to Deleuze's radical provocation to think difference in itself.[104] With the doctrine of the Trinity, we are speaking of 'a profound mystery', as Herbert McCabe writes, 'which we could not hope to know apart from divine revelation'.[105] In Christianity, we are given something like a perspective on the inner life of God, of the '"interpersonal" life within the One'.[106] While the Trinity is revealed to us to a degree, the strange and obviously metaphorical language of Father, Son and Holy Spirit reminds us that, however revealed, we are a long way from getting a handle on the interior life of God – as McCabe writes, it is 'sometimes safer to use clothes that are quite obviously second-hand'.[107]

The Trinity as 'the Christian multiple' as 'an absolute that is itself difference',[108] names 'divine difference', gives 'the trinitarian name of difference'.[109] David Bentley Hart and John Milbank have recently presented the Trinity as an alternative understandings of the ultimacy of difference.[110] In God is an Ur-space, an Ur-time – 'divine differentiation' of 'original distance' and 'primordial displacement'.[111] Christian difference here is not between the infinite One and the finite, plural world, but as itself the infinite 'One' – God is eternally difference and relation, otherness and relation in Himself. Difference is not the product of the origin, but is itself at the origin – as at the beginning of the Gospel of John: the Word was 'with' and 'was' God before all things were made.[112] This difference is not a 'Plotinian descent from unity to plurality', but 'God's perichoresis as unity and difference', as 'situating the infinite emanations of difference within the Godhead itself'.[113] Difference is not a fall from the divine unity, difference is 'at the origin and is the origin', such that 'created difference "corresponds" to God, is analogous to the divine life, precisely in differing from God' – it is, in its very difference, an expression of divine differentiation.[114] Here there are unrecognised affinities between Deleuze's pursuit of difference and Christian theology.[115] 'God', Hart writes, 'is God in supplementation, repetition, variation; and yet the one God'. Thus, 'there is nothing theologically objectionable in, say, Deleuze's desire to speak of difference first and last, or his repeated insistence that there is nothing more "true" than difference'.[116] William Desmond, in his *God and the Between*, sees the ultimate in terms of difference-in-relation – not a mediation that reduces the many to one, but an intermediation as the ultimate.[117] The only 'One' is properly a Between, a Community, a metaxological community – an intermediation 'within the divine' as 'intimately immanent and immanently other, and these all "all at once"' – such that 'if it has a "unity", [it] would be more like a community: manifestation of agapeic love of the plural as plural'.[118] The 'immanent intermediation of Godhead' as a 'social' procession of love is at once personal – for 'to be personal is to be in social relations' – and 'transpersonal' as a community of Persons.[119] With the Christian understanding of the Trinity, relationality takes a central place in a metaphysic informed by orthodox Christian theology. The relational, the between, the 'immanently communicative', instead of the whole (in Desmond's terms, an open whole instead of a closed whole), plays the role of a transcendental principle.[120] For Thomas, the Persons of the Trinity are themselves real, substantive or subsisting (not merely conceptual) relations – though this, as McCabe writes, is something 'mysterious to us; we do not know what it would mean or what it would be like' – our essentialist impulse is to see things as primary and relations as secondary.[121] Thus, as Milbank writes, 'as much as Deleuze, Christianity places in the arche (the Trinity) a multiple which is not set dialectically over against the one, but itself manifests unity'.[122] With the understanding of the Triune God as difference-in-relation, as a between, as a metaxological community, one can see why Hart would observe 'that Christian thought has no metaphysics of the one and the many, the same and the different, because that is a polarity that has no place in the Christian narrative'[123] – we run into paradox, 'the one is many'/'the many are one' for we do not truly understand oneness/unity or manyness/difference/plurality but that they are revealed to us in the Trinity (as in Kierkegaard's *Philosophical Fragments*, where we do not know what God and humans are but that they are revealed to us in Christ). 'Christianity', Hart concludes, 'has no tale to tell of a division or distinction within being between a transcendental unity and a material multiplicity . . . but knows only differentiation and the music of unity, the infinite music of the three persons giving and receiving and giving anew'.[124] The Trinity is a community, 'difference in harmony', 'an infinite differentiation that is also a harmony'.[125] The Trinitarian God as ultimate is not a static, dead eternity. What is eternal, what is changeless, is an original dynamism – not entirely unlike Deleuze's understanding of the eternal return. With an understanding of 'the dynamic God', of 'the dynamism and differentiation that God is',[126] we can affirm with Kierkegaard's pseudonyms that "Eternity is the true repetition" – what is the same, what returns, is an ultimate dynamism.[127] It is a 'peculiarity of trinitarian thought' that God's being or *ousia*, as Hart notes, is 'always determined, by the perichoretic dynamism of the Trinity, as ousia in transit'.[128] In God there is 'no stillness prior to relation'.[129] This eternal movement of the Trinity is a motion of giving and receiving,[130] of 'the divine persons who have being as that gift that passes from each to the other', 'the perpetual handing over in love of all that the Father is to the Son and Spirit, and the perpetual restoration of this gift'.[131] In this 'infinite flow of excessive charitable difference', God is understood as *perichoresis* – 'the God whose life of reciprocal "giving way" and "containing" (*chorein*) is also a kind of "dancing" (*choreuien*), and the God who is *terpsichoros*, delighting in the dance'.[132] Thomas describes the essence of God – not as a property or a 'super-essence' – in terms of action.[133] God's being, his 'to be', *esse*, is conceived 'on the analogy of activity' as a 'pure act'; indeed, the 'act which is the source of all activity'.[134] The being of the Trinity is less understood as a static being than as a dynamic living, as life itself.[135] The 'termless dynamism' of the Trinitarian divine life, as the 'substance' of God that gives being and life to the world,[136] has a certain proximity to Deleuze's thought of 'the powerful, non-organic Life which grips the world' as 'a flow of differing difference' that is the 'unconditioned' foundation and the 'hidden ground' of movement.[137]

The dynamic divine life of the Trinity is supremely characterized as love. God is, in Desmond's terms, an 'agapeic community' – for Thomas, a communicating friendship, an 'adult love' of equals – in Hart, 'eros and agape at once: a desire for the other that delights in the distance of otherness'.[138] The 'gratuitous donation' of love is the binding (com-) and unitive (-unity) force of the metaxological divine community.[139] Trinitarian dwelling together in difference is characterized by porosity, intimacy, embracing, letting be, opening onto - a *perichoresis* or *circumincessio* as 'perfect indwelling, reciprocal "containment", transparency, recurrence, and absolute "giving way"' – a coinherence across 'the interval of appraisal, address, recognition, and pleasure'.[140] The 'motion of divine love', Hart writes, is the 'divine difference, a shared giving and receiving that is the divine life', a 'primordial generosity' as a genuinely productive desire, that does not arise from lack, 'that requires no pathos to evoke it'.[141]

In this vein, the changelessness of the dynamic Trinitarian God is, as Kierkegaard states it, 'changeless in love', an 'eternal love'. What is changeless is the constancy, faithfulness and stability of the original dynamism, the eternal true repetition.[142] The changelessness of God is the constancy of the movement of divine love – 'what stands with (con-stans), rather than what stands under (sub-stans)'.[143] As infinite 'non-identical repetition', God is less substance than 'the infinite play of active . . . self-deriving habit'.[144] The fullness of God, for Desmond, is an infinite reserve – a transcendence completely at home with itself[145] – not lacking, not in need of creation for completion. 'The Trinity', Hart writes, 'is already infinitely sufficient, infinitely "diverse", infinitely at peace' such that 'the "eternal dynamism" of God's immutability, apatheia, and perfect fullness'.[146] Difference and motion for the ultimate is not in terms of opposition, is not negative. God is neither the stasis nor the change that we would commonly understand as defined in opposition to each other, but a changeless, eternally constant movement.[147] God is neither the one nor the many in the way we would commonly understand them, but the one that is three, the different community. To think the aseity of God on the model of eternal return, of repetition, to think the oneness, the community of God as attentive to the thought of difference itself – can we here begin to think of the Triune God as inherent dynamism?

5
Creation, transcendence, immanence

5.1 Deleuze being done with the judgement of God: Immanence over transcendence

Deleuze's atheism announces the death of the transcendent creator God and the hierarchical system of 'exclusionary force' He entails. God's transcendence guarantees 'the limitative order of the world' – 'a centred universe, a fixed hierarchical order, and a substance that is outside of an immanent becoming or evolution'.[1] Deleuze's negative regard for the transcendent God of traditional theology – arising from a commitment to immanence and to avoiding 'the pernicious infiltration' of theology into properly atheistic philosophical thought[2] – is crystallized in his opposition to the judgement of God, the system of God and its organization.

As Protevi writes: 'God has been called many things, but perhaps nothing so strange as the name "Lobster" which he receives in *A Thousand Plateaus*.'[3] What is meant by 'God' for Deleuze commonly entails judgement and organization.[4] As Deleuze and Guattari write:[5]

> The judgment of God, the system of the judgment of God, the theological system, is precisely the operation of He who makes

an organism, an organization of organs called the organism, because He cannot bear the BwO, because He pursues it and rips in apart so He can be first, and have the organism be first.

God, for Deleuze, is a judge that sorts and imposes order, the master organizer 'organizing forms and substances, codes and milieus, and rhythms'[6] – pressing things into conformity, forming strata, a creature fixated around the function of its powerful pinching claws or pincers. A 'guarantor God' produces the divine system as underwriting it and guaranteeing identity within it (holding it together, pincer-like)[7] such that God, 'the immobile organizer of the bricks and of their infinite circuit',[8] *functions to serve order*; 'theology', Deleuze writes, 'is always founded on a teleology (and not the other way round)'.[9] This can be seen most clearly, for Deleuze, in reference to morality 'which always refers existence to transcendent values. Morality is the judgment of God, the *system of Judgment.*'[10] God functions to underwrite a state of infinite debt and man's own self-punishment.[11]

With such an understanding of God as judge and tyrant, one can see why Deleuze might seek 'to be done with the judgement of God' and the horse it rode in on, and anything that has to do with it – any transcendent authority (God as judge), stability (God's law) or persons (as subjects of this law).[12] The God Deleuze is done with – God as dominating tyrant, a voluntarist God, not unlike the Demiurge of Gnosticism – who 'shout[s] at us' from on high 'promising eternal punishment' – is the transcendence, the 'imperial State in the sky or on earth', that would judge the many 'in the name of a higher authority', in terms of 'transcendent values by which they could be compared, selected, and judged relative to one another'.[13] The order of God sets up boundaries, enclosures, organization, stratification – 'the entire system of the judgment of God'[14] – establishes 'the theological body' or 'the body-as-organism' with the transcendent God (as other to the body he forms) as founding, securing, guaranteeing,[15] 'the Christian *simplificatio*' reducing the many to one.[16]

Against the transcendent God as sharply controlling immanence and maintaining stability, identity and order,[17] Deleuze opts for the chaotic life of the immanent divine game/power/creativity, a 'pure ontology' with *'nothing beyond or outside or superior to Being'*[18] – not operating in terms of transcendent judgement but of immanent evaluation in terms of that which is 'increasing the power to live, always opening new "possibilities"' with no 'criteria other than the tenor of existence, the intensification of life'.[19] The transcendent God and the order He underwrites (and presses together with his cosmic-grade pincers) is ultimately itself a function of something immanent, of the human mind's desire 'to reach a position of transcendence vis-à-vis Being in order to be able to dominate it'.[20] Such a God is, as Protevi writes, 'a transcendental illusion produced by an immanent process'.[21] 'The fiction', Deleuze writes, 'of a super-sensible world in opposition to this world, the fiction of a God in contradiction to life', of 'the divine in which life is opposed to life', such a transcendent 'supreme Being' leads to the 'depreciating life'.[22] Deleuze combats this illusion in the name of an 'indomitable will to live', of the 'rebirth of immanence', of a renewed belief in the world.[23] Such an immanent 'life' is put in the place of such a transcendent 'God'.

Entailed in this axiomatic decision for immanence is a decision for and understanding of being as univocal, 'as the basis', writes Hallward, 'and medium for a primordial and unlimited differentiation'.[24] As the dualism or equivocity implied by transcendence supports the hierarchical organization of the world from on high, so does the univocity of being cohere with anti-hierarchical, immanent difference.[25] As Deleuze states in his 1973–4 course lectures: 'those who are between the two [univocity and equivocity] are always those who establish what we call orthodoxy'; speaking of Thomas: 'historically he won'.[26] Analogy – that 'has always been a theological vision, not a philosophical one'[27] – entails an equivocity regarding God: that 'He is not, which means: He is superior to being'; that he is not and he is, 'is' is used in different senses.[28] 'Being', for the theologically orthodox, 'is not univocal because it's scandal; to claim that being is said in one and the same sense of God and of the flea is a terrible thing, we must burn people like that.'[29] Deleuze's critique of analogy is that it is lukewarm, trying to have it both ways: having both the intelligibility of the univocal and the transcendence of God that the equivocal would afford.[30] Deleuze's suspicion is that the equivocity of the analogical serves to secure a more fundamental unity and sameness: 'Univocity signifies that being itself is univocal, while that of which it is said is equivocal, precisely the opposite of analogy'.[31] 'Transcendence', writes Deleuze, 'is preserved by drawing on all the resources of symbolism', and this indirection – maintaining an inexpressibility of the transcendent – is a dissembling equivocation and mystification.[32]

5.2 Deleuzian theologies of immanence

Various theologians and philosophers of religion follow Deleuze's impulse towards an immanent, anti-hierarchical, anti-organizational ontology, seeking a theology of immanence.[33] They explore the possibility of seeing 'Deleuze's atheist philosophy of immanence', his immanent ontology as providing an alternative site to think about God,[34] perhaps to even see 'a religious character of Deleuze's immanence'.[35] Transcendence has alienated us from world – making us able to judge and measure the world in terms of truth or goodness but rendering us 'incapable of believing in this world' for 'as long as we believe in another or better world, we fail to be affected by the world'.[36] What's more, we are better off to give up 'the pretension of a God's eye point of view or transcendent rule' in order to see that it is impossible to have knowledge of what is truly transcendent and that 'all discussions of transcendence must at least be referenced on the plane of immanence, which is the minimum consistency necessary to constitute a shared world of intersubjective experience'.[37] Alternately, if there is a transcendence it is redefined, as Kristien Justaert suggests, as a 'transcendence within immanence' – a transcendence that is the product, a secondary phenomena, of immanence.[38] Transcendence is 'that part within Being that keeps escaping our comprehension'.[39]

A Deleuzian theology of immanence attends to Deleuze's plea for immanence and provides 'an alternative "topos" to think the divine and salvation'.[40] A radical theological thinking as fully immanent would regard this world as something 'independent of any comparison', such that the task of such a theology would be that of 'explicating and implicating the unconditioned power of immanence'.[41]

Deleuze's 'immanent God', as Faber writes, is the immanence of nature naturing – 'the infinite, univocal, affirmative, and self-differentiating essence of God – according to Spinoza, *Deus sive natura naturans*'.[42] In this way, a Deleuzian anti-theology (in the sense of a transcendent God) is 'a "true" *liberation* theology' occupying the affirmative order of Baphomet against the order of judgement, the great chain of being.[43] Against the divine as a 'higher plane or a higher power' from which 'order, harmony and obedience' are imposed, as securing a great chain of Being, a hierarchically ordered universe – against God as 'the supreme principle of philosophical intelligibility'[44] – a Deleuzian theology of immanence would endeavour to be true to a univocity of being in which being 'is equally and immediately present in all beings, without mediation or intermediary' without hierarchy[45] and would so seek to 'unhinge life – the world as it is, or as it becomes – from the transcendent coordinates of the true-good'.[46] Such a theology would resist a transcendent 'theology of dominance' in favour of an 'an infinite intimacy', of 'God' as a 'virtual *potentia*' that encourages and does not constrain us to go to the limit of what we can do.[47] Catherine Keller in her thoughtful and provocative *Face of the Deep* advocates a kind of 'poststructuralist process theology',[48] in which the divine immanence is presented as 'the deep', as a (re)generative, creative and chaotic matrix of possibilities,[49] as the 'divine sea', the process of becoming, 'the godness, *"in" whom unfolds* the universe'.[50]

The immanent God, like Deleuze's virtual life, is immanent excess or surplus[51] ('the capacity of immanence to produce beyond all limits of propriety'[52]) – the divine energy or 'the infinite power of existing' that comes to expression in the strata and actual thoughts and things of this world.[53] These actual expressions are left by the virtual processes. The immanent God is thought in terms of the virtual life or becoming that produces the actual or static elements of our actual experience.[54]

5.3 Degenerative pantheism and the moral lobster

The picture of transcendence that Deleuze rejects in favour of immanence is something of a caricature. In Desmond's terms, it is God as a static, univocal eternity – absolute in its immutability and stasis beyond time and becoming, and so unable to relate to the world – that generates an equivocal oppositional dualism between

God and the world.[55] Deleuze's problem with transcendence as hegemonic is not in relation to an orthodox Christian understanding of transcendence but to something at once 'pre-christian' and a 'recurrent temptation' in the Christian tradition 'to construe divinity over against or parallel to the universe'.[56] The understanding of God as 'the world's infinite contrary' is not the best representation of the Christian tradition but is the product of theological decline – God and creatures are not in competition with each other, for God is not a being – as Hart writes, the 'God who gives of his bounty, not a God at war with darkness'.[57]

Deleuze's 'enthusiastically neo-Spinozist' pantheism reflects an aversion to hierarchy echoing the occultist desire to escape from the judgement of God.[58] Yet in endeavouring to affirm this world by affirming an impersonal and immanent process as ultimate, he ends up with something other than the actual and concrete world of our experience, now subordinated – embracing an immanent monism in order to escape from dualism and transcendence, in the manner Deleuze does, does not ultimately escape another kind of dualism.[59] Deleuze's actual and virtual are both real, but the virtual (as Hallward writes, the 'virtual creating' as 'the reality that lives in any actual creature', like an immortal soul[60]) is ultimately more real, the '"good" transcendental creative factor' having a definite privilege and priority over the '"bad" static and representable created element', over 'the illusory solidity of the actual'.[61] In this way, Deleuze's reversed Platonism yet reflects a neo-Platonic or Gnostic dualism – in Desmond's words, a 'hyperbolic monism' that yet maintains 'a strikingly strong dualistic sense'.[62]

Over against an understanding of God as transcendent creator,[63] Deleuze's immanent, creative God follows the Gnostic narrative of 'the becoming of the perfection of the divine' in the world-affirming variety (or 'modern systematic deformation' in O'Regan's terms).[64] As such, Deleuze's God coheres with Desmond's idea of the dark origin – the apotheosis or 'decomposition' of the 'god' of the autonomous self into a blind Will at the root of the world,[65] a Dionysian origin, a dark 'erotic absolute', 'a blind, insatiable striving' prior to reason.[66] The Gnostic God is such a dark origin, relative to which, 'the world as a counterfeit double or dissembling medium is coupled with an equivocal *agon* both within the divine as such and between the divine and what comes to be relatively "outside" the divine'.[67]

In O'Regan's Gnostic Valentinian narrative grammar, there is a moment in which the pleroma, the divine fullness, creates through its own fault, its own fall. There is, as O'Regan writes, the 'introduction of fault into the realm of divine perfection and fall from the divine that is the fall *of* the divine and the emergence of the creative capacity that parodies the creator God of Genesis' as 'the almighty and good creator of all that is'.[68] The dynamic divine fullness overflows as a kind of fall that yields an ontological deficiency in the lower levels of being – a generation that is a degeneration in which 'the divine itself in the spark of light has become trapped in the dissembling medium of material; hence the lower agonistics is a continuation of the highest breach within divinity'.[69] Deleuze's movement of actualization in which, as Anthony Paul Smith writes, 'identity is formed at the cost of losing the processes from which it arises', represents just such a fall.[70] This complex process of actualization reflects the plural levels of generation or degeneration that are found in Gnostic narratives, such as Boehme's.[71] The unilateral radiation of the virtual, the primary, dynamic 'active or creative *naturans*', generates the actual, the secondary, 'passive or created *naturata*'.[72] Life as virtual power devolves into its actual, material embodiment as an estranged mutant progeny, something that wraps and swaddles and smothers, as something that is to be escaped.[73] This fallenness of the actual, in which things 'fall into their allocated place',[74] reflects the 'negative estimate of the creator' in Gnosticism with its 'negative consequences for an evaluation of the created order'.[75] The virtual here is an abstract, ghostly force that never appears, is never presented or given.[76] When there is a personal God that shows up in Deleuze's writings that is not the positive impersonal God as the power of life, this God, the God of judgement, is something like the Demiurge, the evil creator God that the Gnostics often equated with the Old Testament God. In such a Gnostic disfiguration of the biblical narrative, this tyrannical voluntarist deity is the creator of imprisoned, hierarchical actuality, the enslaving moral master, the monstrous lobster enforcing identity.[77]

Deleuze makes an axiomatic decision for immanence over transcendence. His insistence on the univocity of being follows from and reinforces this choice for immanence. It is from this perspective that Deleuze, in his (in Hart's words) 'excruciatingly unsophisticated' understanding of analogy, then sees analogy as something lukewarm, as trying to have it both ways, both univocity and equivocity – supporting a hierarchy of being, thus equivocity and a stable sameness within that same hierarchy, thus univocity.[78] In fact, Deleuze's disdain for analogy is less a critique of analogy in itself than unfolding the consequences of Deleuze's axiomatic commitment to immanence. As Deleuze writes in *Difference and Repetition*: 'Univocity signifies that being itself is univocal, while that of which it is said is equivocal, precisely the opposite of analogy.'[79] But this simply misses the point of analogy, or, as Milbank writes in response to the above quote: 'Of course, precisely not.'[80] Analogy need not so much be, as Deleuze insists, 'complicit with identity, presence and substance' as it may be rooted in a different understanding of genuine difference. 'Analogy', Milbank writes, 'does not imply "identity", but identity and difference at once' and so recognizes 'the primacy of mixtures, *continua*, overlaps and disjunctions, all subject in principle to limitless transformation'.[81] When Deleuze asserts that 'to claim that being is said in one and the same sense of God and of the flea is a terrible thing, we must burn people like that',[82] he misses that an orthodox Christian understanding of analogy and participation entails just this intimacy – analogy does not function to insulate God in His transcendence; it makes God more immanent to the flea than the flea is to itself. Analogy sees genuine difference in relation as ultimate. Analogy is also an attempt to be true, as Hart writes, to 'the way in which difference concretely occurs, in sequences of positionings, interdependencies, and analogies that make room for one another'.[83] As Milbank writes, Deleuze's 'transcendental univocity, being entirely empty of content, and indeed the medium of a sheerly differentiated content, cannot possibly appear in itself to our awareness, but can only be assumed and exemplified in the phenomena which it organizes. Yet if Being remains in itself unknowable, always absent and concealed, then how do we justify the characterization of Being as univocity?' In the end, 'nothing grounds a preference for this coding'.[84] This reflects the Gnostic Valentinian 'discursive paradoxes of an aporetic kind' in which the dark pleroma, 'the Unknown God is revealed as unrevealed', as unrevealable.[85] The analogical, as with Desmond's metaxological, is the 'middle realm' that 'allows for a space of movement and reversal that escapes the pitfalls Deleuze locates in the dialectic'.[86] The genuine difference that is given is not the pure difference of a relationless dispersal, but an irreducibly plural, different and yet interrelated metaxological between. Without relation, Oliver Davies writes, 'difference retreats into itself and thus withdraws from thinkability. It is only the thinking of a relationality between difference and ourselves . . . that can offer a dialectic in which thinking as a thinking beyond thought becomes meaningful'.[87] The immanent middle of difference in relation need not be dominated or reduced to a flat sameness (a not-difference) by transcendence, and, as Milbank writes, 'in order to avoid monism collapsing into a hierarchical dualism, or else an inverted hierarchical dualism . . . one needs . . . a philosophy of mediation. But mediation is, within immanence, always vanishing'.[88]

5.4 Creation theology: St Thomas saying 'Yes' to the ocean

Deleuze's work can function to help us think through a genuine creation theology – help us reflect on what it might mean for Christian theology to entail a robust and not anemic affirmation of the world. David Burrell comments that such aid may well be needful as certain veins of Christian theology over the centuries have engendered a degraded creation theology, with creation 'as the initial gift of God' being overshadowed by the work of redemption in Christ in the Christian sensibility.[89] Can Christian theology affirm the created world as intrinsically good? Need transcendence eclipse immanence or vice versa?[90]

The Christian doctrine of creation is a revealed doctrine, an article of faith.[91] The hyperbolic thought of creation – that something could come from nothing or 'that anything else should exist outside of God, who is replete Being' – this thought resists our thinking; it is a mystery.[92] Such an understanding of creation and of God as creator as grounded in revelation is consistent with Deleuze's perspective in that a philosophy that disallows revelation is not going to cohere with one that does.[93] From a confessional perspective, immanent philosophy must, as Burrell notes, be 'stretched to serve a revelation whose affirmations exceed its proper reach' and this 'to do the job required of them in elaborating a doctrine of free creation of the universe'.[94] There are, as Robert Sokolowski presents them, fundamental differences between a pagan understanding of the divine – as within the context of an immanent frame, as 'part, the best and governing part, of nature' or the world[95] – and a Christian one in which the gratuitous creation of the world (as intentionally originated from the agapeic community of the immanent life of the Trinity[96]) which 'has no parallel in what we experience in the world'.[97]

The Christian understanding of divine transcendence is thought in terms of a fundamental distinction (Sokolowski and Burrell refer to it as 'the distinction'[98]) between the world and God as, in Desmond's terms, 'the Unequal' or 'transcendence itself'.[99] As such, this kind of distinction between God and the world 'cannot be established by any prior premises' and is part of the content of Christian revelation.[100] The fundamental distinction, an 'infinite qualitative difference', between God and 'all things'[101] is such that 'we cannot speak of God and the world as parallel entities, nor can we use merely contrastive language when speaking of God from the viewpoint of the world', that God is not a part of the world, not one super thing among other things.[102] God – who, as Kierkegaard writes, 'is outside of existence yet in existence', the origin 'whose essence is simply to-be' – is not contained in 'the set of all things' of which it is the origin.[103] This is to be distinguished from a 'classical scheme' of emanation in which 'the great chain of Being' is 'suspended from the First', from the prime mover or first being.[104] Because of this, God and creatures are not in competition with each other; God is not a being among others, and so cannot be a hegemon in competition with creatures.[105] Because this distinction is unlike any other we normally use to understand and distinguish between things in the context of world, 'the names and syntax that are at home within such a context' which we would then use in relation to God 'have to be adapted from their normal use in the element of the identities and differences within the world'; they 'must be properly adjusted if they are to function in the new horizon'.[106]

Analogy is an indirect use of language that arises when we use 'words which have at least a fairly clear sense in a context of creatures' to talk about 'a radically different sort of being'.[107] If we are to speak about God as transcendent, we must speak indirectly, in a species of ambiguity otherwise than the kind of dialectics that would reduce the many to a one, that is not 'complicit with identity, presence and substance',[108] for there is no determinate proportion between creatures and God.[109] The analogical is a metaxological, 'middle' way of speaking 'between identity and difference', Pickstock writes, 'whereby something can be like something else in its very unlikeness'.[110] Analogy can be seen as following from the doctrines of the Trinity and of creation. The 'between' of being other to and yet in relation to God is to be like God – as the divine Persons are different from and yet in relation to one another in the Triune divine communion. The revelation of God as Triune gives forth a capacity for thinking about creation, about God's (who is fundamentally, intrinsically relating) relating to the world[111] – as Milbank writes, 'the analogizing capacity *itself* is "like God"'.[112] 'Created difference', Hart writes, '"corresponds" to God, is analogous to the divine life, precisely in differing from God'.[113]

Analogy operates within the distinction between the world and transcendence as 'original', a transcendence gratuitously and intentionally originating.[114] God, as the answer to 'why everything', McCabe writes, 'cannot be a thing, an existent among others. It is not possible that God and the universe should add up to make two'.[115] And yet God is not made God by the distinction; God is an absolute whole such that 'being creator of the world is not part of what it is to be God'.[116] The theistic God of creation is, for Desmond, the God beyond the whole. As beyond the whole of the world, this God possesses an absoluteness (ab-solo – from itself alone), an asymmetric and 'idiotic' infinity that is beyond any need for completion and so opens the space for otherness apart from itself.[117] Because God 'would be "the same" in greatness and goodness whether He creates or does not create', Sokolowski writes, 'the world and everything in it is appreciated as a gift brought about by generosity that has no parallel in what we experience in the world'.[118] This 'eternal dynamism' and primordial generosity of Trinitarian love – free from desire propelled by lack, an entirely productive desire – coincides with the traditional doctrine of divine *apatheia*,[119] an impassability as 'the utter fullness of an infinite dynamism, the absolutely complete and replete generation of the Son and procession of the Spirit from the Father, the infinite "drama" of God's joyous act of self-outpouring – which is his being as God'.[120]

As such a gratuitous action, creation *ex nihilo* is, as Desmond writes, 'a free giving of the finite other "outside" the divine immanence' – a 'hyperbolic origination', an absolving 'letting be' – such that the arising of the finite world is 'the arising of another as other'.[121] World does not exist necessarily,[122] but is the result of a free giving forth, 'an utterly spontaneous and gracious act',[123] a 'deliberative invention', as Hart writes, 'a kind of play, a kind of artistry for the sake of artistry'.[124] This revealed concept of creation introduced into Western thought 'the radically new idea that an infinite freedom is the "principle" of the world's being'.[125] God as free Creator displays a perspective on the inner life of God, for God's originating freedom is not arbitrary, but wise and loving – always already 'transcendent source, revealing word (wisdom), and nourishing community (love)'.[126]

God, for St Thomas, is to be conceived on the analogy of dynamic, loving activity and so conceived as creator.[127] The creation of the world is a gift – giving forth, as a work of love, the existing contingent world as good and structured towards its own flourishing.[128] God's creative love is the root and origin of every existing thing.[129] The doctrine of *creatio ex nihilo* does not speak of a dominating tyrant's utter control and power over all things, but instead speaks of an agapeic origin 'who gives of his bounty'.[130] 'The reason why there is something rather than nothing', McCabe writes, 'reveals itself as love'.[131] As such, *creatio ex nihilo* is, in Desmond's terms, 'a free giving of the finite other "outside" the divine immanence', a 'hyperbolic origination', an absolving 'letting be', 'the arising of another as other',[132] that gives space, in McCabe's words, 'leaving the world to itself'.[133] The 'hyperbolic asymmetry' between creator and creation – the divine excess, surplus, plenitude,[134] enables a true gift,[135] a 'nonpossesive dispensation' that releases the other as other.[136]

The Trinitarian life within the Agapeic Origin, the eternal movement of giving in the community of God from (plu)perfection to (plu)perfection constitutes a center of creative power complete and full in itself.[137] There is, as Hart writes, an 'analogical interval between Trinitarian infinity and the gift of created glory' – 'all the themes of creation depart from the first theme that is mysteriously unfolded in the Trinity' – in that 'it is precisely Creation's departure from God that approximates God'.[138] God's creation of the world arises from the love that pre-existed the world in the midst of the Trinity; it is thus that God, as St Thomas writes, creates 'on account of the love of His own goodness'.[139] Thus, as Burrell writes, 'the gracious move to creating a universe in the absence of any need whatsoever is best conceived as the One's acquiescing to the One's own inner constitution'.[140]

God's *esse* is the life of the world – the 'act which is the source of all activity'.[141] This *esse* is 'at once the act of existence proper to each being and the proper effect of the creator's action' as God is essentially being and creates and preserves all things;[142] and, as McCabe writes, creation is 'the dependence of all that is, in so far as it is'.[143] Thus, for Thomas, 'there is no difference between God's preserving activity and God's creating' for 'all of God's activity partakes of creating: all that God can do is to create'.[144] God's activity is rendered 'on the model of practical knowing or art'[145] – this is what is behind Kierkegaard's (Climacus') statement: 'God does not think, he creates.'[146] Creatures have being by participation, and this preservation is an intimate continuation of creation.[147] God is the world's intimate other – a distinction without alienating dualism, a community without reduction to unity and cancellation of difference. God is, in Kierkegaard's terms, the power that establishes (not only initially, but continually) and the hidden and sustaining spring of the lake of ourselves, of the world.[148] God as *esse* is a way of thinking of the 'inexpressible intimacy of creature to creator', of God as 'more intimately and profoundly interior to things than anything else'.[149] Here transcendence is not a rival of immanence that would demean this world but something, as Jacob Sherman notes, like 'the superlative form of immanence' in which, as Pickstock writes, 'creatures have no ground in themselves, but perpetually receive themselves from the infinity of God'.[150]

Thus, as Hart writes, 'the Christian God is at once infinitely more transcendent of and, in consequence, infinitely nearer to (within the very being of) finite reality than was the inaccessible God of antique metaphysics, the supreme being set apart on being's summit, the fixed hook from which the cosmos dangled'.[151] There is, in Desmond's terms, a porosity, a 'tense togetherness', an 'intense twinning' of immanence and transcendence – for Teilhard, a 'transparence' and a 'diaphany' between God and the universe.[152] The intimate source of *esse* is 'at the heart of every creature', such that, as McCabe writes, 'God is not, in the relevant sense, other'.[153] God operates in each thing according to its own nature without coercion, such that it, as St Thomas writes, 'has a participation of the Divine goodness'.[154] Teilhard names this communion 'the divine milieu', the sustaining and 'sur-animating' of creatures by 'the divine ocean' in which 'by means of all created things, without exception, the divine assails us, penetrates us, moulds us. We imagined it as distant and inaccessible, whereas in fact we live steeped in its burning layers'.[155] The world that God creates and lets be as intimately other to Himself has its own endowment of goodness, integrity and freedom. 'The wondrousness of creation', Kierkegaard writes, 'the cross which philosophy could not bear but upon which it has remained hanging' is 'not to produce something that is nothing in relation to the Creator, but to produce something that is something' – but 'that God could create beings free over against himself'.[156] Burrell, commenting on St Thomas, echoes this perspective that 'it amounts to an even greater praise to affirm a creator able to constitute creatures to function as agents in their own right, having existence as a gift, to be sure, but *de jure*, as it were'.[157] Far from any Gnostic denigration of the created or the material, orthodox Christian theology such as represented here affirms the goodness of existing things.[158] The integrity of the created order, the 'dignity of causality' is maintained and affirmed'[159] such that 'the believer in the divine *milieu*' often bears 'a striking resemblance to the worshippers of the earth' – the Christian should sympathize with pagan world-worshipers before pagan world-fugitives.[160]

The order affirmed is not the strict stability of the arborescent or the strata, but is rather dynamic and harmonic. The created world is an ever-unfinished between-being, an 'inter-esse',[161] a 'vast "ontogenesis" (a vast becoming of what it is)',[162] a 'glissando of constant variation of species',[163] continual repetition in difference.[164] The orders and stabilities of the world are more on the order of constancies or habits, dispositions that come to be, are constituted – it is natural to acquire natures.[165] This becoming world is a world of interrelation, in Desmond's terms, a metaxological community of being such that the good of creatures is mutual relationship artfully, wisely and benevolently ordered.[166] The goodness of God is made manifest in a multiform and manifold manner in the harmonious plurality of creatures[167] – the '*musica mundana* or *harmonia mundi*' in which, as Hart writes, creation 'is simply another expression or inflection of the music that eternally belongs to God, to the dance and difference, address and response, of the Trinity'.[168] This dynamic ordering of the world, of the immanent, is ordered in relation to the transcendent – the world, like the Divine Persons in the *perichoresis* of the Triune God, is intrinsically extrinsic such that to appropriate the word 'God' is, as McCabe writes, 'to use it to refer to the wisdom by which the world is a story, the singer by which nature is not just sound and fury but music'.[169] Then the material world, the re-enchanted 'sacramental earth',[170] can be seen as 'the scintillating manifestation of the love of God'.[171]

6

The human and the inhuman

For Deleuze, God or 'the order of God' functions as the underwriter and sole guarantor of the identity of the self as an essential, inalienable form[1] – such that 'man must be produced as man by something exterior to nature and to man' to the degree that 'one cannot conserve the self without also holding on to God'.[2] The death of God, then, effects the dissolution of the self[3] – 'Man did not survive God' for 'God's tomb is also tomb of the self'.[4] God and the self as identities do not pass the test of the eternal return for only the different returns.[5] This instals 'an essential dissimilarity' within the self.[6] As Deleuze's vision of the world does not tolerate the subsistence of the self, he wants the work of the death of God as guarantor of identity to be carried through, that man not be put in the 'place' of God as the central organizing identity, but that the underwriting 'place' itself be abolished.[7] The post-theological self is then a 'cracked' or 'fractured I', a self without identity, a schizoid plurality, a function of desire as constructing passing assemblages and aggregates.[8]

Theologies that have appropriated Deleuze's understanding of the self or person see such a dissolved self as a kind of ideal (as the reality of our selves) that we should strive to approximate. To become 'human' in the best sense is to escape or undo the bonds of human organization/identity to find new ways of being as constructed, fluid identities.[9] Such recognizes the unconscious forces as a source of life more fundamental than egoistic thought which shape what we think and do – something unthinkable that causes us to think.[10] Man is seen as part of nature, not as something fundamentally different from nature, as a part of the same network of producing and connecting forces – and not a master over nature, 'swallow[ing] the rest of nature up into our pure form of anthropomorphic death'.[11] The imperative of such theology would be to avoid and give up such dominant and dominating anthropomorphic identity as sinful and to become minoritarian, more closely associated with the unconscious forces operative in acts of creation.[12]

The understanding of the human as something deficient, a kind of prison to be escaped, echoes or coheres the 'the fall of pneumatic being' in Gnosticism.[13] The result, as Desmond writes, is that 'we ourselves are prison, and we are in the prison of ourselves'.[14] The 'fallen' human condition arises in Gnosticism in a manner that 'depends directly or indirectly on the fallen divine',[15] a deficient humanity tied to a deficient divinity. 'Creation devolves from the fallen, disfigured aspect of the pleroma that is the fruit of misrecognition and failure to acknowledge limits.'[16] The cause of the fall of spiritual being within the divine (with the distorted or confused element of the divine) and is maintained in human beings by a forgetfulness – by a striving to be something one cannot be while forgetting the true nature of pleromatic life. For humans, Deleuze's true world – the 'rhizomatic, connected world of pure desire'[17] – is another world, as the anthropological strata of meaning, the human world in which we live, is a degenerate projection. For the human, the unconscious and inhuman life of the world is 'unlived', and indeed, for humans, 'unlivable'.[18] For Deleuze, the human world is a world of illusion, of *doxa*. We are not only ignorant about ourselves and about the world, but our humanity (the illusion of our humanity) seems to be at odds with a genuine appreciation of what we are – such that we are 'trapped in ignorance, impotence and slavery'.[19] Our attachment to the human strata our 'creatural delusions' is so consistently 'obstinate' that it can be said that, for Deleuze, 'humanity is the form that creation takes when it denies or turns against itself'.[20] What we need to do is to become something other than our actual humanity, to escape the judgement of God as the dominion of some evil divinity, such that genuine pneumatic being (Gnostic true humanity) is at once 'superior to the creator and his creation'.[21]

The Christian tradition presents humanity as created in the image of God. However, this revealed understanding is something mysterious;[22] we do not know determinately what the human as *imago Dei* is as the human is defined in relation to the Trinity and the Incarnation – the mysteries of the faith – apart from which we are in the position, as Kierkegaard's Climacus writes, of Socrates, that bewildered 'connoisseur of human nature', who 'no longer knew whether he was a more curious monster than Typhon or whether there was something divine in him'.[23]

Whereas Deleuze's dismissal of the person follows from a particular understanding of the transcendent God – 'as the internalization of transcendent authority'[24] – Christian theology has the resources to present another understanding of God and another understanding of the person. The image of God, Hart writes, 'cannot lend stability to a unified "ego", because it is a trinitarian image'.[25] As Desmond points out, the intermediation of the 'agapeic trinity' as a 'social' procession of love is at once personal – for 'to be personal is to be in social relations' – and 'transpersonal' as a community of Persons.[26] A Trinitarian understanding of the person (as something that has operations in relation to others) is always already transpersonal – a transpersonality 'that less suppresses the personal as fulfills its release into a more ultimate communicative transcending beyond self' in which, as Hart writes, 'a true – that is, selfless – person: a person in communion'.[27] Such a Christian understanding would be sympathetic to Deleuze's critique of the modern self, but would critique the modern self for its dependence upon and encouraging of an anemic theology. The notion of person as a relation stemming from a doctrine of the Trinity – in which 'the term "persons", when applied to the divine *perichoresis*, is governed entirely by the language of relations' – stands opposed to the modern understanding of the person as 'isolated, punctiliar, psychic monad'.[28] The human person, or self as being created in the image of the Trinitarian God is, as Kierkegaard writes, a dependent set of relations – 'a derived, established relation, a relation that relates itself to itself and in relating itself to itself relates itself to another'.[29]

Human being, human nature, is not subsistent in itself, but bears constancies that arise in the midst of becoming. Our very being is habitual, hospitable to second natures, as it 'subsists upon repetition in difference'[30] – repetition that develops a concrete way of being over time.[31] Human life, as Kierkegaard notes, is in a constant process of becoming, of change, for one's being, one's actuality is that of an active relation, an interestedness, a being-between, 'an inter-esse' in relation to God[32] – such that, as Sherman writes, 'a discourse of transcendence does not, by itself, prohibit a robust vision of real becomings'.[33]

Furthermore, from such a Christian perspective, the truly human is a transcending, a becoming inhuman (and so truly human). Our own human good which we naturally seek is to love God as inhuman (as not human) over ourselves.[34] Humans are humans, in such a Christian vision, only as they are elevated beyond humanity in 'that the *esse* of creatures is an *esse-ad-creatorem* (their to-be is to-be-towards-the-creator)'.[35] Our being is not static but fundamentally ecstatic, a being-in-relation-to God as Trinitarian being-in-relation. Our proper being is an unending becoming, as in Gregory of Nyssa's concept of *epektasis* – an 'always outstretched, open, and changing motion'[36] – or in Kierkegaard's understanding of human existence as the 'joining together' of the 'motion' of becoming and the 'motionless' constancy or continuity of motion of the eternal God in one's striving continually forward in relation to something that is not changing.[37] Our 'ecstatic actuality' is such that, Gregory writes, 'the soul rises ever higher and will always make its flight yet higher,' 'and although lifted up through such lofty experiences, he is still unsatisfied in his desire for more. He still thirsts for that which he constantly filled himself to capacity . . . beseeching God to appear to him, not according to his capacity to partake, but according to God's true being'.[38]

This desire (not desire as lack but as already full, productive, fontal) for God as beneath the human is the 'inexpressible intimacy of creature to creator'[39] or, as Teilhard describes it, a welling abyss in our innermost self – 'a bottomless abyss at my feet, and out of it came – arising I know not from where – the current which I dare to call *my* life . . . the profound life, the fontal life, the newborn life, escape our grasp entirely' in which 'my self is given to me far more than it is formed by me'.[40] Regarding this welling desire becoming from and towards God as what a human can do, we are not yet human enough, do not yet go to the limit of our humanity.[41] Humanity as 'what a human can do' is becoming-God – the desirous orientation to know God, to be united to God is at once natural/intrinsic and exceeds us.[42] In Desmond's (Platonic) terms, our eros is both *penia*/poverty that seeks what it wants and *poros*/fullness that is always already given from a prior other.[43] We are our *conatus essendi*, our ecstatic endeavour to be, to urgently ascend to the ultimate. But we are also, and more primordially, our *passio essendi* – created, given to be as a good gift, enabled in our transcending.[44] Humans as relations are both receptive and communicating. Such agapeic desire as 'the energy of our movement' is a productive desire arising from God's 'primordial generosity' as 'the blissful and desiring *apatheia* that requires no pathos to evoke it'.[45]

Sin in this understanding would be corrupted desire as fixation, as seeking 'to possess the things of the world as inert property',[46] to halt, and so stunting our immanent orientation.[47] Hart observes that the modern vision of the person is closer to 'the vicious tendencies of sin' – of self-inclination and self-possession.[48] Kierkegaard portrays the 'inclosing reserve' (*det Indesluttede*) of the self-fixated self, that which 'closes itself up within itself' and 'makes itself prisoner'[49] – 'an inwardness with a jammed lock' that wishes to have 'a world exclusively for itself'.[50] For such a Christian understanding, there is a good order to the universe and to ourselves from which sin is a defection, a dissonance, an aversion from the immutable good and conversion to a mutable good – not willing to be the self that one is, or (what amounts to the same thing) willing to be a self one is not.[51] The difference between good and evil is not the difference between immutability and mutability, but the difference between an order that leads to artificial fixation and a dynamic, *perichoretic* one. Salvation, then, is not 'liberation from mutability', but 'a transition to a changeableness unburdened by sin and death, a perpetual tending forward'.[52] The truly human, what a human can do, is to continually strive beyond itself into the inhuman intimate other of the eternal movement of the divine.

7

The Christ of philosophers

The system of Antichrist (Klossowski's term) is 'opposed', Deleuze writes, 'point for point to the divine order.'[1] This system of anti-originary modification and its implied atheism is not something to be avoided or mourned, 'is not a drama but the philosopher's serenity and philosophy's achievement'.[2] In the face of the death of the transcendent God and the dissolution of the person, there is also the erasure of the priestly concept that men exist in a state of infinite debt and so need a savior.[3] As the order of Antichrist chases away the other order, so does it chase away the need for a Christ, it would seem.

But, as we have seen, God or the divine does not disappear entirely in Deleuze's work. The God that appears in Deleuze's work, with which one must come to terms and be reconciled, for Deleuze, is not the God revealed in Christ but the God 'revealed' by Spinoza. Deleuze's God is Spinoza's God, the creative immanence of nature naturing,[4] such that his thought can be accurately described as Spinozist.[5] Spinoza (who, Deleuze comments, read in paperback, whenever and wherever one can, creates as much emotion as a great musical work[6]) is at once the subject of Deleuze's most extensive meditation on another philosophy (*Expressionism in Philosophy: Spinoza*) and of his most accessible book, an introduction to Spinoza as practical philosophy, a large part of which is a glossary (*Spinoza: Practical Philosophy*). Spinoza functions, for Deleuze, as a prophet of immanence – as the only one who consistently 'succeeded', Justaert writes, 'in barring transcendence from his thinking completely and putting the plane of immanence forward as the core of his philosophy'.[7] The liberation that Spinoza's teaching enables is a liberation from subjectification supported by transcendence – an opportunity to think differently about ourselves and the world. As Deleuze and Guattari note in *What is Philosophy?*, all concepts have names attached to them, 'made by' tags, as it were. The God that lurks in Deleuze's corpus is not the God of Abraham, Isaac and Jacob – not the God of Jesus – but the God of Spinoza. There is no transcendent God, but there is but one God (or Nature or Life or Dionysius) and its prophet is Spinoza (or Nietzsche, Spinoza *sive* Nietzsche). Spinoza – 'the infinite becoming-philosopher' relative to which 'the greatest philosophers are hardly more than apostles who distance themselves from or draw near to this mystery' – revealed the plane of immanence. He showed and pointed to what is available to all, to what one can do. It is in this sense that, for Deleuze, 'Spinoza is the Christ of philosophers'.[8]

Clayton Crockett expands on this connection in the constructive context of a secular theology. Spinoza emerges as 'the first quintessentially modern philosopher', Clayton writes, 'due to his consistent identification of God and Nature' – instituting a new era characterized by a new understanding of God and God's relation to the world.[9] Crockett's Deleuzian project in his *Radical Political Theology* is that of a theology 'for which Spinoza would serve as a saint, if not the Christ' – a political theology based on the gospel of Spinoza.[10] Mindful of Badiou's work on Paul, Crockett looks to 'assemble a Paul-effect for Deleuze' of seeing Deleuze as the philosophical apostle that 'provides important theoretical resources to think the event'.[11]

Deleuze's understanding of Spinoza as the Christ of philosophers follows the nineteenth-century esoteric impulse in figures such as Warrain towards a 'rational' (not revealed) religion.[12] Such a rational, Spinozist religion, which has no need for atonement, follows the Gnostic refusal 'to understand the passion and death [of Jesus Christ] as the mystery of atonement'.[13] But more deeply, the function of the Deleuzian Christ of philosophers resembles the fifth narrative episode of the O'Regan's Gnostic Valentinian narrative grammar in which 'a divine being, either explicitly or implicitly associated with Jesus Christ, enters the extrapleromatic world to recall human being to their true destiny'.[14] Deleuze's philosophy is faithful to Spinoza as an immanent Gnostic savior whose philosophy is the secret liberating knowledge that the world is not as we think it is. Here the gnosis is the philosophy of Spinoza as the Christ of philosophers whose *Ethics* awakens us from 'the spell of ourselves' and recalls us to the virtual plane of immanence, the domain of spirit, of divine life – the good news of the crowned anarch-ingdom.[15] Here Spinoza resembles the Socratic teacher in Kierkegaard's *Philosophical Fragments* – the teacher that does not uniquely reveal something that one could not have come to otherwise, but is merely the passing occasion for one's realization of the answer that is immanent, was always in one's midst. The immanent gnosis/gospel (the gospel of Spinoza according to Deleuze) is such that, as Hallward notes, 'redemption from the human', the overcoming and undoing of the human strata, 'is the task of the human alone'.[16] Philosophy, philosophers – and therefore supremely Spinoza, the Christ of philosophers – provides immanent assistance in seeing through the illusions of the actual.[17] Associated with Christ, but as a parodic reversal of the work of Christ, Spinoza stands to recall humanity to its true, inhuman destiny – only a philosopher can save us.

The incarnation in orthodox theology seems to be something impossible, something revealed to us beyond our horizons of expectation.[18] The incarnate savior is not the immanent teacher who only 'reveals' what was immanently 'within' us, but is one who truly reveals, gives something we lack. The transcendent and yet immanent teacher is the divine-human healer or physician who seeks to transform, renew, re-create us – a 're-making' that cannot be fully worked out in terms of self-creation.[19] This 'condescending' revelation of the transforming divine life in the incarnate God-Man, Jesus Christ, coheres with the perichoretic moving and giving forth of the Trinity such that, as Herbert McCabe writes, 'the story of Jesus is what the eternal trinitarian life of God looks like when it is projected upon the screen of history'.[20]

Likewise, the orthodox belief in the two natures of creator God and created humanity united (but not confused) in the person of Christ – as truly different and united, in communion – brings the Christian distinction, the 'infinite qualitative difference' between God and the world into precise focus, precisely in the thought of their communion, of their being related in 'one' without the difference being cancelled out, being reduced to one, without the creator-creature distinction in the Christological paradox being obscured.[21] Chalcedonian Christology reflects the metaxological communion both within the Trinitarian Godhead and between the God and the world. This conjunction is not a denial of, or escape from, the world, but a declaration of the intimacy of God and the world such that the affirmation of the reality of creation, as Pieper reads in St Thomas, surges 'from reverence for the reality of the Incarnation of God'.[22] Even the crucifixion, in the Christian tradition, is an affirmation of human life – death is dolorous because life is good.[23]

In Christ's transforming work, he makes new connections, new communions, between humans and God and other humans. In Justaert's terms, Christ is a deterritorializing assemblage that presses us to give up our falsely static subjectivities and to become a part of, a partaker in the divine life through such a 'Christ-assemblage'.[24] Humans in Christ share in Christ's union with God – such that, as Teilhard writes, 'across the immensity of time and the disconcerting multiplicity of individuals, one single operation is taking place: the annexation to Christ of his chosen; one single thing is being made: the mystical body of Christ'.[25] In Christ, as the way given to us through life with and unto God, 'we are taken up,' McCabe writes 'into the exchange of love between the Father and the incarnate and human Son, we are filled with the Holy Spirit, we become part of the divine life'.[26]

8

The Divine Life II: Salvation, affirmation and becoming-God

8.1 Deleuze's salvation from/in the world

If Deleuze has anything like a religious vision of salvation, it is at once one of escape from the world (its static actual forms, their subject and their God) and an affirmation of the world. Deleuze's anti-theology is, in Judith Poxon's words, 'a "true" *liberation* theology' that seeks to escape from the world of the divine distribution of boundaries, barriers and enclosures – the order of God that would establish identity.[1] Against the divine distribution and the exclusionary force that forms the theological body is the demonic distribution and 'the inclusive force of the order of the Antichrist' that forms a 'perverse body'.[2]

Salvation, for Deleuze, entails the dissolution of the self, a becoming inhuman. As the unity of God is the self's only guarantee (as a 'product' of God),[3] the death of God brings about a cracking of the self that fractures and 'installs and interiorises within' the self an 'essential dissimilarity'.[4] Instead of an essential unity, the self liberated from the judgement of God is 'carried away by the verbs of pure becoming and slides into the language of events'.[5] Against the 'faith' that would resurrect or heal the self, Deleuze could be seen as advocating another 'theological' self, a self resting in the dead God (a mad self waiting and dreaming with dead Cthuhlu), where 'a different and more mortuary betrothal between the dead God and the dissolved self forms the true condition by default and the true metamorphosis of the agent'.[6] Such a transformation of the self – where a traditional theology would allow no such transformations, no werewolves[7] – is an imperative to becoming-nonhuman, becoming-impersonal, becoming transparent to the plane of immanence in which, as Justaert writes, 'nothing is fixed; no fixed identities, but only intensities that move at different speeds'.[8] This transcending of the static self/ego/personality and its supporting hierarchy is a 'thinking beyond the human condition'[9] – a becoming-imperceptible that 'is at the same time a becoming-divine'.[10] This 'new man' is liberated from the chains of categories such that there is nothing preventing one from doing what one can do, from realizing one's force. In this breaking down of the self there is a 'tuning-in', an attaining to a sense or vision of 'life in all its force, in all its beauty'.[11]

The other side of salvific transformation for Deleuze is the affirmation of life – the belief in the world. Whereas Christianity, on Deleuze's Nietzschean accounting 'Christian nihilism', would judge life to either justify it or to accuse it,[12] Deleuze's Nietzschean-Spinozist ethic of immanent modes of existence works to increase the power to live.[13] Such immanent ethical evaluation entails 'evaluating every being, every action and passion, even every value, in relation to the life which they involve' where 'the good is outpouring, ascending life, the kind which knows how to transform itself, to metamorphose itself according to the forces it encounters, and which forms a constantly larger force with them, always increasing the power to live, always opening new "possibilities"'.[14] The Deleuzian good is not other than the world; it is the life of the world – full of potential and possibility. Deleuzian saving faith is belief in the world; this 'conversion of thought' is the one thing needful, for we lack, Marrati writes, 'belief in the possibility of creating new forms of existence, of experimenting with new forms of life'.[15] The beatitude of Deleuzian faith, as passing beyond the human, is the awareness that we are living, lived by, the immanent and impersonal divine life of the world.[16]

8.2 Worldly spirituality and immanent liberation

Deleuzian reconceptions of salvation and spirituality take various forms but emphasize certain common points. Clayton Crockett proposes a radical theology as a theological materialism, a nondualist understanding of the material and spiritual that would serve 'to restore our belief in the world, this world'.[17] Such a religious belief in the world is, as Barber notes, 'becoming part of the world', being affected by it as opposed to believing in another world that would remove us from relations to this world.[18] This is an affirmation of immanence that 'calls forth powers from this world so that we may believe in this world and act in it', in Anthony Paul Smith's terms, 'as custodians tending to the machines of the universe'.[19]

Goodchild presents a Deleuzian spirituality in terms of an ethics of thinking. Such imbues thought with religious pathos, affirmation and creativity – maximizing active, joyful passions judged by immanent criteria – and, in so doing, elevating thought to a level that is divine.[20] Deleuzian faith is a faith in immanence, an affirmation of the repetition of pure dynamism – and so a selective affirmation of that which is most true to virtual becoming.[21] Barber likewise frames an immanent spirituality or style of being religious that would be a 'properly Deleuzean spirituality' as one focused on the task of re-expressing the world. Such 'a presumptionless spirituality' would escape from the 'insipid conformity' of the 'devotee of transcendence'.[22]

Several theologians have explored the possibilities of using Deleuze towards the project of a postmodern kind of liberation theology. Justaert sees Deleuze's redemptive project as echoing some of the main themes of liberation theology.[23] First, Deleuze supports liberation theologies in presenting identities as constructed and fluid and seeking the deconstruction of falsely fixed identities[24] on the way 'towards Being as a purely immanent dynamic' towards life as it is 'in terms of movements, intensity, velocity and power'.[25] This would be a revolution as a 'liberation of life' and the liberation of assemblages of desire from the power and mastery involved in humanism.[26] Second, Deleuze echoes liberation theology's concern of resisting the repressive force of the state.[27] Along these lines, Deleuzian theologies present a different conception of God to help develop a different understanding of politics[28] – a 'vision', Keller writes, 'of a liberated Being' opposed to *dominology* in 'a world in which there are no longer hierarchies'.[29] Instead of thinking of God *vis-à-vis* the *postestas* of a transcendent God that enforces a politics of obedience, Crockett suggests that 'God' names 'the virtual *potentia* that makes it possible to restore belief'.[30] Third, a Deleuzian theology focuses on minorities echoing liberation theology's passion for the marginalized.[31] Such a focus intends to escape the imposed molar order of harmony and obedience from reigning orthodoxy – to undo human organization and to create new non-majoritarian ways of becoming human[32] – to encourage a micropolitics that, in Justaert's words, 'doesn't consist of decisions that need to be implemented, but of lines of desire, of intensities, of flows'.[33] A liberation theology conceived along these Deleuzian lines would seek to create open spaces for difference, for the virtual in new actual forms,[34] allowing for an unceasing project of the 'constant arrivals of revolution' – the arrival, as Anthony Paul Smith observes, of 'the immeasurable itself' as generating ruptures in 'the current molar state of affairs'.[35] The proximity and attendance to the virtual's immanent energy of creation 'resists the actual and always threatens to dissolve it'.[36]

A Deleuzian spirituality and ethics would seek to experiment to see what the mind and body can do and so to elevate thought to the level of the virtual divine life.[37] This kind of Deleuzian faith resembles a Nietzschean *amor fati* as, in Justaert's words, 'a kind of *trust* that the flow will go where it has to'.[38] Such a spiritual ethics without teleology, without judging the world, is not, Barber maintains, merely accepting or simply tolerating the world as it is,[39] but is a work of continually transforming and so transcending ourselves and our modes of existence[40] in an immanent mutual transformation between the world and ourselves.[41] In this way we seek to '*intensify* our affective, immanent relation to this world' – to bring about healing through a process like sympathetic magic – healing through a renewed encounter with that which causes the suffering.[42] Here there is a tension between, as Barber states, 'refus[ing] every attempt to reduce the world to our demands of what it should or could be'[43] and the dual ethical impulse that Anthony Paul Smith recognizes, on the one hand, to 'foster ecosystems that promote the further divergence and creation of life' and, on the other, to avoid 'swallow[ing] the rest of nature up into our pure form of anthropomorphic death'[44] – a transforming that is a letting-be that lets things be as they are according to their fluid nature and changes things when they are not. This is to go with the inhuman flow and resist human impulse to transform the flow into something it is not; rather transform the human in accord with this flow – intentionally reterritorialize in such a way as to allow for 'the most radical deterritorializations'.[45]

8.3 Stuck in the desert, saying 'Yes' to the ocean

As Deleuze's philosophy develops, especially in his partnership with Guattari, the actual world comes to be viewed as pervaded by structures of illusion and oppression that are to be escaped. Hallward sees in this 'subtractive' move something implicitly mystical – a 'mechanics of *dis*-embodiment and *de*-materialisation' that continually leads out of the actual world as the site of entrapment towards the virtual as the site of life and creation.[46] We humans must transcend the actual as we experience it to achieve non-human immanence.[47] Philosophy, for Deleuze, is to serve as a vehicle for spirit's escape from its confinement matter.[48] This reflects the Gnostic understanding of the world with its smothering intermediate layers/strata as a place of estrangement – in which 'spiritual' humanity is enclosed and would escape.[49] Here the spiritual, true humanity, in a reversal of the biblical narrative, would show a superiority to the creator and his creation.[50]

Indeed, in affirming the virtual, and advocating a return to the living, creative virtual, Deleuze reflects the final narrative episode of the Gnostic Valentinian narrative grammar, that of 'the fullscale reconstitution of divine perfection' – the 'narrative closure or *synclasis* a wished-for symmetry between narrative alpha and omega, such that ontotheological narrative essentially shapes a circle'.[51] To gain access to reality, we must dissolve the obstructions of actuality, to see through them and so return to their virtual, generative origin.[52] To overcome man and to return to the divine creativity as 'a kind of becoming-God of the human'[53] is quite similar to a Gnostic salvation as, in Desmond's terms, 'an "awakening" to one's identity with the divine'.[54]

The liberation and affirmation that are the substance of Deleuzian salvation have a spectral quality. Justaert argues that Deleuze's 'liberation' – as seeing through the illusion of consciousness and discovering the true nature of unconscious reality – is not unlike Western consumer 'Buddhist' conception of liberation as a 'going with the flow'.[55] This liberation is an idealized liberation – an infinite resistance, a continuous deterritorialization, a permanent revolution that seems to be, by definition, non-concrete.[56] Deleuze's affirmation, as well, comes off as abstract – as Hart writes, his 'joyous affirmation of the world' is the kind that 'can be accomplished only upon the mountaintops, from an impossibly sublime perspective'; this affirmation is only the most general evaluation such that, as Hallward writes, 'preoccupation with the world as such, let alone a concern with the orderly representation of the things of the world, serves only to inhibit any such affirmation'.[57] Contrariwise, to be true to the world as experienced, to make a judgement about such, can be a critique that is true to the world and yet seeks to change it – surely this is what it means to be a part of the world, to be involved in it. From this perspective, pure acceptance or affirmation would be a turn into renunciation – a white night in which all cows are white. An affirmation that absolves one of relation to the actual world (and of oneself as well) – a 'dissipation of the actual', an 'intensive disembodiment'.[58]

Deleuze's immanent philosophical religiosity would 'complete the human adventure by escaping it' through the invention of 'forms of transformative subtraction or purification'.[59] This philosophical religiosity is an austere renouncer path that is a strange asceticism or self-dissolution.[60] Justaert again draws parallels between Deleuze (and Spinoza behind him) with Western consumer Buddhism: a discovery of the very nature of reality, understanding the subject and consciousness as an illusion, an immanent vision of the world and denial of world of representation.[61] Deleuze echoes Desmond's observation that Gnosticism can embrace both extreme asceticism and antinomic liberty, for in Deleuze, the more actively (freely, unconstrainedly) creative one is, the more spiritual one is – those that tend towards the virtual are the Deleuzian *pneumatachoi*.[62] The result, as René Girard commented upon the publication of *Anti-Oedipus*, is, 'appearances notwithstanding, a new form of particularly ethereal piety'.[63]

The redemptive re-orientation towards dissolution, in the more specific context of the human, entails a redemption from the human as the task of the human – the gospel of Spinoza according to Deleuze.[64] This abandonment of the subject, of actors, is an abandonment of the active development of persons and a mysticism in which the self/soul is dispersed into a micropolitics that has nothing to say to individuals but to cease to be – 'to de-personalise or counter-actualise themselves and thereby become an adequate channel for creation as such'.[65] The result, Justaert concludes, is an 'indifferent, noncommittal world-view' in that 'Deleuze's philosophy of uncertainty, contingency and of ungrounded Being does not seem to offer much of an answer to the question of how to act'.[66] In rejecting 'all forms of moral valuation or strategic judgement' and preferring an at best untenable 'anti-normative' view of justice the subject, the actor is paralysed[67] for the Deleuzian preference for the minority, for example, ends up being arbitrary.[68] While Anthony Paul Smith reasserts that 'immanence does not name a flight from this world, but calls forth powers from this world so that we may believe in this world and act in it, not under the illusion that we are its masters, but as custodians tending to the machines of the universe',[69] we are left with the pointed question of just who this 'we' is. One cannot graft responsibility and ethical agency (not to mention something that looks a lot like a Christian understanding of stewardship) onto an immanent frame that would see, at the very least, a kind of ethical imperative in the dissolution of the illusion of agents with subjective consciousness that can be reasonably responsible for anything.[70] Smith himself recognizes something like this in a more recent essay, observing that Deleuze and Guattari's thought 'appears also to lack a mechanism by which to select the best organization of power other than vague suggestions at cautious experimentation'.[71] It is difficult to escape the thought that the theorist, as Pickstock writes, 'is simply the spectator of fated conflicts – between territorial politicisms and presidents, on the one hand, and deterritorializing terrorists and mavericks, on the other'.[72]

With his emphasis on intensive, non-relational difference – virtual difference but no actual others (or selves for that matter) – Deleuze is left with little room for relationships between individuals, be they of conflict or solidarity. This rejection, in Hallward's terms, of 'any viable theory of inter-individual relation' again leaves Deleuze 'essentially indifferent to the politics of this world' and without any account of what could make any particular organization of power preferable to another.[73] He is left seeing political realities, human realities, like all realities, as little more than an unending 'violent interplay between stasis and movement'.[74] In Hart's judgement, this is due to the fact that Deleuze, 'fails to attend to the way in which difference concretely occurs' in actuality, dealing instead with an overly idealized virtual pure difference.[75] It is thus, in Justaert's appraisal, that Deleuze's politics fails due to its lack of concrete political strength.[76]

Deleuzian spirituality as an ethical way of being is one of affirmation, but an ideal affirmation. In the concrete context, it is unclear what is to be affirmed in actual human life – the affirmation is in danger of being drown in his nay-saying – an odd yea-saying. This, again, echoes the upside down and equivocal nature of Gnosticism – in particular, the world-affirming systematic deformation of the Valentinian narrative grammar.[77] There is little surprise that Deleuze is left with a tragic equivocity: seeking to affirm the world but, in the end, having the difficulty of believing in the world. Deleuze wants to affirm the world – 'this', Hart writes, 'is the first wisdom.'[78] But there are two voices in Deleuze's thought: the Nietzschean, pagan, Dionysian voice that would affirm the world as it is, and the Gnostic voice that would seek to escape it and so leave one without a world to be found to believe in. With the virtual as associated with what is to be affirmed and the actual with what is to be escaped, we are to escape what we are at pains to see as bad rather than innocent and to affirm what we are at pains to see as good. We are to affirm a life that is and yet is not this life. In so doing, are we affirming a world that does not exist?

8.4 Agapeic communion, becoming-God and ecclesial assemblage

Love, as Deleuze and Guattari note, operates by joining multiplicities.[79] Revolutionary love moves in the opposite direction of the love that would fixate on a self-identical self and its accretions.[80] In a Christian confessional frame, we can see that our being, in

Desmond's terms, is the promise of agapeic being[81] – porous to that from which it came to be (the power that establishes it) and opening to beyond itself, seeking to unite with others as a 'binding force', as friendship communicating.[82] Such being, reflecting our origin and that to which we are ordered, is, in Hart's words 'an expression of the superabundant joy and agape of the Trinity, joy and love are its only grammar and its only ground; one therefore must learn a certain orientation, a certain charity and a certain awe'.[83] In the Christian vision, it is God who endows the metaxological community of creation with the promise of agapeic being – intimately empowering, energizing, communicatively enabling a fuller agapeic community in its midst and with its Origin.[84] Such agapeic being as a promise, as a becoming between presence and absence, follows the impulse, the productive yet ordered desire of a love uniting, bringing together the lover to the beloved – as giving a kind of self-transcending unity to the self.[85] In the promise of our agapeic being, the good to which such love is oriented is not an alien imposition but an 'inbuilt goal' – the Trinitarian God that is the good/goal of our agapeic being is the one that created us, endowed us with such an orientation – we are made as loving by, after and towards God as Trinitarian love.[86]

In the confessional context of the Christian faith – which, as Hart describes it, 'came as an evangel promising newness of life, and that in all abundance, preaching creation, divine Incarnation, resurrection of the flesh, and the ultimate restoration of heavens and earth' – a 'pagan' belief in and celebration of the world can function as a sacrament, as a 'sacred gratitude' towards God in the things of the world and not an opposition between the two.[87] In the light of the Christian doctrines of creation and of the Incarnation, the sacred comes to permeate and saturate the world – such the world becomes a divine milieu in which nothing is profane.[88] 'The believer in the divine *milieu*', Teilhard writes, often bears 'a striking resemblance to the worshippers of the earth' in that the Christian multiplies their contacts with the world but 'prolongs them along their common axis, which links them to God: and, by the same token, the universe is thus unified for him, although it is only attainable at the final centre of its consummation'.[89] Such a Christian vision preserves Deleuze's 'project of cosmological and metaphysical re-enchantment'.[90] The world as it appears, the very aesthetics of happening, in its marvelous intricacy, its immanent excess and its 'fugitive' beauty is, in Desmond's terms, a hyperbole of being, an excessive and over-full given in immanence.[91] Christian theology then need not demean the world, but indeed may serve to help us to believe in this world, to help us to see the world as it exists as something good and beautiful.[92] Thus can a theologian like St Thomas, in Pieper's words, contribute towards 'the saving of creation as a visible reality from any attempt at reduction, devaluation, or sheer annihilation'.[93]

The Christian path of salvation is one of transformation in relation to God. This becoming of a fluid self in and as a community is the development of the self not as a static thing, but as a habit of being in relation. Such a habit (the 'natural' habit of taking on habits[94]) is repetition – not as the univocal return of the same or an equivocal return of the different – but a developing coherence in the midst of becoming and plurality, a developing community between the pure becoming of difference and static unity.[95] As one becomes in relation to God the habitual quality that develops is (not unlike Deleuze's ethics) a greater transparency or porosity of the self to the divine life. Such becoming, as Hart writes, 'a true – that is, selfless – person: a person in communion' entails a relation between such a person and God is one of intimate communion – as Desmond writes: 'a union that sustains otherness [singularity and particularity] in togetherness and is not a self-mediating unity but an intermediating metaxu'.[96] As this progressively porous and intimate divine communion 'sur-animates' us – in Teilhard's terms, 'introduces a higher principle of unity into our spiritual life' – we go to the limit of what we can do.[97] We are not yet human enough, for we do not yet go to the limit of our humanity, for humans are humans only as they are elevated beyond humanity, transformed with and unto God.[98] Thus the human on the path of salvation is essentially a wayfarer – 'indeed', Sherman writes, 'as a *theologia viatorum* the intent of theology is all about becoming'.[99] Christian theology as a *theologia viatorum* is for those in the world who would walk in the world towards beatitude truly (not escaping this world for another).[100]

The negative side of the Christian way is not a negation of the world or becoming or the finite as such, but an escape from, a repentance from, a 'dying to' what imprisons, to established order. The 'slopes' of matter, Teilhard writes, can become for us an impulse towards failure (because of original sin and its passed down historical and cultural accretions and distortions) and can also become for us 'the spur or the allurement to be our accomplice towards heightened being' (because of creation and the Incarnation).[101] Walking with Deleuze, the Christian should seek to escape from false absolutizations of the way things are, established orders – to not let oneself or the church be determined by the way it is now. Repentance, *metanoia*, is turning from, seeking to dissolve the bad coherence, the 'misplaced concreteness' one has come to be a part of, come to be.[102] This process is not escape as such but a transformation, a deterritorialization of oneself, a detachment – one must, as Teilhard writes, 'go beyond himself, tear himself away from himself', must persist in a 'migrating, and dying partially in what one loves' such that 'we can set no limits to the tearing up of roots that is involved on our journey into God'.[103] In this renunciation along the way of life is a paradoxical movement in which one both 'takes leave' of oneself (as falsely calcified in the strata of the established order) and also thereby begins to 'take possession' of oneself (as one is, as an ontological wayfarer).[104] Thus, the Christian way of salvation is neither an escape from all relation and coherence and stability into a non-existent realm of pure difference nor a 'liberation from mutability' but, paradoxically, as Hart writes, 'a transition to a changeableness unburdened by sin and death, a perpetual tending forward'.[105]

A Christian understanding of the way of salvation is a being human as an *epektasis*, a constant movement and transcending in the world towards God.[106] Instead of just going beyond the human or the self *per se*, Christian theology would see this way as going beyond the human and so being human, as dynamic being in relation. This becoming (in)human as becoming towards God is also understood in the Christian tradition in terms of *theosis*, of becoming-God – 'inscribing a becoming-divine within the very heart of the human being'.[107] What 'we can do' from the perspective of Christian theology, from the perspective of creation and grace, is God – our restless hearts can find their rest in God (if a 'rest' or beatitude of perpetual movement). We are called in our very being – in the given promise of agapeic being – to join in the divine life of the blessed community of the Trinitarian God. We can become transparent, porous, diaphanous to God, sur-animated by God, divinized, taken up into the divine life of the Trinity and so, as McCabe writes, 'God will simply be the life of mankind'.[108] Thus, Sherman writes that 'indeed, for Christian theology at least as much as for Deleuze, the trajectory of becoming aims at nothing less than becoming-divine, theosis, or deification'.[109]

We are always already community, always being as being with – from the community 'within' the self to the rhizomal web of nano-communities in which we participate – extending from in the midst of oneself to the whole of reality. 'We do not open ourselves'; Desmond writes, 'being opened, we are as an opening', and an open wholeness of plural singularities in relation is the basic reality of the world around us, within us.[110] Even in the intimacy of our secret selves we are with another, never alone, always already in communion with another before and with and after us.[111]

Becoming the church as body of Christ, as a living, fluid community in the world, is an extension between the becoming of the self and the divine milieu of the world in communion with, sur-animated by, the Triune God. *Ecclesia* in this frame is a coming or bringing together, an *arrangement*, an assemblage – a sympathetic symbiosis, a life together, a multiplicity 'made up of many heterogeneous terms and which establishes liaisons, relations between them, across ages, sexes and reigns – different natures'.[112] The church is (or can, should be) the Christ-assemblage[113] – as something that happens and continues to happen 'which brings into play within us and outside us populations, multiplicities, territories, becomings, affects, events'[114] – bringing together in the evolving body of Christ, knitting together, a series of binding and unbinding knots and nodes and packs and constellations (selves, friendships, congregations, holy 'orders') throughout the world and throughout history.[115]

The 'agapeics' of such a community, in Desmond's terms, would be another hyperbole of being, a reflection of the divine life of the Trinity, communicating 'a surplus generosity not only in being receptive to the gift of the other but in freeing us to give beyond ourselves to others'.[116] – we can, as Hart writes, 'see in the communality and interdependency of the church, the peaceful participation of Christians in one body, a true if vastly inexact image of how God is forever a God dwelling in and with'.[117] Such is manifest in Christianity's Eucharistic symbols of the church, of the body of Christ, the Christ assemblage, of the life of Christ in which we participate now and in the future – 'the cardinal signs of fellowship, feasting, and joy: bread and wine'.[118]

Thinking of church in terms of the dynamic, rhizomal growth emphasizes its fluid 'radical relationality' as nano-church – wherever two or three are gathered. A church constituted as micropolitical entity, as Carl Raschke writes, by 'microresponses to the revelatory character of the Christian message in its complete kinesthetic setting and to its incarnation in the relational matrix of marriages, families, and friends' so 'ceases to be anchored merely in either the charismatic or structural authority of the religious leader, the preacher, or the board of elders'.[119] This would be another kind of kingdom (a kingdom with a poor servant king that would look relatively anarchic) not restricted by the strata of blood, sex, culture or political power – and the enslaving pincers of the Lobster-God shall not prevail against it.[120]

NOTES

Chapter 1

1. Dosse, *Intersecting Lives*, 88–90, 95, 98.
2. Dosse, *Intersecting Lives*, 99.
3. Deleuze also read Wronski and Warrain, referring to them in *Difference and Repetition*. The connection to this esoteric tradition is presented further below (3.3.2.).
4. Gutting, *Thinking the Impossible*, 7.
5. Dosse, *Intersecting Lives*, 99–100, 102, 104.
6. Dosse, *Intersecting Lives*, 100–1, 105–7.
7. *David Hume, sa vie, son oeuvre* (Paris: Presses Universtaires de France, 1952).
8. *Empirisme et subjectivité* (Paris: Presses Universtaires de France, 1953).
9. Dosse, *Intersecting Lives*, 116.
10. Dosse, *Intersecting Lives*, 106.
11. Gutting, *Thinking the Impossible*, 22–3.
12. Dosse, *Intersecting Lives*, 109. Gutting notes how the French turn to the German 'H's had 'a devastating effect on French philosophical style', with Hegel being 'a strikingly bad influence', resulting in a steep decline in lucidity from Bergson on. While Deleuze largely resisted the three 'H's and looked for philosophical inspiration to some of the great examples of clarity and style in the history of philosophy (Spinoza, Nietzsche and Bergson), he never escaped a certain 'hermetic' – if often a beautiful – obscurity (Gutting, *Thinking the Impossible*, 65, 187, 200).
13. Dosse, *Intersecting Lives*, 112.
14. *Nietzsche et la philosophie* (Paris: Presses Universitaires de France, 1962).
15. *La philosophie critique de Kant* (Paris: Presses Universtaires de France Vendôme, 1963).
16. *Proust et les signes* (Paris: Presses Universtaires de France, 1964).
17. Dosse, *Intersecting Lives*, 135.

18 *Nietzsche* (Paris: Presses Universtaires de France, 1965).
19 *Le Bergsonisme* (Paris: Presses Universtaires de France, 1966).
20 Gilles Deleuze and Leopold von Sacher-Masoch, *Présentation de Sacher-Masoch*, (Paris: Éditions de Minuit, 1967).
21 Gutting, *Thinking the Impossible*, 41; Baugh, 'Hegel', 130.
22 Dosse, *Intersecting Lives*, 129–33.
23 *Nietzsche et la philosophie* (Paris: Presses Universitaires de France, 1962).
24 *Nietzsche: sa vie, son oeuvre, avec un exposé de sa philosophie* (Paris: Presses Universtaires de France, 1965).
25 Deleuze, *Nietzsche and Philosophy*, 34.
26 Dosse, *Intersecting Lives*, 97–8, 101, 103, 137.
27 'La conception de la différence chez Bergson', in *Les etudes bergsoniennes* (1956) 4:77–122. This essay is translated and included in *Desert Islands and Other Texts, 1953–74*, 32–51.
28 'Bergson, 1859–1941', in *Les philosophes célèbres*, ed. by Maurice Merleau-Ponty (Paris: Lucien Mazenod, 1956): 292–9. This essay is translated and included in *Desert Islands and Other Texts, 1953–74*, 22–31.
29 *Le Bergsonisme* (Paris: Presses Universitaires de France, 1966).
30 Gutting, *Thinking the Impossible*, 41, 63; Deleuze, *Negotiations*, 140; Deleuze, *Expressionism in Philosophy: Spinoza*, 11; Deleuze, *What is Philosophy?*, 60.
31 Dosse, *Intersecting Lives*, 101–3.
32 *Spinoza et le problème de l'expression* (Paris: Éditions de Minuit,1968).
33 *Spinoza textes choisis*, Collection Philosophes (Paris: Presses Universitaires de France, 1970).
34 *Spinoza – Philosophie pratique* (Paris: Editions de Minuit, 1981); Dosse, *Intersecting Lives*, 143.
35 More accurately, the first quotation is from Deleuze and Guattari. Deleuze and Guattari, *What is Philosophy?*, 48; Deleuze, *Spinoza: Practical Philosophy*, 26.
36 *Différence et répétition* (Paris: Presses Universitaires de France, 1968).
37 Dosse, *Intersecting Lives*, 165–6.
38 Deleuze, *Difference and Repetition*, xv.
39 *Spinoza et le problème de l'expression* (Paris: Éditions de Minuit, 1968).
40 Dosse, *Intersecting Lives*, 177–8.
41 *Logique du sens* (Paris: Éditions de Minuit, 1969).

NOTES

42 Dosse, *Intersecting Lives*, 344–5, 347, 354–5.
43 *L'Anti-Oedipe: Capitalisme et Schizophrenie* (Paris: Éditions de Minuit, 1972).
44 *Capitalisme et Schizophrénie, tome 2: Mille Plateaux* (Paris: Éditions de Minuit, 1980).
45 *Kafka: Pour une Littérature Mineure* (Paris: Éditions de Minuit, 1975).
46 Dosse, *Intersecting Lives*, 250.
47 *Francis Bacon: Logique de la sensation* (Paris: Éditions de la Difference, 1981).
48 Dosse, *Intersecting Lives*, 397.
49 *Cinéma, tome 1. L'Image-mouvement* (Paris: Éditions de Minuit, 1983).
50 *Cinéma, tome 2. L'Image-temps* (Paris: Éditions de Minuit, 1985).
51 *Foucault* (Paris: Éditions de Minuit, 1986).
52 *Le pli: Leibniz et le baroque* (Paris: Éditions de Minuit, 1988).
53 *Périclès et Verdi: La philosophie de François Châtelet* (Paris: Éditions de Minuit, 1988).
54 *Qu'est-ce que la philosophie?* (Paris: Éditions de Minuit, 1991).
55 Dosse, *Intersecting Lives*, 492.
56 Dosse, *Intersecting Lives*, 497.
57 Dosse, *Intersecting Lives*, 454–5.
58 'Immanence, A Life' is translated in *Pure Immanence*.
59 'The Actual and the Virtual' is translated in *Dialogues II*.

Chapter 2

1 Deleuze, *Desert Islands*, 107; Deleuze, *Difference and Repetition*, 284–5.
2 Deleuze, *Difference and Repetition*, 123–4, 279–80; Deleuze, *Desert Islands*, 98.
3 Deleuze, *Difference and Repetition*, 115; Deleuze, *Negotiations*, 31–2.
4 Deleuze, *Negotiations*, 149; Deleuze, *Cinema 1*, 76.
5 Deleuze, *Cinema 1*, 11, 17.
6 Deleuze, *Difference and Repetition*, 182.
7 Dosse, *Intersecting Lives*, 165; Alliez, *The Signature of the World*, 105.
8 D. Smith, 'Univocity,' 175.

114 NOTES

9 D. Smith, 'Univocity,' 175.
10 May, 'Philosophy as a Spiritual Exercise,' 229.
11 Deleuze, *Difference and Repetition*, 304.
12 *Collapse III* 42. Dosse, *Intersecting Lives*, 434.
13 Dosse, *Intersecting Lives*, 165; Goodchild, *Deleuze and Guattari*, 144.
14 Hardt, *An Apprenticeship in Philosophy*, 79; Alliez, *The Signature of the World*, 105, 111. Christian Kerslake details Deleuze's interest (to be examined in Chapter 3) in the esoteric nineteenth-century mixture of occult traditions, German Idealism and differential calculus found in the work of Hoëne Wronski, Johann Malfatti de Montereggio and Francis Warrain. See Kerslake, 'Wronski' and 'The Somnambulist and the Hermaphrodite'.
15 Deleuze, *Nietzsche and Philosophy*, 9, 189; Deleuze, *Bergsonism*, 46; Deleuze, *Difference and Repetition*, 53–5, 206, 267; Bogue, *Deleuze and Guattari*, 32.
16 Deleuze, *Nietzsche and Philosophy*, 36, 189, 194, 197; Deleuze, *Pure Immanence*, 74, 84–5; Deleuze and Guattari, *Anti-Oedipus*, 42.
17 Deleuze, *Nietzsche and Philosophy*, xi–xii, 36, 72, 189, 194, 197; Deleuze, *Pure Immanence*, 84–5.
18 Deleuze, *Nietzsche and Philosophy*, 36, 189, 194, 197; Deleuze, *Difference and Repetition*, 198.
19 Hardt, *An Apprenticeship in Philosophy*, 66; Deleuze, *Nietzsche and Philosophy*, 190. Deleuze, *Nietzsche and Philosophy*, 186; Deleuze, *Difference and Repetition*, 58; Deleuze, *Expressionism in Philosophy: Spinoza*, 167; Hardt, *An Apprenticeship in Philosophy*, xiii–xiv.
20 Deleuze, *Expressionism in Philosophy: Spinoza*, 173–4. Deleuze, *Expressionism in Philosophy: Spinoza*, 55, 60–1, 67, 167.
21 Deleuze, *Difference and Repetition*, xx. Deleuze, *Difference and Repetition*, xix, 52, 235, 243, 266.
22 Hardt, *An Apprenticeship in Philosophy*, xiii. Deleuze, *Nietzsche and Philosophy*, 179; Deleuze, *Difference and Repetition*, 54–5, 207; Hardt, *An Apprenticeship in Philosophy*, 116–17.
23 Deleuze, *Pure Immanence*, 83; Deleuze, *Spinoza: Practical Philosophy*, 12; Deleuze, 'Responses to a Series of Questions', 42.
24 Deleuze, *Dialogues II*, 45.
25 Deleuze, *Nietzsche and Philosophy*, 147; Deleuze, *Pure Immanence*, 68; Deleuze, *Spinoza: Practical Philosophy*, 12–13, 26; Deleuze, *Desert Islands*, 144.
26 Deleuze, *Nietzsche and Philosophy*, 13, 16, 100; Deleuze, *Pure Immanence*, 68, 70; Deleuze, *Spinoza: Practical Philosophy*, 25; Deleuze and Guattari, *Anti-Oedipus*, 332; Deleuze, *Cinema 2*, 137, 141.

NOTES   115

27 Deleuze, *Nietzsche and Philosophy*, 34; Deleuze, *Spinoza: Practical Philosophy*, 12; Deleuze and Guattari, *Anti-Oedipus*, 334.
28 Deleuze, *Pure Immanence*, 66, 68; Deleuze, *Spinoza: Practical Philosophy*, 13.
29 Deleuze, *Nietzsche and Philosophy*, 68, 71–2; Deleuze, *Pure Immanence*, 68, 74; Deleuze, *Expressionism in Philosophy: Spinoza*, 320.
30 Deleuze, *Empiricism and Subjectivity*, 85–6; Deleuze, *Nietzsche and Philosophy*, xiv; Deleuze, *Dialogues II*, vi.
31 Deleuze, *Expressionism in Philosophy: Spinoza*, 321; Deleuze, *Negotiations*, 136; Deleuze and Guattari, *What is Philosophy?*, 5, 7, 11.
32 Deleuze, *Bergsonism*, 97, 100; Deleuze, *Difference and Repetition*, 212.
33 Deleuze, *Difference and Repetition*, xvi, 126–30; Deleuze, *Negotiations*, 148.
34 Deleuze, *Difference and Repetition*, xvi; Deleuze and Guattari, *A Thousand Plateaus*, 379.
35 Deleuze, *Difference and Repetition*, 131, 134, 167; Deleuze and Guattari, *What is Philosophy?*, 199–204.
36 Deleuze, *Difference and Repetition*, xv–xvi, 131–2, 265, 301.
37 Deleuze, *Pure Immanence*, 70; Deleuze, *The Logic of Sense*, 259; Deleuze, *Negotiations*, 148.
38 Deleuze, *Difference and Repetition*, 59, 66, 127.
39 Deleuze, *Nietzsche and Philosophy*, 76; Deleuze, *Desert Islands*, 95–6.
40 Deleuze, *Difference and Repetition*, 2, 60, 66, 126–7; Deleuze, *The Logic of Sense*, 253–7; Deleuze and Guattari, *What is Philosophy?*, 30.
41 Deleuze, *Difference and Repetition*, 62; Deleuze, *The Logic of Sense*, 255.
42 Deleuze, *Dialogues II*, vi; Alliez, *The Signature of the World*, 116.
43 Deleuze and Guattari, *A Thousand Plateaus*, 374–6; Deleuze, *Negotiations*, 147–9.
44 Colebrook, *Gilles Deleuze*, 15; Deleuze, *Dialogues II*, 18.
45 Deleuze, *Difference and Repetition*, 227; Deleuze, *The Logic of Sense*, 74.
46 Alliez, *The Signature of the World*, 116; Deleuze, *Difference and Repetition*, xix; Deleuze and Guattari, *What is Philosophy?*, 47.
47 Williams, *Gilles Deleuze's* Difference and Repetition, 79.
48 Deleuze, *Difference and Repetition*, 59, 66; Deleuze, *Cinema 2*, 130.
49 Deleuze, *Difference and Repetition*, 66; Deleuze, *The Logic of Sense*, 262, 53.

116   NOTES

50 Deleuze, *Pure Immanence*, 27; Dosse, *Intersecting Lives*, 100.
51 Deleuze, *Negotiations*, 143; Alliez, *The Signature of the World*, 114; Dosse, *Intersecting Lives*, 131. Alliez described his philosophy as a 'biophilosophy' (Alliez, *The Signature of the World*, 116).
52 Deleuze and Guattari, *Anti-Oedipus*, 96; Deleuze and Guattari, *A Thousand Plateaus*, 254–5; Hardt, *An Apprenticeship in Philosophy*, 14.
53 Deleuze, *Nietzsche and Philosophy*, 184; Deleuze, *Bergsonism*, 100, 112–13; Deleuze and Guattari, *Anti-Oedipus*, 285–6.
54 Deleuze, *Bergsonism*, 94–5, 98; Deleuze, *Cinema 2*, 141–2; Alliez, *The Signature of the World*, 114; Hardt, *An Apprenticeship in Philosophy*, 14; Colebrook, *Gilles Deleuze*, 5, 13–14, 96–7, 121, 126.
55 Deleuze, *Bergsonism*, 16; Deleuze, *Spinoza: Practical Philosophy*, 123; Deleuze, *Dialogues II*, 43; Deleuze, *Cinema 2*, 140; Colebrook, *Gilles Deleuze*, 16.
56 Deleuze and Guattari, *A Thousand Plateaus*, 503; Deleuze, *Cinema 2*, 81; Deleuze, *Negotiations*, 67, 143; Albert, 'Impersonal, hylozoic cosmology', 187.
57 Deleuze, *Cinema 1*, 58, 68, 81; Deleuze and Guattari, *Anti-Oedipus*, 35; Deleuze, *Cinema 2*, 40.
58 Deleuze, *Cinema 1*, 58. Deleuze and Guattari, *Anti-Oedipus*, 78, 96; Bogue, *Deleuze and Guattari*, 150.
59 Deleuze, *Difference and Repetition*, 20; Deleuze, *Cinema 2*, 141; Deleuze and Guattari, *What is Philosophy?*, 39; Colebrook, *Gilles Deleuze*, 125; Williams, *Gilles Deleuze's Difference and Repetition*, 13, 68; DeLanda, *Intensive Science and Virtual Philosophy*, 106.
60 Deleuze, *Nietzsche and Philosophy*, 189; Deleuze, *Bergsonism*, 55; Deleuze and Guattari, *Anti-Oedipus*, 3–7, 19; Deleuze, *Cinema 2*, 142; Hardt, *An Apprenticeship in Philosophy*, xiv, 16, 61–2, 67, 93; Colebrook, *Gilles Deleuze*, 14, 96–7.
61 Deleuze, *Difference and Repetition*, 258; Deleuze, *The Logic of Sense*, 107.
62 Deleuze and Guattari, *Anti-Oedipus*, 4–5, 35; Deleuze, *Negotiations*, 146, 150.
63 Deleuze, *Nietzsche and Philosophy*, 6, 50; Deleuze and Guattari, *A Thousand Plateaus*, 249–50; Deleuze, *Cinema 2*, 140, 142; Deleuze, *Negotiations*, 146–7.
64 Deleuze and Guattari, *A Thousand Plateaus*, 272, 275, 292.
65 Deleuze, *The Logic of Sense*, 2; Deleuze, *Negotiations*, 146; Deleuze, *Desert Islands*, 101.
66 Deleuze, *Spinoza: Practical Philosophy*, 123; Deleuze and Guattari, *A Thousand Plateaus*, 293; Deleuze, *Negotiations*, 121.

NOTES

67 Deleuze, *Dialogues II*, 22–5; Deleuze and Guattari, *A Thousand Plateaus*, 238; Deleuze, *Cinema 2*, 142; Deleuze, *Negotiations*, 146.
68 Deleuze, *Dialogues II*, 2; Deleuze and Guattari, *A Thousand Plateaus*, 239, 305.
69 Deleuze, *Cinema 1*, 10; Deleuze, *Cinema 2*, 17; Deleuze, *Negotiations*, 55.
70 Deleuze, *Bergsonism*, 37, 94–5; Deleuze, *Cinema 2*, 37, 271.
71 Deleuze, *Cinema 2*, 81–2, 98; Deleuze, *Negotiations*, 66; Colebrook, *Gilles Deleuze*, 45.
72 Deleuze and Guattari, *A Thousand Plateaus*, 281; Deleuze, *Cinema 1*, 1, 23–4; Deleuze, *Negotiations*, 157.
73 Deleuze, *Negotiations*, 122, 146; Deleuze and Guattari, *What is Philosophy?*, 47.
74 Deleuze and Guattari, *Anti-Oedipus*, 96; Deleuze, *Cinema 1*, 9–10, 18; Deleuze, *Negotiations*, 55.
75 Deleuze, *Difference and Repetition*, xv, 29–30, 40–1, 116–17; Deleuze, *The Logic of Sense*, 261–2; Deleuze and Guattari, *Anti-Oedipus*, 42.
76 Deleuze, *Difference and Repetition*, 67; Dosse, *Intersecting Lives*, 138.
77 Deleuze, *Difference and Repetition*, 56–8, 64, 304.
78 Hardt, *An Apprenticeship in Philosophy*, 6–7, 63; Williams, *Gilles Deleuze's* Difference and Repetition, 70.
79 Hardt, *An Apprenticeship in Philosophy*, 14, 63.
80 Deleuze, *Difference and Repetition*, 57, 266–7.
81 D. Smith, 'Univocity', 175.
82 Deleuze, *Difference and Repetition*, 29, 32, 138, 262, 264.
83 Deleuze, *Difference and Repetition*, xv, 34–5, 115, 137–8, 266, 270.
84 Deleuze, *Difference and Repetition*, 133, 243, 266.
85 Deleuze, *Difference and Repetition*, xix, 55, 270; Deleuze, *The Logic of Sense*, 262.
86 Deleuze, *Pure Immanence*, 84; Deleuze, *Negotiations*, 145–6.
87 Deleuze, *Nietzsche and Philosophy*, 4, 8, 17; Deleuze, *Pure Immanence*, 74.
88 Deleuze, *Nietzsche and Philosophy*, 23–4; Deleuze, *Difference and Repetition*, 50; Deleuze and Guattari, *A Thousand Plateaus*, 254.
89 Deleuze, *Dialogues II*, vii.
90 Deleuze, *Pure Immanence*, 86; Deleuze, *Difference and Repetition*, 203; Deleuze and Guattari, *Anti-Oedipus*, 42; Deleuze, *Dialogues II*, 19, 43; Hardt, *An Apprenticeship in Philosophy*, 47–8.
91 Deleuze and Guattari, *A Thousand Plateaus*, 20–1.

92 Deleuze, *Difference and Repetition*, 51, 202–4, 236; Deleuze and Guattari, *A Thousand Plateaus*, 292.
93 Deleuze, *Dialogues II*, 19; Deleuze and Guattari, *A Thousand Plateaus*, 21, 71, 211, 328.
94 Deleuze, *Difference and Repetition*, 51.
95 Deleuze, *Difference and Repetition*, 278; Deleuze, *The Logic of Sense*, 262.
96 Deleuze, *Difference and Repetition*, 37, 41, 278, 304; Deleuze, *The Logic of Sense*, 263; Deleuze, *Desert Islands*, 143.
97 Deleuze, *Expressionism in Philosophy: Spinoza*, 48–9, 165–6.
98 Deleuze, *Difference and Repetition*, 35, 304. Univocity, Daniel Smith notes, is not mentioned in Deleuze's work before 1968 and 'equally abruptly . . . disappears . . . almost without a trace'. D. Smith, 'Univocity', 168.
99 Deleuze, *Difference and Repetition*, 35, 304; Deleuze, The Logic of Sense, 179; Deleuze and Guattari, *A Thousand Plateaus*, 254; Deleuze, *Expressionism in Philosophy: Spinoza*, 66.
100 Deleuze, *Difference and Repetition*, 39, 58.
101 Deleuze, *Difference and Repetition*, 33, 36, 304; Williams, *Gilles Deleuze's* Difference and Repetition, 68.
102 Deleuze, *Difference and Repetition*, 37–9, 304; Deleuze, *Expressionism in Philosophy: Spinoza*, 167, 173, 175.
103 D. Smith, 'Univocity', 180.
104 'Field of immanence' is perhaps synonymous with 'plane of immanence'. Deleuze and Guattari, *A Thousand Plateaus*, 154–7; Deleuze, *Negotiations*, 145. 'Plane of consistency' seems to be a synonym in *Spinoza: Practical Philosophy* while it acquires different meanings in *A Thousand Plateaus* and *What is Philosophy?*, usually having to do with the particularities of the virtual. Deleuze, *Spinoza: Practical Philosophy*, 122, 128; Deleuze and Guattari, *A Thousand Plateaus*, 254–5, 262–6; Deleuze and Guattari, *What is Philosophy?*, 35, 45, 118.
105 Deleuze, *Spinoza: Practical Philosophy*, 122, 128; Deleuze and Guattari, *What is Philosophy?*, 45–9; Deleuze, *Pure Immanence*, 26–7; DeLanda, *Intensive Science and Virtual Philosophy*, 153.
106 Deleuze and Guattari, *A Thousand Plateaus*, 14, 20–1; Deleuze, *Expressionism in Philosophy: Spinoza*, 174.
107 Deleuze, *Spinoza: Practical Philosophy*, 124; Deleuze and Guattari, *A Thousand Plateaus*, 254, 266; Alliez, *The Signature of the World*, 76–7.
108 Deleuze, *Cinema 1*, 59, 61; Deleuze, 'Responses to a Series of Questions', 39; Hardt, *An Apprenticeship in Philosophy*, xiii.

NOTES

109 Deleuze, *Spinoza: Practical Philosophy*, 128; Deleuze, *Dialogues II*, 25; Deleuze, *Negotiations*, 145–7. While in Deleuze and Guattari's last book together, the plane of immanence as 'THE plane of immanence' is 'interleaved' – entailing a multiplicity of varied and distinct planes of immanence or 'layers' – these later (virtual) planes are understood in a different manner than 'THE plane of immanence' as 'the base of the planes' which is maintained as the single plane that is not immanent 'to' anything else. Deleuze and Guattari, *What is Philosophy?*, 50, 57–60; Deleuze, *Dialogues II*, 113.

110 Hardt, *An Apprenticeship in Philosophy*, 74–80, 114; Deleuze and Guattari, *Anti-Oedipus*, 22, 75. In one of his last writings, Deleuze refers to this plane of immanence as 'A LIFE'. Deleuze, *Pure Immanence*, 27–30; Alliez, *The Signature of the World*, 110.

111 Deleuze and Guattari, *What is Philosophy?*, 47, 59; Deleuze and Guattari, *A Thousand Plateaus*, 18–19; Deleuze, *Pure Immanence*, 31.

112 Deleuze and Guattari, *What is Philosophy?*, 47; Deleuze, *Negotiations*, 146; Hardt, *An Apprenticeship in Philosophy*, xv.

113 Deleuze, *Expressionism in Philosophy: Spinoza*, 173; Hardt, *An Apprenticeship in Philosophy*, 69.

114 Deleuze, *Pure Immanence*, 68; Deleuze, *Difference and Repetition*, xv, 33–5, 138–9, 269; Deleuze, *Cinema 2*, 141; Goodchild, *Deleuze and Guattari*, 34.

115 Deleuze, *Difference and Repetition*, 33, 36, 304; Deleuze, *Cinema 2*, 137.

116 Deleuze, *Difference and Repetition*, 29, 139, 271; Deleuze, *Expressionism in Philosophy: Spinoza*, 173.

117 Deleuze, *Difference and Repetition*, 271.

118 Deleuze, *Difference and Repetition*, 20–4, 84, 287.

119 Deleuze, *Difference and Repetition*, 57, 202.

120 Deleuze, *Difference and Repetition*, 19, 25, 27, 289.

121 Deleuze, *Difference and Repetition*, 13–15, 24–5.

122 Deleuze, *Difference and Repetition*, 17.

123 Deleuze, *Difference and Repetition*, 1–3, 11–13.

124 Deleuze, *Difference and Repetition*, 21–3, 289.

125 Deleuze, *Difference and Repetition*, 23, 289, 303.

126 Deleuze, *Difference and Repetition*, 136; Deleuze, *Negotiations*, 161; Colebrook, *Gilles Deleuze*, 63.

127 Deleuze, *Nietzsche and Philosophy*, 46, 48, 189; Deleuze, *Difference and Repetition*, 57, 126, 243.

128 Deleuze, *Difference and Repetition*, 301.

129 Deleuze, *Nietzsche and Philosophy*, xi–xii, 24, 48, 71–2, 189; Deleuze, *Pure Immanence*, 87; Deleuze, *Difference and Repetition*, 41, 55, 67.
130 Deleuze, *Difference and Repetition*, 67, 125, 241.
131 Deleuze, *Difference and Repetition*, 67; Deleuze, *The Logic of Sense*, 264.
132 Deleuze, *Nietzsche and Philosophy*, xi; Deleuze, *The Logic of Sense*, 64.
133 Deleuze, *Pure Immanence*, 88–9, 91; Deleuze, *Difference and Repetition*, 90.
134 Deleuze, *Nietzsche and Philosophy*, 71–2, 86, 189; Deleuze, *Pure Immanence*, 88–9; Deleuze, *Difference and Repetition*, 6, 41, 54–5.
135 Deleuze, *Cinema 1*, 131; Colebrook, *Gilles Deleuze*, 60, 63.
136 Deleuze, *Difference and Repetition*, 90–1.
137 Deleuze, *Nietzsche and Philosophy*, 189; Deleuze, *Pure Immanence*, 87; Deleuze, *Difference and Repetition*, 115, 126, 300.
138 Deleuze, *Difference and Repetition*, 116.
139 Deleuze, *Difference and Repetition*, 1–3, 116–17, 270; Deleuze, *The Logic of Sense*, 123, 261–2.
140 Deleuze, *Difference and Repetition*, 127, 265; Deleuze, *Desert Islands*, 101.
141 Deleuze, *The Logic of Sense*, 176; Deleuze and Guattari, *A Thousand Plateaus*, 6; Deleuze, *Difference and Repetition*, 69.
142 Deleuze, *Cinema 1*, 61; Deleuze and Guattari, *What is Philosophy?*, 51.
143 Deleuze, *Difference and Repetition*, 242–3; Deleuze and Guattari, *A Thousand Plateaus*, 313.
144 Deleuze and Guattari, *What is Philosophy?*, 204; Bogue, *Deleuze and Guattari*, 77.
145 Deleuze, *The Logic of Sense*, 266; Deleuze and Guattari, *A Thousand Plateaus*, 313, 322, 337.
146 Deleuze, *Difference and Repetition*, 57, 68, 227; Deleuze and Guattari, *What is Philosophy?*, 42.
147 Deleuze, *Difference and Repetition*, 57, 123, 128, 199, 219, 299; Deleuze, *The Logic of Sense*, 176.
148 Alliez, *The Signature of the World*, 109.
149 Deleuze, *Kant's Critical Philosophy*, 40.
150 Deleuze, *Nietzsche and Philosophy*, 4; Deleuze, *Empiricism and Subjectivity*, 87–8; Deleuze, *Dialogues II*, 43.
151 Colebrook, *Gilles Deleuze*, 6.

NOTES 121

152 Deleuze and Guattari, *What is Philosophy?*, 204; Colebrook, *Gilles Deleuze*, 34, 88; Goodchild, *Deleuze and Guattari*, 65.
153 Deleuze, *Difference and Repetition*, 68, 285; Deleuze and Guattari, *What is Philosophy?*, 160–1; DeLanda, *Intensive Science and Virtual Philosophy*, 76; Williams, *Gilles Deleuze's Difference and Repetition*, 17–18; Colebrook, *Gilles Deleuze*, 36.
154 Deleuze, *Difference and Repetition*, 56–7, 266.
155 Deleuze, *Difference and Repetition*, 199; Bogue, *Deleuze and Guattari*, 78.
156 Deleuze, *Difference and Repetition*, 278; Deleuze and Guattari, *What is Philosophy?*, 157, 160; Williams, *Gilles Deleuze's Difference and Repetition*, 198.
157 Williams, *Gilles Deleuze's Difference and Repetition*, 182.
158 Hardt, *An Apprenticeship in Philosophy*, 14; Williams, *Gilles Deleuze's Difference and Repetition*, 199.
159 Deleuze, *Difference and Repetition*, 209–10; Williams, *Gilles Deleuze's Difference and Repetition*, 9; Colebrook, *Gilles Deleuze*, 126. There is perhaps a parallel distinction in Deleuze and Guattari's work in *Anti-Oedipus* between desire (29, 287) – the metaphysical (358), 'desiring-production' (30) – and the social (29, 358) – 'environments, fields, forms of herd instinct' (287), 'social production' (30). They are both productions of the real (32).
160 Deleuze, *Difference and Repetition*, 101; Deleuze, *Dialogues II*, 112–15; Deleuze, *Cinema 2*, 68–70;
161 Deleuze, *Difference and Repetition*, 229.
162 Deleuze, *The Logic of Sense*, 64, 86, 94, 124–6; Deleuze and Guattari, *What is Philosophy?*, 156–60.
163 Deleuze, *The Logic of Sense*, 165, 175; Deleuze and Guattari, *What is Philosophy?*, 157, 160.
164 Deleuze, *Difference and Repetition*, 100, 102; Williams, *Gilles Deleuze's Difference and Repetition*, 17–18, 197–200.
165 Deleuze, *Difference and Repetition*, 229–30.
166 Deleuze, *Difference and Repetition*, 10, 100; Deleuze, *The Logic of Sense*, 150–2, 178–9; Deleuze, *Dialogues II*, vi; Deleuze and Guattari, *What is Philosophy?*, 159–61; Alliez, *The Signature of the World*, 29; Bogue, *Deleuze and Guattari*, 150; DeLanda, *Intensive Science and Virtual Philosophy*, 123, 134, 210.
167 Hardt, *An Apprenticeship in Philosophy*, 17.
168 Deleuze and Guattari, *What is Philosophy?*, 118, 155–6, 160–1; Hardt, *An Apprenticeship in Philosophy*, 18; Williams, *Gilles Deleuze's Difference and Repetition*, 7–8, 200; Alliez, *The Signature of the World*, 40; Goodchild, *Deleuze and Guattari*, 206.

169 Deleuze, *Difference and Repetition*, 209; DeLanda, *Intensive Science and Virtual Philosophy*, 41, 60–76; Colebrook, *Gilles Deleuze*, 99; Williams, *Gilles Deleuze's* Difference and Repetition, 146–7, 173, 199.
170 Deleuze, *Difference and Repetition*, 102; Bogue, *Deleuze and Guattari*, 59.
171 Deleuze, *Bergsonism*, 96–100; Deleuze, *Difference and Repetition*, 208, 279–80; Deleuze, *Dialogues II*, 41; Deleuze and Guattari, *What is Philosophy?*, 156; Deleuze, *Dialogues II*, 101. Deleuze does seem to refer to the virtual as unreal in *Negotiations* but this is unusual (Deleuze, *Negotiations*, 65).
172 Deleuze, *Difference and Repetition*, 211, 279; Deleuze, *Desert Islands*, 101; Alliez, *The Signature of the World*, 106–7.
173 Deleuze, *Difference and Repetition*, 100–2, 106–7, 278, 299.
174 Deleuze, *Difference and Repetition*, 209, 221, 279–80; Deleuze, *Desert Islands*, 100, 102.
175 Deleuze, *Bergsonism*, 93, 96, 104; Deleuze, *Dialogues II*, 112–13; Deleuze, *Cinema 1*, 18.
176 Deleuze, *Bergsonism*, 60–1, 100; Deleuze, *Cinema 1*, 103, 105, 109.
177 Deleuze, *Difference and Repetition*, 119, 126, 279–81; Deleuze, *The Logic of Sense*, 103, 241; Deleuze, *Desert Islands*, 94, 97, 102–3, 108, 111.
178 Deleuze, *Bergsonism*, 100, 55–6; Deleuze, *Difference and Repetition*, 83, 101–3; Deleuze, *Cinema 2*, 56, 79–80, 109, 122–3, 130.
179 Deleuze, *Bergsonism*, 55–6, 71; Deleuze, *Difference and Repetition*, 68, 83; Deleuze, *Dialogues II*, 112; Deleuze, *Cinema 2*, 79–80; Bogue, Deleuze and Guattari, 58. 'Man', for Bergson, if not Deleuze, has a capacity for self-consciousness in which 'the actual becomes adequate to the virtual' (Deleuze, *Bergsonism*, 106, 112–13).
180 Deleuze, *The Logic of Sense*, 130–2; Bogue, *Deleuze and Guattari*, 151.
181 Deleuze, *The Logic of Sense*, 19, 70–1, 86, 94, 182–3.
182 Deleuze, *The Logic of Sense*, 4–8, 165–6, 182–3; Deleuze and Guattari, *A Thousand Plateaus*, 88, 507; Deleuze and Guattari, *What is Philosophy?*, 156.
183 Deleuze, *The Logic of Sense*, 23, 61, 130, 216.
184 Deleuze, *The Logic of Sense*, 64, 80, 125, 166.
185 Deleuze, *The Logic of Sense*, 125, 93, 95, 104.
186 Deleuze, *The Logic of Sense*, 167, 182; Bogue, *Deleuze and Guattari*, 73, 151.
187 Deleuze, *The Logic of Sense*, 86.

188 Deleuze, *The Logic of Sense*, 88.
189 Deleuze and Guattari, *Anti-Oedipus*, 19, 326–7, 352; Deleuze and Guattari, *A Thousand Plateaus*, 31, 40, 153; Bogue, *Deleuze and Guattari*, 93.
190 Goodchild, *Deleuze and Guattari*, 70.
191 Deleuze, *The Logic of Sense*, 88.
192 Goodchild, *Deleuze and Guattari*, 156.
193 Deleuze and Guattari, *Anti-Oedipus*, 19, 84, 281; Deleuze and Guattari, *A Thousand Plateaus*, 153.
194 Deleuze and Guattari, *A Thousand Plateaus*, 43, 72, 157–8, 270, 507, 511; Goodchild, *Deleuze and Guattari*, 144.
195 Deleuze, *Spinoza: Practical Philosophy*, 122, 128; Deleuze and Guattari, *A Thousand Plateaus*, 157.
196 Deleuze and Guattari, *Anti-Oedipus*, 15; Deleuze and Guattari, *A Thousand Plateaus*, 262, 479, 507; DeLanda, *Intensive Science and Virtual Philosophy*, 78; Goodchild, *Deleuze and Guattari*, 45.
197 Deleuze and Guattari, *Anti-Oedipus*, 11, 15, 325–9.
198 Deleuze and Guattari, *Anti-Oedipus*, 326, 329; Deleuze and Guattari, *A Thousand Plateaus*, 4, 30, 158–9. 'A *body (corps)* is not reducible to an *organism*' (Deleuze and Guattari, *A Thousand Plateaus*, 366).
199 Deleuze and Guattari, *A Thousand Plateaus*, 40–5, 163, 270.
200 Deleuze and Guattari, *Anti-Oedipus*, 257; Deleuze and Guattari, *A Thousand Plateaus*, 4, 71, 145, 270.
201 The term *précurseur sombre* is translated as 'dark precursor' in *Difference and Repetition*, but as 'obscure precursor' in *The Logic of Sense* and elsewhere.
202 Deleuze, *The Logic of Sense*, 56, 95, 166, 168, 183; DeLanda, *Intensive Science and Virtual Philosophy*, 132.
203 Deleuze, *Difference and Repetition*, 144; Deleuze, *The Logic of Sense*, 60.
204 Deleuze, *Difference and Repetition*, 144, 200; Deleuze, *The Logic of Sense*, 80, 103, 241; Bogue, *Deleuze and Guattari*, 75, 80.
205 Deleuze, *The Logic of Sense*, 41, 50, 66, 68, 166.
206 Deleuze, *The Logic of Sense*, 64–6.
207 Deleuze, *Difference and Repetition*, 119, 145, 291; Deleuze, *The Logic of Sense*, 40, 50–1; Deleuze, *Desert Islands*, 97: 'A lightning bolt flashes between different intensities, but it is preceded by an *obscure precursor*, invisible, imperceptible, which determines in advance the inverted path as in negative relief, because this path is first the agent of communication between series of differences.'

208 Deleuze, *The Logic of Sense*, 40; Bogue, *Deleuze and Guattari*, 75, 154.
209 Deleuze, *The Logic of Sense*, 53, 56, 176.
210 Deleuze, *The Logic of Sense*, 167, 176, 183, 241.
211 This is reminiscent of the Derrida's quasi-transcendental infrastructures in Rodolphe Gasché's *The Tain of the Mirror*.
212 DeLanda, *Intensive Science and Virtual Philosophy*, 210.
213 Deleuze and Guattari, *A Thousand Plateaus*, 141, 510–11.
214 Deleuze and Guattari, *A Thousand Plateaus*, 72–3, 141, 144, 213, 252, 511, 513; DeLanda, *Intensive Science and Virtual Philosophy*, 212.
215 Deleuze and Guattari, *A Thousand Plateaus*, 9, 21, 32, 72, 270, 504–5.
216 Deleuze and Guattari, *A Thousand Plateaus*, 72–3, 145, 270, 336–7; Deleuze, *Dialogues II*, 53–4.
217 Deleuze and Guattari, *A Thousand Plateaus*, 55–6, 72, 134, 282.
218 Deleuze and Guattari, *A Thousand Plateaus*, 11.
219 E.g. Williams, *Gilles Deleuze's* Difference and Repetition, 11, 21, 176, 197–200.
220 Deleuze and Guattari, *A Thousand Plateaus*, 72.
221 Deleuze and Guattari, *A Thousand Plateaus*, 9; Deleuze, *Negotiations*, 145–7.
222 Deleuze, *Difference and Repetition*, 182–3, 191, 193, 203–4, 267, 279; Deleuze and Guattari, *What is Philosophy?*, 33; Deleuze, *Desert Islands*, 96.
223 Deleuze, *Difference and Repetition*, 183; Alliez, *The Signature of the World*, 109.
224 Deleuze, *Bergsonism*, 38, 80; Alliez, *The Signature of the World*, 109.
225 Deleuze and Guattari, *A Thousand Plateaus*, 484, 505–7.
226 Deleuze and Guattari, *Anti-Oedipus*, 85; Deleuze and Guattari, *A Thousand Plateaus*, 33.
227 Williams, *Gilles Deleuze's* Difference and Repetition, 7–8, 167, 173, 176.
228 Deleuze, *Difference and Repetition*, 50–1, 231.
229 Deleuze and Guattari, *A Thousand Plateaus*, 153, 479, 507; Deleuze and Guattari, *Anti-Oedipus*, 19, 84.
230 Deleuze and Guattari, *A Thousand Plateaus*, 33.
231 Deleuze, *Difference and Repetition*, 144; Deleuze, *Desert Islands*, 97.
232 Deleuze, *Difference and Repetition*, 222, 252.
233 Deleuze, *Difference and Repetition*, 144–5, 236.
234 Deleuze, *Difference and Repetition*, 222–3, 228; Deleuze, *Dialogues II*, 23.

NOTES

235 Deleuze, *Bergsonism*, 93–5; Deleuze, *Difference and Repetition*, 56.
236 Deleuze, *Difference and Repetition*, 50–1, 266–7; Deleuze, *The Logic of Sense*, 262; Deleuze, *Desert Islands*, 96–7.
237 Deleuze, *Difference and Repetition*, 56–7.
238 Deleuze, *Difference and Repetition*, 232, 237, 240–1, 259; Bogue, *Deleuze and Guattari*, 63.
239 Deleuze, *Nietzsche and Philosophy*, 63; Deleuze, *Difference and Repetition*, 96, 144–5, 222; Deleuze and Guattari, *What is Philosophy?*, 211.
240 Deleuze and Guattari, *What is Philosophy?*, 212.
241 Deleuze, *Difference and Repetition*, 56–7, 236, 266–7.
242 Deleuze, *Empiricism and Subjectivity*, 87; Deleuze, *Difference and Repetition*, 226–7.
243 Deleuze, *Difference and Repetition*, 227, 230–1, 236.
244 Deleuze, *Difference and Repetition*, 139–40, 144–5, 285.
245 Deleuze, *Bergsonism*, 26–7; Deleuze, *Difference and Repetition*, 141, 237.
246 Deleuze, *Difference and Repetition*, 80.
247 Deleuze, *Difference and Repetition*, 70, 74–5; Deleuze and Guattari, *What is Philosophy?*, 212.
248 Deleuze, *Empiricism and Subjectivity*, 66, 68; Deleuze, *Difference and Repetition*, 75, 108.
249 Deleuze, *Empiricism and Subjectivity*, 44; Deleuze, *Nietzsche and Philosophy*, 133.
250 Deleuze, *Difference and Repetition*, 71, 78–9, 84, 108.
251 Deleuze, *Difference and Repetition*, 70–1, 79, 82, 85.
252 Deleuze, *Difference and Repetition*, 79–80.
253 Deleuze, *Difference and Repetition*, 79.
254 Deleuze, *Difference and Repetition*, 80, 94; Bogue, *Deleuze and Guattari*, 66.
255 Deleuze, *Difference and Repetition*, 80–2.
256 Deleuze, *Difference and Repetition*, 79–80, 94.
257 Deleuze, *Cinema 2*, 54–6, 122–3.
258 Deleuze, *Cinema 2*, 80.
259 Deleuze, *Bergsonism*, 27, 55.
260 Deleuze, *Bergsonism*, 55–6; Deleuze, *Dialogues II*, 112.
261 Deleuze, *Bergsonism*, 60; Deleuze, *Cinema 2*, 68–9, 109, 123; Deleuze, *Dialogues II*, 112.
262 Deleuze, *Bergsonism*, 94–5, 105–6; Deleuze, *Cinema 1*, 9–11, 18, 23, 27–8; Alliez, *The Signature of the World*, 111.
263 Deleuze, *Bergsonism*, 38, 112–13.

264 Deleuze, *The Logic of Sense*, 5.
265 Deleuze, *The Logic of Sense*, 4–5, 61–4, 162–5; Deleuze, *Dialogues II*, 114.
266 Deleuze, *The Logic of Sense*, 74.
267 Deleuze and Guattari, *A Thousand Plateaus*, 262–3; Deleuze, *Cinema 2*, 81–3, 99; DeLanda, *Intensive Science and Virtual Philosophy*, 106.
268 Deleuze, *Dialogues II*, 114; Deleuze, *Cinema 2*, 82–3, 130; DeLanda, *Intensive Science and Virtual Philosophy*, 106.
269 Deleuze, *The Logic of Sense*, 5, 61–4, 77, 164–7; Deleuze and Guattari, *A Thousand Plateaus*, 262.
270 Deleuze, *The Logic of Sense*, 77.
271 Deleuze, *The Logic of Sense*, 5, 53, 62, 241; Deleuze and Guattari, *A Thousand Plateaus*, 263.
272 Deleuze, *The Logic of Sense*, 62, 100–1.
273 Deleuze, *The Logic of Sense*, 64, 180.
274 Deleuze, *The Logic of Sense*, 53, 165.
275 Deleuze, *The Logic of Sense*, 77, 88, 166.
276 Deleuze, *The Logic of Sense*, 64, 166–7, 180.
277 Deleuze, *The Logic of Sense*, 52–3; Deleuze, *Desert Islands*, 94.
278 Deleuze, *The Logic of Sense*, 4–11, 61, 132, 136, 175; Deleuze, *Cinema 1*, 106; Deleuze and Guattari, *What is Philosophy?*, 156.
279 Deleuze, *The Logic of Sense*, 6, 24, 37–8, 52–3, 136, 151, 182, 184; Deleuze and Guattari, *What is Philosophy?*, 21–2, 33–4, 159.
280 Deleuze, *The Logic of Sense*, 52–4, 116, 136, 152, 177; Deleuze, *Desert Islands*, 100; Deleuze, *Pure Immanence*, 29, 31.
281 Deleuze and Guattari, *A Thousand Plateaus*, 479, 507; Deleuze, *Negotiations*, 141; Deleuze and Guattari, *What is Philosophy?*, 21; Goodchild, *Deleuze and Guattari*, 57.
282 Deleuze, *The Logic of Sense*, 3, 8; Deleuze, *Nietzsche and Philosophy*, xi; Deleuze and Guattari, *A Thousand Plateaus*, 261, 275.
283 Deleuze, *Difference and Repetition*, 187–9; Deleuze, *The Logic of Sense*, 54, 56.
284 Deleuze, *The Logic of Sense*, 116; Deleuze, *Desert Islands*, 100.
285 Deleuze, *Negotiations*, 34; Deleuze, *The Logic of Sense*, 5, 24, 175, 184.
286 Deleuze, *The Logic of Sense*, 63.
287 Deleuze and Guattari, *What is Philosophy?*, 156.
288 Deleuze, *The Logic of Sense*, 56, 180.
289 Deleuze, *Negotiations*, 143; Deleuze, *Pure Immanence*, 28–9, 31.

NOTES

290 Deleuze, *Difference and Repetition*, 126, 265; Deleuze, *The Logic of Sense*, 7, 216, 261–3.
291 Deleuze, *Difference and Repetition*, 67.
292 Deleuze, *The Logic of Sense*, 262–3.
293 Deleuze, *Difference and Repetition*, 128; Deleuze, *The Logic of Sense*, 258.
294 Deleuze, *The Logic of Sense*, 124–5.
295 Deleuze, *The Logic of Sense*, 69–73, 81, 86, 95, 141, 176, 241.
296 Deleuze, *The Logic of Sense*, 77, 141, 166.
297 Deleuze, *The Logic of Sense*, 70–2, 104, 125, 133; Bogue, *Deleuze and Guattari*, 70–3.
298 Deleuze, *The Logic of Sense*, 28, 35, 80–1, 86, 166.
299 Deleuze, *Difference and Repetition*, 162, 256, 278; Deleuze, *The Logic of Sense*, 104, 121.
300 Deleuze, *Difference and Repetition*, 146, 194, 214; Deleuze, *The Logic of Sense*, xiii, 3, 70, 75, 78–9.
301 Deleuze, *Difference and Repetition*, 155; Deleuze, *The Logic of Sense*, 28, 31, 36, 75.
302 Deleuze, *The Logic of Sense*, 19, 22, 107, 149, 166–7, 180.
303 Deleuze, *The Logic of Sense*, 24, 125, 241.
304 Deleuze, *The Logic of Sense*, 81, 125, 167, 241.
305 Deleuze, *Difference and Repetition*, 154; Deleuze, *Expressionism in Philosophy: Spinoza*, 335; Deleuze, *The Logic of Sense*, 19, 86, 149, 167, 180.
306 Deleuze, *Difference and Repetition*, 246, 251, 279–80.
307 Alliez, *The Signature of the World*, 114.
308 Deleuze, *Difference and Repetition*, 245; Deleuze, *Desert Islands*, 102.
309 Deleuze, *Difference and Repetition*, 207, 210, 221, 252, 279–80; Deleuze, *Desert Islands*, 94, 99–100.
310 Deleuze, *Difference and Repetition*, xvi, 246; Deleuze, *Desert Islands*, 99.
311 Deleuze, *Difference and Repetition*, 1, 84, 201.
312 Deleuze, *Difference and Repetition*, xvi, xx, 17, 20, 23–5.
313 Deleuze, *Difference and Repetition*, 284.
314 Deleuze, *Difference and Repetition*, 123; Deleuze, *Expressionism in Philosophy: Spinoza*, 18; Hardt, *An Apprenticeship in Philosophy*, 69.
315 Deleuze, *Difference and Repetition*, 78.
316 Deleuze, *Difference and Repetition*, 66.
317 Deleuze, *Difference and Repetition*, 200–1; Deleuze, *The Logic of Sense*, 56–7.

318 Deleuze, *Difference and Repetition*, 196, 207; Deleuze, *The Logic of Sense*, 56.
319 Deleuze, *Difference and Repetition*, 198, 207, 209, 280; Deleuze, *Desert Islands*, 95.
320 Deleuze, *The Logic of Sense*, 56.
321 Deleuze, *Difference and Repetition*, 168; Bogue, *Deleuze and Guattari*, 59.
322 Deleuze, *Difference and Repetition*, 163, 202–3, 267; Deleuze, *The Logic of Sense*, 123.
323 Deleuze, *Difference and Repetition*, 259, 267; Alliez, *The Signature of the World*, 113; Williams, *Gilles Deleuze's* Difference and Repetition, 57.
324 Deleuze, *Difference and Repetition*, 187, 280.
325 Deleuze, *Difference and Repetition*, 187–9; Deleuze, *The Logic of Sense*, 54.
326 Deleuze, *Difference and Repetition*, 157; Deleuze, *The Logic of Sense*, 104, 121.
327 Deleuze, *Difference and Repetition*, 108, 267–8, 280.
328 Deleuze, *Difference and Repetition*, 123–4, 259.
329 Deleuze, *Difference and Repetition*, 64.
330 Deleuze, *Difference and Repetition*, 267.
331 Deleuze, *Difference and Repetition*, 162–3; Williams, *Gilles Deleuze's* Difference and Repetition, 142.
332 Deleuze, *Difference and Repetition*, 162.
333 Deleuze, *Difference and Repetition*, xx, 207, 209, 267.
334 Deleuze, *Difference and Repetition*, 155, 192, 194, 267–8; Williams, *Gilles Deleuze's* Difference and Repetition, 112.
335 Deleuze, *Difference and Repetition*, 187, 280; Deleuze, *The Logic of Sense*, 7.
336 Deleuze, *Difference and Repetition*, 155, 183, 191. Early on, Deleuze describes the idea as 'a governing principle, a schema, a rule of construction' (Deleuze, *Empiricism and Subjectivity*, 64).
337 Deleuze, *Difference and Repetition*, 182, 203, 267, 288.
338 Deleuze, *Difference and Repetition*, 209.
339 Deleuze, *Difference and Repetition*, 278.
340 Deleuze, *Desert Islands*, 99.
341 Deleuze, *Difference and Repetition*, 183, 267, 278, 280.
342 Deleuze, *Difference and Repetition*, 194; Deleuze, *Desert Islands*, 99; Williams, *Gilles Deleuze's* Difference and Repetition, 112.
343 Deleuze, *Difference and Repetition*, 183, 279–80; Deleuze, *Desert Islands*, 99–100, 111.

NOTES

344 Deleuze, *Difference and Repetition*, 278–82; Deleuze, *Desert Islands*, 99–100.
345 Deleuze, *Difference and Repetition*, 186–7, 203.
346 Deleuze, *Difference and Repetition*, 162–3, 168.
347 Deleuze, *Difference and Repetition*, 259.
348 Deleuze, *Difference and Repetition*, 198, 201, 209; Alliez, *The Signature of the World*, 113.
349 Deleuze and Guattari, *What is Philosophy?*, 27–9, 33.
350 Deleuze, *Negotiations*, 25; Deleuze and Guattari, *What is Philosophy?*, 159; Goodchild, *Deleuze and Guattari*, 57.
351 Deleuze and Guattari, *What is Philosophy?*, 199.
352 Deleuze and Guattari, *What is Philosophy?*, 16, 23, 35.
353 Deleuze and Guattari, *What is Philosophy?*, 16, 18, 80–1.
354 Deleuze and Guattari, *What is Philosophy?*, 118.
355 Deleuze and Guattari, *What is Philosophy?*, 21–2; Colebrook, *Gilles Deleuze*, 36.
356 Deleuze and Guattari, *Anti-Oedipus*, 100, 167, 183.
357 Deleuze and Guattari, *Anti-Oedipus*, 98, 108, 920; Deleuze and Guattari, *A Thousand Plateaus*, 29, 33; Deleuze, *Negotiations*, 144; Deleuze, *Desert Islands*, 221, 232.
358 Deleuze and Guattari, *Anti-Oedipus*, 54, 183, 290; Deleuze, *Negotiations*, 13; Deleuze, *Desert Islands*, 232–3.
359 Deleuze, *Difference and Repetition*, 78–9; Deleuze, *The Logic of Sense*, 263; Deleuze and Guattari, *Anti-Oedipus*, 1–2, 5.
360 Deleuze and Guattari, *Anti-Oedipus*, 1, 6, 9, 26–7, 33, 315, 325; Deleuze, *Desert Islands*, 219.
361 Deleuze and Guattari, *Anti-Oedipus*, 1, 6, 246, 315.
362 Deleuze and Guattari, *A Thousand Plateaus*, 40, 43, 72, 161, 372.
363 Deleuze and Guattari, *Anti-Oedipus*, 33, 130–1, 144, 246.
364 Deleuze and Guattari, *Anti-Oedipus*, 2, 283–6; Deleuze, *Negotiations*, 144; Colebrook, *Gilles Deleuze*, 55–7.
365 Deleuze, *Desert Islands*, 219, 232–3.
366 Deleuze and Guattari, *Anti-Oedipus*, 32, 289, 327; Bogue, *Deleuze and Guattari*, 93.
367 Deleuze and Guattari, *Anti-Oedipus*, 6, 8–11.
368 Deleuze and Guattari, *Anti-Oedipus*, 5, 24, 35, 53, 289.
369 Deleuze and Guattari, *Anti-Oedipus*, 26–7, 33, 54, 180, 183, 290; Deleuze, *Desert Islands*, 232–3.
370 Deleuze and Guattari, *Anti-Oedipus*, 30, 181, 286.
371 Deleuze and Guattari, *Anti-Oedipus*, 1–2, 5, 36, 39–40, 294; Deleuze, *Desert Islands*, 219.

130   NOTES

372 Deleuze and Guattari, *Anti-Oedipus*, 41, 315, 338, 366–7; Deleuze, *Negotiations*, 144; Deleuze, *Desert Islands*, 219, 232–3.
373 Deleuze, *The Logic of Sense*, 102, 105, 123; Bogue, *Deleuze and Guattari*, 78.
374 Deleuze, *Difference and Repetition*, 279; Deleuze, *The Logic of Sense*, 99; Deleuze, *Pure Immanence*, 26, 28, 32; Alliez, *The Signature of the World*, 108.
375 Deleuze, *Desert Islands*, 102.
376 Deleuze, *Pure Immanence*, 29.
377 Deleuze, *Difference and Repetition*, 201–2.
378 Deleuze, *Cinema 1*, 68.
379 Deleuze, *Difference and Repetition*, 1, 5, 25; Deleuze, *The Logic of Sense*, 109; Deleuze, *Negotiations*, 146, 150; Williams, *Gilles Deleuze's* Difference and Repetition, 161.
380 Deleuze, *Difference and Repetition*, 118, 276–7, 286; Colebrook, *Gilles Deleuze*, 74.
381 Deleuze, *The Logic of Sense*, 104.
382 Deleuze, *The Logic of Sense*, 99, 102–3, 107, 109; Deleuze, *Desert Islands*, 143.
383 Deleuze, *Difference and Repetition*, 163, 191, 246, 279–80; Deleuze, *Desert Islands*, 111.
384 Deleuze, *Difference and Repetition*, 277.
385 Deleuze, *The Logic of Sense*, 103, 107; Deleuze, *Spinoza: Practical Philosophy*, 128.
386 Deleuze and Guattari, *A Thousand Plateaus*, 254, 261.
387 Deleuze, *Desert Islands*, 102.
388 Deleuze, *Difference and Repetition*, 246.
389 Deleuze, *Dialogues II*, 113.
390 Deleuze, *Difference and Repetition*, 252, 257, 259, 280–1.
391 Deleuze, *Difference and Repetition*, 281; Deleuze, *Expressionism in Philosophy: Spinoza*, 92, 175.
392 Deleuze, *Difference and Repetition*, 228, 237, 258–9.
393 Deleuze, *Difference and Repetition*, 244.
394 Colebrook, *Gilles Deleuze*, 99, 126.
395 Deleuze, *Pure Immanence*, 32.
396 Deleuze, *Bergsonism*, 97–100; Alliez, *The Signature of the World*, 108; Hardt, *An Apprenticeship in Philosophy*, 17–18.
397 Deleuze and Guattari, *What is Philosophy?*, 155–6, 160; Alliez, *The Signature of the World*, 40.
398 Deleuze, *Bergsonism*, 97.
399 Deleuze, *The Logic of Sense*, 63, 167–8.

400 Deleuze, *The Logic of Sense*, 136; Deleuze, *Cinema 1*, 98, 105; Deleuze and Guattari, *What is Philosophy?*, 155–60; Deleuze, *Pure Immanence*, 31.
401 Deleuze, *Difference and Repetition*, 183; Deleuze, *The Logic of Sense*, 110, 117.
402 Deleuze, *The Logic of Sense*, 124–5, 141.
403 Deleuze, *Difference and Repetition*, 252; Deleuze, *The Logic of Sense*, 110; Williams, *Gilles Deleuze's* Difference and Repetition, 186, 199–200; Colebrook, *Gilles Deleuze*, 97.
404 Deleuze, *Difference and Repetition*, 101, 183, 189, 267; Deleuze, *The Logic of Sense*, 63.
405 Deleuze, *Difference and Repetition*, 251.
406 Williams, *Gilles Deleuze's* Difference and Repetition, 6, 186, 204; Alliez, *The Signature of the World*, 42.
407 Deleuze, *Difference and Repetition*, 251, 279–80.
408 Deleuze, *Difference and Repetition*, 246, 251.
409 Deleuze, *Difference and Repetition*, 246; Bogue, *Deleuze and Guattari*, 61; Alliez, *The Signature of the World*, 108; Williams, *Gilles Deleuze's* Difference and Repetition, 188.
410 DeLanda, *Intensive Science and Virtual Philosophy*, 61; Williams, *Gilles Deleuze's* Difference and Repetition, 206.
411 Deleuze, *Difference and Repetition*, 38, 246, 257, 259.
412 Deleuze, *Difference and Repetition*, 247, 251, 269, 276–7, 279; Deleuze, *Desert Islands*, 97.
413 Deleuze, *Difference and Repetition*, 246, 253, 257–9, 276–7, 280–1.
414 Deleuze and Guattari, *A Thousand Plateaus*, 261–3, 507; Deleuze, *Negotiations*, 141.
415 Deleuze, *Difference and Repetition*, 247, 279; Deleuze, *Desert Islands*, 97.
416 Deleuze, *Difference and Repetition*, 38; DeLanda, *Intensive Science and Virtual Philosophy*, 106; Bogue, *Deleuze and Guattari*, 62.
417 Deleuze, *Spinoza: Practical Philosophy*, 126; Deleuze, *Dialogues II*, 44–5; Deleuze and Guattari, *A Thousand Plateaus*, 254; DeLanda, *Intensive Science and Virtual Philosophy*, 153.
418 Bogue, *Deleuze and Guattari*, 63.
419 Deleuze, *Difference and Repetition*, 56–7, 244–6; Bogue, *Deleuze and Guattari*, 63–4; Alliez, *The Signature of the World*, 108; Williams, *Gilles Deleuze's* Difference and Repetition, 200.
420 Deleuze, *Difference and Repetition*, 237, 244, 258–9, 280–1.
421 Deleuze, *Difference and Repetition*, 237, 253; Williams, *Gilles Deleuze's* Difference and Repetition, 199, 201.

NOTES

422 Deleuze, *The Logic of Sense*, 110–13.
423 Deleuze, *Difference and Repetition*, 217–18, 245; Deleuze, *Dialogues II*, 114.
424 Deleuze, *Desert Islands*, 108.
425 Deleuze, *Difference and Repetition*, 214, 216, 218; Deleuze, *Desert Islands*, 94.
426 Deleuze, *Difference and Repetition*, 118; Deleuze, *Desert Islands*, 96–7, 102–3, 108.
427 Deleuze, *Desert Islands*, 96.
428 Deleuze, *Difference and Repetition*, 217–18.
429 Deleuze, *Difference and Repetition*, 207.
430 Deleuze, *Difference and Repetition*, 211–12, 279. See Deleuze, *Desert Islands*, 111 where Deleuze calls 'actualization' what he later, in DR, calls 'differenciation.'
431 Deleuze, *Difference and Repetition*, 212, 254–5; Deleuze, *Bergsonism*, 97, 100–1 (read here 'differentiate' as 'differenciate').
432 Deleuze, *Difference and Repetition*, 123–4, 207, 284.
433 Deleuze, *Difference and Repetition*, 246, 254–5, 281.
434 Deleuze, *Difference and Repetition*, 228, 230, 255.
435 Deleuze, *Difference and Repetition*, 245–7, 258, 284.
436 Deleuze, *Difference and Repetition*, 217, 221.
437 Deleuze, *Difference and Repetition*, 245, 280; Deleuze, *Desert Islands*, 96.
438 Deleuze, *Difference and Repetition*, 207, 210–14, 217, 245–7, 251, 254, 277–81; Deleuze, *Desert Islands*, 96, 100, 102, 111.
439 Deleuze, *Difference and Repetition*, 207, 209, 211, 279–80.
440 The use of 'individual' here follows DeLanda and Alliez in breaking a bit with Deleuze's terminology. DeLanda, *Intensive Science and Virtual Philosophy*, 153, 211, 221; Alliez, *The Signature of the World*, 108.
441 Deleuze and Guattari, *A Thousand Plateaus*, 142–3.
442 Deleuze and Guattari, *What is Philosophy?*, 156, 160–1.
443 Deleuze, *Bergsonism*, 97; Deleuze, *Desert Islands*, 101, 110.
444 Deleuze, *Bergsonism*, 80–1; Alliez, *The Signature of the World*, 109.
445 Hardt, *An Apprenticeship in Philosophy*, 14; Williams, *Gilles Deleuze's* Difference and Repetition, 200.
446 Deleuze, *Difference and Repetition*, 221; Deleuze, *Pure Immanence*, 32.
447 Deleuze, *The Logic of Sense*, 63–4, 168.
448 Deleuze, *The Logic of Sense*, 63–4, 184; Deleuze and Guattari, *A Thousand Plateaus*, 262; DeLanda, *Intensive Science and Virtual Philosophy*, 106; Bogue, *Deleuze and Guattari*, 68.

NOTES

449 Deleuze, *Cinema 2*, 129–30, 133.
450 Deleuze, *The Logic of Sense*, 4, 6–7, 37, 53, 63, 136, 150, 167–8, 182; Deleuze, *Dialogues II*, 50; Deleuze, *Cinema 1*, 106; Deleuze and Guattari, *What is Philosophy?*, 155–6, 159; Deleuze, *Pure Immanence*, 31.
451 Deleuze, *The Logic of Sense*, 22, 24, 37–8, 64, 167, 182, 241; Deleuze, *Cinema 1*, 99.
452 Deleuze, *The Logic of Sense*, 52, 64–6, 96, 167, 182, 241; Deleuze, *Cinema 1*, 99; Deleuze and Guattari, *What is Philosophy?*, 22.
453 Deleuze, *The Logic of Sense*, 24.
454 Deleuze and Guattari, *A Thousand Plateaus*, 484.
455 Deleuze and Guattari, *A Thousand Plateaus*, 5, 18.
456 Deleuze, *Dialogues II*, 19; Deleuze and Guattari, *A Thousand Plateaus*, 5–6, 15, 292–3, 327, 505.
457 Deleuze, *Dialogues II*, 19; Deleuze and Guattari, *A Thousand Plateaus*, 212, 292, 328, 505.
458 Deleuze and Guattari, *A Thousand Plateaus*, 506.
459 Deleuze and Guattari, *A Thousand Plateaus*, 12, 239.
460 Deleuze and Guattari, *A Thousand Plateaus*, 190, 212.
461 Deleuze and Guattari, *A Thousand Plateaus*, 8, 10, 33, 371, 505–7.
462 Deleuze and Guattari, *A Thousand Plateaus*, 239, 294; Deleuze, *Negotiations*, 146.
463 Deleuze, *Dialogues II*, 4, 19; Deleuze and Guattari, *A Thousand Plateaus*, 8–9, 294–5, 336.
464 Deleuze, *Dialogues II*, vii, 21; Deleuze and Guattari, *A Thousand Plateaus*, 21, 25, 263.
465 Deleuze and Guattari, *A Thousand Plateaus*, 7–8, 17.
466 Deleuze, *Negotiations*, 31–2, 149.
467 Deleuze and Guattari, *A Thousand Plateaus*, 6–7, 358.
468 Deleuze and Guattari, *A Thousand Plateaus*, 14–15, 20, 34, 506; Deleuze, *Negotiations*, 146.
469 Deleuze, *Difference and Repetition*, 36–7, 269, 282; Deleuze, *The Logic of Sense*, 102–3; Deleuze and Guattari, *A Thousand Plateaus*, 380.
470 Deleuze and Guattari, *A Thousand Plateaus*, 370, 474.
471 Deleuze and Guattari, *A Thousand Plateaus*, 381–2, 385, 474; Goodchild, *Deleuze and Guattari*, 165–6.
472 Deleuze and Guattari, *A Thousand Plateaus*, 361–2, 377, 477–9.
473 Deleuze and Guattari, *Anti-Oedipus*, 340.
474 Deleuze, *Difference and Repetition*, 36–7, 304; Deleuze, *The Logic of Sense*, 75, 102–3; Deleuze and Guattari, *A Thousand Plateaus*, 380.

475 Deleuze and Guattari, *A Thousand Plateaus*, 371, 379–82, 474, 482, 505–6.
476 Deleuze, *Difference and Repetition*, 36–7; Deleuze and Guattari, *A Thousand Plateaus*, 159–60.
477 Deleuze, *Dialogues II*, 23; Deleuze and Guattari, *A Thousand Plateaus*, 380.
478 Deleuze and Guattari, *Anti-Oedipus*, 340; Deleuze and Guattari, *A Thousand Plateaus*, 482.
479 Deleuze and Guattari, *A Thousand Plateaus*, 474–5, 500, 506.
480 Deleuze, *Difference and Repetition*, 206, 282, 285; Deleuze, *The Logic of Sense*, 60, 77, 102–3, 107; Deleuze, *Desert Islands*, 143.
481 Deleuze and Guattari, *A Thousand Plateaus*, 479, 507.
482 Deleuze and Guattari, *A Thousand Plateaus*, 371, 486.
483 Deleuze and Guattari, *A Thousand Plateaus*, 72, 145, 270.
484 DeLanda, *Intensive Science and Virtual Philosophy*, 209.
485 Deleuze and Guattari, *A Thousand Plateaus*, 314–15, 322–3.
486 Deleuze and Guattari, *A Thousand Plateaus*, 315.
487 Deleuze and Guattari, *A Thousand Plateaus*, 9, 40, 53, 159–60, 322, 337.
488 Deleuze and Guattari, *A Thousand Plateaus*, 270; DeLanda, *Intensive Science and Virtual Philosophy*, 209.
489 Deleuze, *Difference and Repetition*, 36; Deleuze and Guattari, *A Thousand Plateaus*, 72, 319, 322–3.
490 Deleuze, *Dialogues II*, 52–3.
491 Deleuze and Guattari, *A Thousand Plateaus*, 508.
492 Deleuze and Guattari, *Anti-Oedipus*, 221, 228, 232.
493 Deleuze and Guattari, *Anti-Oedipus*, 67, 222, 224, 314–16; Deleuze and Guattari, *A Thousand Plateaus*, 220–1.
494 Deleuze and Guattari, *A Thousand Plateaus*, 54, 508.
495 Deleuze and Guattari, *Anti-Oedipus*, 102; Deleuze and Guattari, *A Thousand Plateaus*, 303.
496 Deleuze and Guattari, *Anti-Oedipus*, 257–8, 316; Deleuze and Guattari, *A Thousand Plateaus*, 10, 54, 72, 221, 303, 509; Deleuze and Guattari, *What is Philosophy?*, 86.
497 Deleuze and Guattari, *Anti-Oedipus*, 199, 222, 261; Deleuze and Guattari, *A Thousand Plateaus*, 54, 220–1, 295.
498 Deleuze and Guattari, *A Thousand Plateaus*, 57, 71–2.
499 Deleuze and Guattari, *A Thousand Plateaus*, 141, 502; DeLanda, *Intensive Science and Virtual Philosophy*, 209.
500 Deleuze and Guattari, *A Thousand Plateaus*, 159, 270, 502.

NOTES

501 Deleuze, *Cinema 2*, 99; DeLanda, *Intensive Science and Virtual Philosophy*, 209.
502 Deleuze and Guattari, *A Thousand Plateaus*, 40–1, 158–9, 211, 505; Deleuze, *Spinoza: Practical Philosophy*, 23; Deleuze, *Cinema 2*, 133.
503 Deleuze and Guattari, *A Thousand Plateaus*, 134, 159–61; Goodchild, *Deleuze and Guattari*, 147, 160. Deleuze and Guattari alternately identify the physicochemical, organic and anthropomorphic as the 'three major strata'. See Deleuze and Guattari, *A Thousand Plateaus*, 502; DeLanda, *Intensive Science and Virtual Philosophy*, 208; Bogue, *Deleuze and Guattari*, 127.
504 Deleuze and Guattari, *A Thousand Plateaus*, 159–61; Goodchild, *Deleuze and Guattari*, 156.
505 Goodchild, *Deleuze and Guattari*, 153.
506 Deleuze, *The Logic of Sense*, 125–6.
507 Deleuze, *Difference and Repetition*, 79–81, 101; Deleuze, *The Logic of Sense*, 102–3.
508 Deleuze and Guattari, *A Thousand Plateaus*, 134, 159; Goodchild, *Deleuze and Guattari*, 147.
509 Deleuze and Guattari, *A Thousand Plateaus*, 336.
510 Goodchild, *Deleuze and Guattari*, 158.
511 Deleuze and Guattari, *Anti-Oedipus*, 321, 381.
512 Deleuze and Guattari, *A Thousand Plateaus*, 292.
513 Deleuze and Guattari, *A Thousand Plateaus*, 11, 24.
514 Deleuze and Guattari, *A Thousand Plateaus*, 15.
515 Deleuze, *Dialogues II*, 21; Deleuze and Guattari, *A Thousand Plateaus*, 15.
516 Deleuze and Guattari, *A Thousand Plateaus*, 24.
517 Alliez, *The Signature of the World*, 116; Williams, *Gilles Deleuze's* Difference and Repetition, 31.
518 Deleuze, *Difference and Repetition*, 36–7; Deleuze and Guattari, *A Thousand Plateaus*, 37.
519 Deleuze, *Difference and Repetition*, 243; Deleuze and Guattari, *A Thousand Plateaus*, 376.
520 Deleuze, *Pure Immanence*, 26; Colebrook, *Gilles Deleuze*, 72ff.
521 Colebrook, *Gilles Deleuze*, 125.
522 Deleuze, *Difference and Repetition*, 257–8.
523 Deleuze, *Empiricism and Subjectivity*, 26, 31, 64, 87, 104, 113.
524 Deleuze, *Difference and Repetition*, 258; Deleuze, *The Logic of Sense*, 102–3; Deleuze and Guattari, *Anti-Oedipus*, 358, 362; Deleuze, *Desert Islands*, 145.

525 Deleuze and Guattari, *Anti-Oedipus*, 362; Deleuze and Guattari, *A Thousand Plateaus*, 3.
526 Deleuze, *Negotiations*, 26.
527 Deleuze, *Difference and Repetition*, 276–7; Deleuze, *The Logic of Sense*, 102–3; Deleuze, *Negotiations*, 145–6; Deleuze and Guattari, *What is Philosophy?*, 48.
528 Deleuze and Guattari, *Anti-Oedipus*, 2, 4–5, 8.
529 Deleuze and Guattari, *Anti-Oedipus*, 72.
530 Deleuze and Guattari, *Anti-Oedipus*, 17, 26–7.
531 Deleuze and Guattari, *Anti-Oedipus*, 20–1.
532 Deleuze, *Difference and Repetition*, xxi, 58, 145, 254, 259; Deleuze, *The Logic of Sense*, 141.
533 Deleuze, *Difference and Repetition*, 145, 259, 276–7; Deleuze, *The Logic of Sense*, 3, 141, 175–6.
534 Deleuze and Guattari, *A Thousand Plateaus*, 3.
535 Deleuze and Guattari, *Anti-Oedipus*, 311, 362, 366.
536 Deleuze, *The Logic of Sense*, 102–3, 107.
537 Deleuze, *Nietzsche and Philosophy*, 41; Deleuze, *Spinoza: Practical Philosophy*, 17–20.
538 Deleuze, *Spinoza: Practical Philosophy*, 21.
539 Deleuze, *Difference and Repetition*, 68, 138.
540 Deleuze, *Difference and Repetition*, 74.
541 Deleuze, *Empiricism and Subjectivity*, x; Deleuze and Guattari, *What is Philosophy?*, 48. Deleuze, *Empiricism and Subjectivity*, 92–3; Deleuze, *Difference and Repetition*, 73–4, 79, 276–7; Deleuze and Guattari, *A Thousand Plateaus*, 3; Deleuze and Guattari, *What is Philosophy?*, 48, 212–13; Williams, *Gilles Deleuze's* Difference and Repetition, 93, 202–3.
542 Deleuze, *Difference and Repetition*, 75, 118, 254, 286.
543 Deleuze, *Difference and Repetition*, 78–9; Deleuze, *The Logic of Sense*, 117.
544 Deleuze and Guattari, *Anti-Oedipus*, 4.
545 Deleuze and Guattari, *Anti-Oedipus*, 362, 366; Deleuze and Guattari, *A Thousand Plateaus*, 18, 203.
546 Deleuze and Guattari, *A Thousand Plateaus*, 190, Colebrook, *Gilles Deleuze*, 5.
547 Deleuze and Guattari, *A Thousand Plateaus*, 3, 24, 29, 37, 239–42.
548 Deleuze and Guattari, *Anti-Oedipus*, 53, 113, 130–1, 318, 379.
549 Deleuze, *Difference and Repetition*, 58, 148.
550 Deleuze and Guattari, *Anti-Oedipus*, 7, 19, 35, 87.
551 Deleuze and Guattari, *Anti-Oedipus*, 5, 24, 102, 130.

552 Deleuze and Guattari, *Anti-Oedipus*, 35, 86–7, 131.
553 Deleuze and Guattari, *Anti-Oedipus*, 34, 40, 102, 246.
554 Colebrook, *Gilles Deleuze*, 66, 69, 126.
555 Deleuze and Guattari, *A Thousand Plateaus*, 32.
556 Deleuze and Guattari, *A Thousand Plateaus*, 171, 190.
557 Deleuze and Guattari, *A Thousand Plateaus*, 503; Deleuze, *Cinema 1*, 68, 81; Goodchild, *Deleuze and Guattari*, 65, 213.
558 Deleuze and Guattari, *A Thousand Plateaus*, 159, 270.
559 Goodchild, *Deleuze and Guattari*, 150–1.
560 Deleuze, *Pure Immanence*, 25, 29.
561 Deleuze and Guattari, *A Thousand Plateaus*, 238, 280; Goodchild, *Deleuze and Guattari*, 213.
562 Colebrook, *Gilles Deleuze*, 13.
563 Williams, *Gilles Deleuze's* Difference and Repetition, 210; Colebrook, *Gilles Deleuze*, 55, 79.
564 Deleuze, *Difference and Repetition*, 144–5, 196, 227.
565 Deleuze and Guattari, *A Thousand Plateaus*, 279.
566 Deleuze and Guattari, *A Thousand Plateaus*, 361–3.
567 Deleuze and Guattari, *A Thousand Plateaus*, 24, 239, 249.
568 Deleuze and Guattari, *A Thousand Plateaus*, 33, 371, 505–7.
569 Deleuze, *Dialogues II*, 20; Deleuze and Guattari, *A Thousand Plateaus*, 161, 295; Deleuze, *Negotiations*, 133.
570 Deleuze and Guattari, *A Thousand Plateaus*, 9, 11, 21, 24, 55, 506.
571 Deleuze and Guattari, *A Thousand Plateaus*, 9, 32, 204, 508.
572 Deleuze and Guattari, *A Thousand Plateaus*, 9, 21, 134, 506; Deleuze, *Negotiations*, 33.
573 Deleuze and Guattari, *A Thousand Plateaus*, 106, 291–2.
574 Deleuze and Guattari, *A Thousand Plateaus*, 171, 252, 279.
575 Spinoza (in Portuguese '*espinoza*' meaning 'thorny') designed a signet ring with his initials on the top, a thorny rose in the middle and the Latin word '*Caute*', his personal motto, at the bottom.
576 Deleuze and Guattari, *A Thousand Plateaus*, 163, 165, 503.
577 Deleuze and Guattari, *A Thousand Plateaus*, 160–1.
578 Deleuze, *Spinoza: Practical Philosophy*, 22.
579 Deleuze, *Spinoza: Practical Philosophy*, 18, 23; Goodchild, *Deleuze and Guattari*, 35.
580 Deleuze, *Difference and Repetition*, 6; Deleuze and Guattari, *A Thousand Plateaus*, 154; Deleuze, *Cinema 2*, 141.
581 Deleuze, *Difference and Repetition*, 6.
582 Deleuze, *Cinema 2*, 141.

583 Deleuze, *Spinoza: Practical Philosophy*, 23; Williams, *Gilles Deleuze's* Difference and Repetition, 202.
584 Goodchild, *Deleuze and Guattari*, 41.
585 Deleuze, *Pure Immanence*, 68; Deleuze, *Spinoza: Practical Philosophy*, 25; Bogue, *Deleuze and Guattari*, 18; Goodchild, *Deleuze and Guattari*, 206.
586 Deleuze, *Nietzsche and Philosophy*, 186, 190; Hardt, *An Apprenticeship in Philosophy*, xiv.
587 Deleuze, *Nietzsche and Philosophy*, 16; Deleuze, *Pure Immanence*, 83; Deleuze, *Spinoza: Practical Philosophy*, 12.
588 Deleuze, *Nietzsche and Philosophy*, 13, 16.
589 Deleuze, *Spinoza: Practical Philosophy*, 13; Deleuze, *Dialogues II*, 45; Deleuze, *Desert Islands*, 144.
590 Deleuze, *Pure Immanence*, 69; Deleuze, *Cinema 2*, 142, 147; Goodchild, *Deleuze and Guattari*, 206.
591 Deleuze, *Nietzsche and Philosophy*, 197; Deleuze, *Difference and Repetition*, 116, 198; Deleuze, *The Logic of Sense*, 60.
592 Deleuze, *Nietzsche and Philosophy*, 23; Deleuze, *Difference and Repetition*, 116, 198.
593 Deleuze, *The Logic of Sense*, 149–52.
594 Deleuze, *Difference and Repetition*, 7, 88, 94.
595 Deleuze, *Pure Immanence*, 91; Deleuze, *Difference and Repetition*, 41–2, 300; Deleuze, *Cinema 1*, 131, 133.
596 Deleuze, *Difference and Repetition*, 57, 243.
597 Deleuze, *Difference and Repetition*, 6.
598 Deleuze and Guattari, *Anti-Oedipus*, 25–7, 30, 111; Deleuze and Guattari, *A Thousand Plateaus*, 154, 157; Bogue, *Deleuze and Guattari*, 89; Goodchild, *Deleuze and Guattari*, 33.
599 Deleuze and Guattari, *Anti-Oedipus*, 347.
600 Deleuze and Guattari, *Anti-Oedipus*, 111, 116; Deleuze and Guattari, *A Thousand Plateaus*, 154, 157; Goodchild, *Deleuze and Guattari*, 11.
601 Deleuze and Guattari, *A Thousand Plateaus*, 155.
602 Deleuze and Guattari, *Anti-Oedipus*, 29, 33, 183, 287, 358; Deleuze and Guattari, *A Thousand Plateaus*, 14; Goodchild, *Deleuze and Guattari*, 56, 69; Colebrook, *Gilles Deleuze*, 91.
603 Deleuze and Guattari, *Anti-Oedipus*, 105, 167, 180, 271; Deleuze and Guattari, *A Thousand Plateaus*, 203.
604 Deleuze and Guattari, *Anti-Oedipus*, 40, 130, 167.
605 Deleuze and Guattari, *Anti-Oedipus*, 116, 271.
606 Deleuze, *Nietzsche and Philosophy*, 84–5; Deleuze, *Negotiations*, 133–4; Bogue, *Deleuze and Guattari*, 34.

607 Deleuze, *Cinema 2*, 141–2, 147; Deleuze, *Negotiations*, 133.
608 Deleuze, *Cinema 2*, 146–7.
609 Deleuze, *Cinema 2*, 142, 147.
610 Deleuze, *Difference and Repetition*, 41; Deleuze, *Cinema 2*, 141–2.
611 Deleuze, *Cinema 2*, 171–2.
612 Deleuze, *Cinema 2*, 177, 183, 201–2.
613 Deleuze, *Cinema 2*, 189; Deleuze and Guattari, *What is Philosophy?*, 74–5, 92.
614 Deleuze, *Cinema 2*, 172–3, 189, 201–3.
615 Deleuze, *Expressionism in Philosophy: Spinoza*, 271; Deleuze, *Spinoza: Practical Philosophy*, 14, 28; Hardt, *An Apprenticeship in Philosophy*, 117.
616 Deleuze, *Expressionism in Philosophy: Spinoza*, 272; Deleuze, *Spinoza: Practical Philosophy*, 29; Deleuze, *Desert Islands*, 144; Deleuze, *Pure Immanence*, 84; Hardt, *An Apprenticeship in Philosophy*, 117.
617 Hardt, *An Apprenticeship in Philosophy*, 96.
618 Deleuze and Guattari, *A Thousand Plateaus*, 155.
619 Deleuze, *Pure Immanence*, 27, 30.
620 Deleuze, *Nietzsche and Philosophy*, 84–5; Deleuze, *Expressionism in Philosophy: Spinoza*, 262; Deleuze, *Spinoza: Practical Philosophy*, 28.

Chapter 3

1 Goodchild, 'Why is philosophy so compromised with God?', 165n. 7.
2 Dosse, *Intersecting Lives*, 101.
3 Dosse, *Intersecting Lives*, 168.
4 Dosse, *Intersecting Lives*, 471.
5 Barber, 'Immanence and Re-expression', 38.
6 Goodchild, 'Theological Passion', 357.
7 Poxon, 'Embodied anti-theology', 49.
8 Deleuze, *Abécédaire*.
9 Goodchild, 'Why is philosophy so compromised with God?', 156.
10 Deleuze, *The Logic of Sense*, 281.
11 Caputo, 'Open Theology', 45, 47; Crockett, *Theology of the Sublime*, 1–2.
12 Crockett, *Radical Political Theology*, 128.
13 Crockett, 'Post-Secular Spinoza', 3.
14 Smith and Whistler, 'What is Continental Philosophy of Religion Now?', 3.

NOTES

15 Crockett, 'Post-Secular Spinoza', 3; *Theology of the Sublime*, 5.
16 Smith and Whistler, 'What is Continental Philosophy of Religion Now?', 14–15, 17.
17 Crockett, 'Secular Theology', 37; 'Post-Secular Spinoza', 2; *Theology of the Sublime*, 1–2; Smith and Whistler, 'What is Continental Philosophy of Religion Now?', 3.
18 Crockett, 'Post-Secular Spinoza', 2.
19 Crockett, *Theology of the Sublime*, 7 – quoting the first volume of Tillich's *Systematic Theology*.
20 Crockett, 'Secular Theology', 38; Robbins, 'Theses on Secular Theology', 34.
21 Keller, *Face of the Deep*, xvii.
22 Crockett, *Interstices of the Sublime*, 131; Crockett, 'the Sublime Fold of Religion'.
23 Smith and Whistler, 'What is Continental Philosophy of Religion Now?', 4.
24 Altizer and Hamilton, *Radical Theology*, 46; Gilkey, *Naming the Whirlwind*, 113–15.
25 Crockett, *Radical Political Theology*, 75; 'Post-Secular Spinoza', 2.
26 Altizer and Hamilton, *Radical Theology*, 29–30.
27 Crockett, *Theology of the Sublime*, 3, 5.
28 Barber, 'Secularism', 169.
29 Goodchild, 'Deleuze and Philosophy of Religion', 145; 'Theological Passion', 363.
30 Crockett, *Theology of the Sublime*, ix, 4–5.
31 Barber, 'Immanence and Re-expression', 38.
32 Bonta, 'Rhizome', 62.
33 A. Smith, 'Believing in this World', 103; Goodchild, 'Philosophy as a Way of Life', 27.
34 Goodchild, 'Philosophy as a Way of Life', 24–5; See Hadot, *Philosophy as a Way of Life*.
35 Betcher, 'Take my Yoga upon You', 60.
36 Goodchild, 'Theological Passion', 357–60; 'Why is philosophy so compromised with God?', 157–8.
37 Goodchild, 'Theological Passion', 363–4.
38 Crockett, *Radical Political Theology*, 157.
39 Justaert, 'Liberation Theology', 155.
40 Smith and Whistler, 'What is Continental Philosophy of Religion Now?', 21.
41 A. Smith, 'The Judgment of God and the Immeasurable', 79
42 Sherman, 'No Werewolves In Theology?', 20.

43 Hart, *The Beauty of the Infinite*, 107.
44 See Sherman, 'No Werewolves In Theology?', 5: 'Certainly, after Hallward, we cannot fail to recognize the prevalence of religious, mystical, and contemplative themes throughout the Deleuzean corpus, but I think it fair to say that Hallward exaggerates the extent to which these particular themes necessarily lead Deleuze and his readers in acosmic, apolitical, and incorporeal directions.'
45 Crockett, *Radical Political Theology*, 135. For the record, Crockett is speculating about another genealogy.
46 Deleuze, *Abécédaire*.
47 Kerslake, 'The Somnambulist and the Hermaphrodite'; Bonta, 'Rhizome', 62–3; D. Smith, 'Univocity', 167–8.
48 Martinism 'originat[ed] in the thought of Martinès de Pasqually (?–1774), and his follower Louis Claude Saint-Martin (1743–1803). The former, a Spanish or Portuguese Jew, had inaugurated a number of secret societies in France devoted to theurgic ritual, while his follower Saint-Martin was the author of mystical tracts (including one entitled *L'Homme du désir*) which gave primacy to the mystical task of interior transformation over ritual . . . By the end of the nineteenth century, a number of Rosicrucians, Freemasons, Illuminati and theosophists inhabited Paris and assembled to form a new movement of French Martinism, in which Papus and Stanislas de Guaita were the intellectually dominant figures. The theoretical foundations of late French Martinism were provided by Malfatti and Hoëne Wronski' (Kerslake, 'The Somnambulist and the Hermaphrodite').
49 Kerslake, 'The Somnambulist and the Hermaphrodite'.
50 Kerslake, 'Wronski', 168–9.
51 Kerslake, 'Wronski', 168.
52 Kerslake, 'Wronski', 178.
53 Kerslake, 'Wronski', 170.
54 Kerslake, 'Wronski', 170–1, 183.
55 Kerslake, 'Wronski', 171–2.
56 Kerslake writes of Malfatti (an Austrian physician, highly respected in his time, who was Beethoven's doctor, and perhaps his poisoner – either unintentionally, by using alchemical elements such as arsenic and lead medicinally, or intentionally, as an agent of the Austrian government): 'his ideas are frankly so strange that a basic reality-check on his existence and movements needs to be carried out before any further examination of his work' (Kerslake, 'The Somnambulist and the Hermaphrodite').
57 Kerslake, 'The Somnambulist and the Hermaphrodite'.

58 'Malfatti is more reckless in suggesting that there is one universal philosophy which emanates first of all from Indian mysticism, and then repeats itself in different forms throughout the history of religion, through the Neo-Platonism of Proclus and Dionysius the Areopagite, down to Böhme [Boehme] and Saint-Martin. This conviction that something eternal is repeated by various 'initiates' throughout history is a background assumption of Malfatti's book, as well as of the esoteric and occult traditions in general' (Kerslake, 'The Somnambulist and the Hermaphrodite').
59 Bonta, 'Rhizome', 62–3, 66; Kerslake, 'The Somnambulist and the Hermaphrodite'.
60 O'Regan, *Gnostic Return*, 8.
61 Albert, 'Impersonal, hylozoic cosmology', 193.
62 Kerslake, 'The Somnambulist and the Hermaphrodite'.
63 Hart, *The Beauty of the Infinite*, 91.
64 See my *Religion, Metaphysics, and the Postmodern: William Desmond and John D. Caputo*, Chapter 1.
65 Hart, *The Beauty of the Infinite*, 92.
66 O'Regan, *Gnostic Return*, 12.
67 While O'Regan sees something of twentieth-century Gnosticism in the radical, secular theology of Altizer and Tillich, Deleuze is not mentioned in the book (O'Regan, *Gnostic Return*, 5, 36).
68 My reading of Deleuze along these lines coheres, at least in part, with Hallward's reading. Having come to Hallward's book late after my own systematic reading (after the initial draft of Chapter 2), my general stance is that while Deleuze is more equivocal or plurivocal than Hallward presents him, there is a strong and consistent component of Deleuze's thought that reflects Hallward's reading.
69 O'Regan, *Gnostic Return*, 138, 141.
70 O'Regan, *Gnostic Return*, 138.
71 O'Regan, *Gnostic Return*, 101. On William Desmond's understanding of the counterfeit double see Simpson, *Religion, Metaphysics and the Postmodern*, 103.
72 O'Regan, *Gnostic Return*, 133, 138.
73 O'Regan, *Gnostic Return*, 45.
74 Hart, *The Beauty of the Infinite*, 38.
75 Balthasar, *Cosmic Liturgy*, 45.
76 Burrell, *Freedom and Creation*, 1.
77 Burrell, *Faith and Freedom*, 43, 64, 135. McCabe, *God Still Matters*, 39.
78 Sokolowski, *The God of Faith and Reason*, 13, 15, 31.

79 Sokolowski, *The God of Faith and Reason*, xi, 11, 18, 19, 33.
80 Sokolowski, *The God of Faith and Reason*, 116; Burrell, *Freedom and Creation*, 21.
81 Simpson, *The Truth is the Way*, 39.
82 Thomas Aquinas, *Summa Theologica*, II-II.1.4; II-II.1.5ad1.
83 Thomas Aquinas, *Summa Theologica*, II-II.2.10; II-II.4.1.
84 Kierkegaard, *Upbuilding Discourses in Various Spirits*, 259.
85 Westphal, *Overcoming Onto-Theology*, 76.
86 See Martin Palmer's account of eighth- and ninth-century (Nestorian and Syrian) Christianity in China in *The Jesus Sutras: Rediscovering the Lost Scrolls of Taoist Christianity* (New York: Wellspring/Ballantine, 2001).
87 Burrell, *Faith and Freedom*, 120.
88 McCabe, *God Still Matters*, 3.
89 Westphal, *Overcoming Onto-Theology*, 76; Hart, *The Beauty of the Infinite*, 11.
90 David Tracy, *Blessed Rage for Order: The New Pluralism in Theology* and *Plurality and Ambiguity: Hermeneutics, Religion, Hope*.
91 Burrell, *Freedom and Creation*, 42.
92 Hart, *The Beauty of the Infinite*, 31.
93 Desmond, *God and the Between*, 114.
94 Desmond, *God and the Between*, 5, 10, 117.
95 Desmond, *God and the Between*, 109.
96 Dosse, *Intersecting Lives*, 112.

Chapter 4

1 Clark, 'A Whiteheadian Chaosmos', 180.
2 Deleuze and Guattari, *A Thousand Plateaus*, 383.
3 Clark, 'A Whiteheadian Chaosmos', 190; Milbank, *Theology and Social Theory*, 301, 306.
4 D. Smith, 'Univocity', 175.
5 Milbank, *Theology and Social Theory*, 260, 279; Justaert, 'Évaluation Théologique', 533.
6 Justaert, 'Transcendence'.
7 D. Smith, 'Univocity', 179.
8 Hallward, *Out of this World*, 12; Milbank, *Theology and Social Theory*, 306.
9 D. Smith, 'Univocity', 180.

10 Baugh, 'Hegel', 130.
11 Dosse, *Intersecting Lives*, 139.
12 Sherman, 'No Werewolves In Theology?', 2.
13 Deleuze, *Nietzsche and Philosophy*, 125, 158, 184.
14 Dale, 'Knowing', 135. God, for Deleuze, is like Morgoth in Tolkein's *Silmarillion*: the great enemy of the world.
15 Milbank, 'The Mystery of Reason', 74; Milbank, 'Immanence and Life', 15; Poxon, 'Embodied anti-theology', 49.
16 Hart, *The Beauty of the Infinite*, 96.
17 Deleuze, *Essays Critical and Clinical*, 133.
18 Pearson, 'Pure Reserve', 149.
19 D. Smith, 'Univocity', 179; Pearson, 'Pure Reserve', 153; Clark, 'A Whiteheadian Chaosmos', 192.
20 Clark, 'A Whiteheadian Chaosmos', 190. '"Paradoxical instances", "aleatory points", "dark precursors": these, I would suggest, are the only divine elements in the Deleuzian chaosmos, "primitives" in both a methodological and metaphysical sense' (191).
21 Dosse, *Intersecting Lives*, 152; Deleuze, *Abécédaire*.
22 Milbank, 'Immanence and Life', 4; Sherman, 'No Werewolves In Theology?', 3.
23 Sherman, 'No Werewolves In Theology?', 3.
24 Albert, 'Impersonal, hylozoic cosmology', 187.
25 Deleuze, *The Logic of Sense*, 107.
26 Milbank, 'Immanence and Life', 21.
27 Deleuze, *The Logic of Sense*, 297.
28 Justaert, 'Évaluation Théologique', 532–3.
29 Deleuze, *The Logic of Sense*, 297.
30 Deleuze, *Difference and Repetition*, 116, 282–3.
31 Goodchild, 'Deleuze and Philosophy of Religion', 150, 156–7.
32 Goodchild, 'Theological Passion', 359.
33 Albert, 'Impersonal, hylozoic cosmology', 188.
34 Bonta, 'Rhizome', 67.
35 Keller, *Face of the Deep*, 191, 238.
36 A. Smith, 'Believing in this World', 111–13.
37 Barber, 'Secularism', 169; Goodchild, 'Deleuze and Philosophy of Religion', 16.
38 A. Smith, 'Believing in this World', 112.
39 Goodchild, 'Theological Passion', 359.
40 Crockett, *Theology of the Sublime*, 111.
41 Clark, 'A Whiteheadian Chaosmos', 187.

42 Clark, 'A Whiteheadian Chaosmos', 189.
43 Clark, 'A Whiteheadian Chaosmos', 192; See Albert, 'Impersonal, hylozoic cosmology', 188.
44 Clark, 'A Whiteheadian Chaosmos', 190–1.
45 Bonta, 'Rhizome', 62, 73.
46 Keller, *Face of the Deep*, 7, 13, 190.
47 Keller, *Face of the Deep*, 169.
48 Keller, *Face of the Deep*, xviii.
49 Keller, *Face of the Deep*, 28, 38, 198.
50 Keller, *Face of the Deep*, 216; Bonta, 'Rhizome', 66. Keller presents 'Tehom, Elohim, Ruach' as a kind of trinity – 'The Deep, the Difference and the Spirit. The godness of our depths, our differences, our spirits' – 'Womb, Word and Wind. Tiamat, Sophia and Shekhinah' (Keller, *Face of the Deep*, 231, 235).
51 Albert, 'Impersonal, hylozoic cosmology', 190.
52 Barber, 'Secularism', 169–71.
53 Goodchild, 'Deleuze and Philosophy of Religion', 153.
54 Faber, 'De-Ontologizing God', 216, 219, 223; Albert, 'Impersonal, hylozoic cosmology', 190.
55 Keller, *Face of the Deep*, xvii, 170.
56 Keller, *Face of the Deep*, 170, 182, 226.
57 Keller, *Face of the Deep*, 10, 172–3, 177.
58 Justaert, 'Liberation Theology', 156.
59 Albert, 'Impersonal, hylozoic cosmology', 188.
60 Justaert, 'Évaluation Théologique', 543; Justaert, 'Transcendence'.
61 Crockett, *Radical Political Theology*, 69–75.
62 Crockett, *Radical Political Theology*, 61, 75.
63 Keller, *Face of the Deep*, 168.
64 Barber, 'Immanence and Creation', 140; Barber, 'Immanence and Re-expression', 39, 42.
65 A. Smith, 'The Judgment of God and the Immeasurable', 72. The bracketed terms are mine, not Smith's.
66 Goodchild, 'Deleuze and Philosophy of Religion', 161, 163.
67 Goodchild, 'Deleuze and Philosophy of Religion', 154.
68 Goodchild, 'Theological Passion', 360.
69 Goodchild, 'Theological Passion', 364.
70 Hallward, *Out of this World*, 30; See the *OED* for definitions of 'virtual' and 'virtue'.
71 Pickstock, *After Writing*, 123; Milbank, *Theology and Social Theory*, 381.

72 Desmond, 'From Under the Ground of the Cave'.
73 Kerslake, 'Wronski', 176, 182.
74 Hallward, *Out of this World*, 16–17.
75 Hallward, *Out of this World*, 54, 143.
76 Desmond, *God and the Between*, 106.
77 Desmond, *God and the Between*, 92.
78 Hallward, *Out of this World*, 4, 10.
79 Deleuze, Bergsonism, 29. Hallward writes: 'one of the most characteristic features of Deleuze's work is his tendency to present what initially appears as a binary relation in such a way as to show that this relation is in fact determined by only one of its two "terms"' (Hallward, *Out of this World*, 156).
80 Kerslake, 'The Somnambulist and the Hermaphrodite'; Bonta, 'Rhizome', 68.
81 O'Regan, *Gnostic Return*, 141, 136.
82 Davies, 'Thinking Difference', 84.
83 Hart, *The Beauty of the Infinite*, 52, 56.
84 Clark, 'A Whiteheadian Chaosmos', 190.
85 Milbank, *Theology and Social Theory*, xiii, 301, 306, 314. Milbank notes that Deleuze's philosophy of difference cannot so easily (as with Heidegger or Derrida) fit the claim it is an ontology of violence (Milbank, *Theology and Social Theory*, 314).
86 O'Regan, *Gnostic Return*, 2.
87 Hallward, *Out of this World*, 152–3.
88 Hallward, *Out of this World*, 156. 'By "relation" I mean a process that operates between two or more minimally discernible terms, in such a way as to condition or inflect (but not fully to generate) the individuality of each term. A relation is only a relation in this sense if its terms retain some limited autonomy with respect to each other. A relation is only a relation if it is between terms that can be meaningfully discerned, even if the means of this discernment proceed at the very limit of indiscernment. In other words, the question is: can Deleuze's theory of difference provide a coherent theory of relation between terms' (Hallward, *Out of this World*, 152).
89 Bonta, 'Rhizome', 7.
90 Desmond is here referring to Christopher Janaway's work.
91 Desmond, 'From Under the Ground of the Cave'. Desmond, *God and the Between*, 24–6.
92 Desmond, 'From Under the Ground of the Cave'; Hallward, *Out of this World*, 36; Davies, 'Thinking Difference', 85.
93 Desmond, 'From Under the Ground of the Cave'.

94 Desmond, 'From Under the Ground of the Cave'.
95 Hart, *The Beauty of the Infinite*, 57; Balthasar, *Cosmic Liturgy*, 45.
96 Hart, *The Beauty of the Infinite*, 64; Milbank, *Theology and Social Theory*, 278–9; Sherman, 'No Werewolves In Theology?', 13–14.
97 Desmond, *God and the Between*, 218.
98 O'Regan, *Gnostic Return*, 133.
99 O'Regan, *Gnostic Return*, 131.
100 Kerslake, 'Wronski', 170–1, 185. 'On Warrain's Wronskian architectonic, life is composed of a series of levels of reality, each a rhythmical and dynamic compromise between continuity and discontinuity, each with its own "universal problem" [*problème universel*] (how to find a dynamic equilibrium for opposing forces), each with its own secret harmonies. For Warrain, this "life" is the true matter of the transcendental calculus' (Kerslake, 'Wronski', 185).
101 Clark, 'A Whiteheadian Chaosmos', 192; Bonta, 'Rhizome', 65. Kerslake writes: 'Warrain's metaphysics of vibration and rhythm appears to be both immanently philosophical and esoteric, and suggests a way in which the potential clash of principles between philosophy and the "esoteric" might be resolved. Warrain illustrated his chapter on Wronski's Law of Creation in Concrete Synthesis with a diagram which correlates the elements of Wronski's system one-by-one with the cabbalistic sephiroth of Jewish mysticism' (Kerslake, 'Wronski', 171).
102 Hallward, *Out of this World*, 1, 4, 8, 10.
103 Hallward, *Out of this World*, 16, 55, 164.
104 Milbank, *Theology and Social Theory*, 279; Balthasar, *Cosmic Liturgy*, 46.
105 McCabe, *God Still Matters*, 36.
106 Burrell, *Faith and Freedom*, 131.
107 McCabe, *God Still Matters*, 3.
108 Milbank, *Theology and Social Theory*, 381, 437.
109 Hart, *The Beauty of the Infinite*, 181, 185.
110 Hart, *The Beauty of the Infinite*, 8; Milbank, *Theology and Social Theory*, 435–6.
111 Hart, *The Beauty of the Infinite*, 186, 192, 212.
112 Hart, *The Beauty of the Infinite*, 180, 183.
113 Hart, *The Beauty of the Infinite*, 183; Milbank, *Theology and Social Theory*, 435.
114 Hart, *The Beauty of the Infinite*, 180, 183.
115 Davies, 'Thinking Difference', 85.

116 Hart, *The Beauty of the Infinite*, 180–1.
117 Milbank, 'The Mystery of Reason', 77, 102.
118 Desmond, *God and the Between*, 113, 160, 179.
119 Desmond, *God and the Between*, 191–2, 291.
120 Milbank, 'Immanence and Life', 23, 25; Desmond, *God and the Between*, 160.
121 Thomas Aquinas, *Summa Theologica*, 1.28.1; Thomas Aquinas, *Compendium of Theology*, I.53; McCabe, *God Still Matters*, 49, 52.
122 Milbank, *Theology and Social Theory*, 381.
123 Hart, *The Beauty of the Infinite*, 180.
124 Hart, *The Beauty of the Infinite*, 180.
125 Milbank, *Theology and Social Theory*, 434, 438.
126 Hart, *The Beauty of the Infinite*, 188, 192.
127 Kierkegaard, *Repetition*, 221, 305; Kierkegaard, *The Concept of Anxiety*, 18, 151; Simpson, *The Truth is the Way*, 90.
128 Hart, *The Beauty of the Infinite*, 181, 252.
129 Hart, *The Beauty of the Infinite*, 185.
130 Desmond, *God and the Between*, 289–90; Hart, *The Beauty of the Infinite*, 185; Milbank, *Theology and Social Theory*, 381.
131 Hart, *The Beauty of the Infinite*, 184, 252.
132 Milbank, *Theology and Social Theory*, 381; Hart, *The Beauty of the Infinite*, 175.
133 Thomas Aquinas, *Summa Theologica*, I.13.7ad1; Burrell, *Knowing the Unknowable God*, 44.
134 Burrell, *Knowing the Unknowable God*, 32, 59; Burrell, *Knowing the Unknowable God*, 32; Burrell, *Freedom and Creation*, 70.
135 Thomas Aquinas, *Summa Theologica*, I.18.2, I.3.3 sed contra; McCabe, *God Still Matters*, 50.
136 Hart, *The Beauty of the Infinite*, 177, 185.
137 Deleuze, *Cinema 2*, 81–2, 98; N 66; Colebrook 45.
138 Desmond, *God and the Between*, 301; Thomas Aquinas, *Summa Theologica*, I.20.2ad3; McCabe, *God Still Matters*, 7; Hart, *The Beauty of the Infinite*, 20.
139 Thomas Aquinas, *Summa Theologica*, I.20.1ad3, I.38.2.
140 Hart, *The Beauty of the Infinite*, 173, 175.
141 Hart, *The Beauty of the Infinite*, 180, 185, 167.
142 Kierkegaard, *Late Writings*, 268, 271–2; *Upbuilding Discourses in Various Spirits*, 268.
143 Desmond, 'Wording the Between'.
144 Milbank, *Theology and Social Theory*, 309; Milbank, 'The Mystery of Reason', 110.

145 Desmond, *God and the Between*, 107, 160.
146 Hart, *The Beauty of the Infinite*, 157, 159.
147 'To attribute stasis to God', McCabe writes, 'is as mistaken as to attribute change to him' (McCabe, *God Still Matters*, 43).

Chapter 5

1 Shaviro, 'God', 19; Ansell-Pearson, 'Pure Reserve', 141.
2 Justaert, 'Évaluation Théologique', 531; Protevi, 'Organism', 39; Albert, 'Impersonal, hylozoic cosmology', 184.
3 Protevi, 'Organism', 30; TP 40.
4 Deleuze, *Abécédaire*.
5 Deleuze and Guattari, *A Thousand Plateaus*, 158–9.
6 Deleuze, *The Logic of Sense*, 293; Deleuze and Guattari, *A Thousand Plateaus*, 502; Poxon, 'Embodied anti-theology,' 47.
7 Deleuze, *Difference and Repetition*, 57; Poxon, 'Embodied anti-theology', 42.
8 Deleuze and Guattari, *Anti-Oedipus*, 200.
9 Deleuze, *Kant's Critical Philosophy*, 72.
10 Deleuze, *Spinoza: Practical Philosophy*, 23.
11 Deleuze, *Abécédaire*; Dale, 'Knowing,' 127, 133.
12 Deleuze, *The Logic of Sense*, 292.
13 Deleuze, *The Logic of Sense*, 277; Deleuze and Guattari, *What is Philosophy?*, 43; Deleuze, *Cinema 2*, 144; Deleuze and Guattari, *What is Philosophy?*, 74.
14 Deleuze, *Difference and Repetition*, 37; Deleuze and Guattari, *A Thousand Plateaus*, 40.
15 Poxon, 'Embodied anti-theology', 45; Deleuze, *The Logic of Sense*, 292–3.
16 Deleuze, *The Logic of Sense*, 297.
17 Deleuze, *The Logic of Sense*, 71, 78; Justaert, 'Transcendence'.
18 Deleuze and Guattari, *What is Philosophy?*, 51; D. Smith, 'Univocity', 174.
19 Deleuze, *Cinema 2*, 141; Deleuze and Guattari, *What is Philosophy?*, 74.
20 Justaert, 'Transcendence'.
21 Protevi, 'Organism', 39.
22 Deleuze, *Nietzsche and Philosophy*, 125, 158, 184.
23 Deleuze, *Essays Critical and Clinical*, 133; Pearson, 'Pure Reserve', 141.

24 Hallward, *Out of this World*, 12; Justaert, 'Transcendence'; Milbank, *Theology and Social Theory*, 306.
25 Justaert, 'Transcendence'.
26 Kaufman, 'Klossowski, Deleuze, and Orthodoxy', 54.
27 Deleuze, *The Logic of Sense*, 179.
28 Kaufman, 'Klossowski, Deleuze, and Orthodoxy', 51; Deleuze, *Expressionism in Philosophy: Spinoza*, 46.
29 Kaufman, 'Klossowski, Deleuze, and Orthodoxy', 54.
30 Kaufman, 'Klossowski, Deleuze, and Orthodoxy', 54.
31 Deleuze, *Difference and Repetition*, 304; Milbank, *Theology and Social Theory*, 306.
32 Deleuze, *Expressionism in Philosophy: Spinoza*, 178.
33 Goodchild, 'Why is philosophy so compromised with God?', 159.
34 Goodchild, 'Why is philosophy so compromised with God?', 157; Justaert, 'Topologies', 254.
35 Barber, 'Immanence and Re-expression', 41.
36 Barber, 'Immanence and Re-expression', 43–5.
37 Goodchild, 'Meaningless Suffering'; Crockett, 'Post-Secular Spinoza', 7; Crockett, *Radical Political Theology*, 91.
38 Justaert, 'Topologies', 241, 253.
39 Justaert, 'Topologies', 253.
40 Goodchild, 'Why is philosophy so compromised with God?' 157; Justaert, 'Topologies', 254; Justaert, 'Transcendence.'
41 Crockett, 'Post-Secular Spinoza', 6; Barber, 'Immanence and Re-expression', 44; Barber, 'Immanence and Creation', 140.
42 Faber, 'De-Ontologizing God', 216, 219, 223.
43 Poxon, 'Anti-theology', 50; Shaviro, 'God', 19.
44 Crockett, 'Post-Secular Spinoza', 8; D. Smith, 'Univocity', 174; Goodchild, 'Why is philosophy so compromised with God?', 159.
45 D. Smith, 'Univocity', 174.
46 Barber, 'Immanence and Re-expression', 44.
47 Keller, *Face of the Deep*, 26, 230–1; Crockett, *Radical Political Theology*, 75; Goodchild, 'Deleuze and Philosophy of Religion', 154.
48 Keller, *Face of the Deep*, 170.
49 Keller, *Face of the Deep*, 12, 21, 169, 226.
50 Keller, *Face of the Deep*, 218–19.
51 Barber, 'Immanence and Re-expression', 40; Barber, 'Secularism', 170–1.
52 Barber, 'Secularism', 169.
53 Barber, 'Immanence and Re-expression', 40–2; Goodchild, 'Deleuze and Philosophy of Religion', 154.

54 A. Smith, 'The Judgment of God and the Immeasurable', 80; A. Smith, 'Believing in this World', 108.
55 Simpson, *Religion, Metaphysics, and the Postmodern*, 103–4; Desmond, *Ethics and the Between*, 42–4.
56 Burrell, *Freedom and Creation*, 60; McCabe, *God Still Matters*, 6–7.
57 Hart, *The Beauty of the Infinite*, 258; Burrell, *Freedom and Creation*, 62. Hart writes: 'And this state of theological decline was so precipitous and complete that it even became possible for someone as formidably intelligent as Calvin, without any apparent embarrassment, to regard the fairly lurid portrait of the omnipotent despot of book III of his *Institutes* . . . as a proper depiction of the Christian God.' (Hart, *The Beauty of the Infinite*, 134).
58 Hallward, *Out of this World*, 4, 10, 12, 156; Kerslake, 'The Somnambulist and the Hermaphrodite'.
59 Milbank, 'Immanence and Life', 18, 21.
60 Hallward, *Out of this World*, 35.
61 Milbank, 'Immanence and Life', 16–17; Hallward, *Out of this World*, 32; Justaert, '*Évaluation Théologique*', 532.
62 Desmond, *God and the Between*, 211; Pickstock, 'Theology and Post-modernity', 77; Milbank, *Theology and Social Theory*, 380.
63 Hallward, *Out of this World*, 3, 6, 12–14, 54.
64 O'Regan, *Gnostic Return*, 45, 141.
65 Desmond, *God and the Between*, 24–6.
66 Desmond, *Art, Origins, Otherness*, 165; Desmond, *God and the Between*, 25.
67 Desmond continues: 'Immanent divine agonistics: Sophia, emanation of the Alien God as absolutely pleromatic, beyond pleroma, so hyperbolic in light as to be, in a way, a dark origin' (Desmond, *God and the Between*, 218).
68 O'Regan, *Gnostic Return*, 138, 162.
69 Desmond, *God and the Between*, 59, 218.
70 A. Smith, 'The Judgment of God and the Immeasurable', 80.
71 Bonta, 'Rhizome', 65, 70; Desmond, *God and the Between*, 221.
72 Hallward, *Out of this World*, 1, 29–30, 37, 47, 162.
73 Hallward, *Out of this World*, 25; Desmond, *God and the Between*, 221.
74 Hallward, *Out of this World*, 31.
75 O'Regan, *Gnostic Return*, 151.
76 Hallward, *Out of this World*, 22, 27.
77 O'Regan, *Gnostic Return*, 150–1; McCabe, *God Matters*, 17.

78 Hart, *The Beauty of the Infinite*, 62; Kaufman, 'Klossowski, Deleuze, and Orthodoxy', 54. Deleuze sees the supporters of analogy as 'those who are between the two [univocity and equivocity]' who are also 'always those who establish what we call orthodoxy' – regarding St Thomas: 'historically he won' (Kaufman, 'Klossowski, Deleuze, and Orthodoxy,' 54). But is this true? Perhaps he 'won' until only shortly after his death in 1277. When his work was reinstated, it was with a modern univocal framework towering in the background.
79 Deleuze, *Difference and Repetition*, 304.
80 Milbank, 'The Soul of Reciprocity (Part Two)', 505.
81 Milbank, *Theology and Social Theory*, 306–7.
82 Kaufman, 'Klossowski, Deleuze, and Orthodoxy', 54.
83 Hart, *The Beauty of the Infinite*, 281.
84 Milbank, *Theology and Social Theory*, 306.
85 O'Regan, *Gnostic Return*, 146–8.
86 Kaufman, 'Klossowski, Deleuze, and Orthodoxy', 47.
87 Davies, 'Thinking Difference', 84.
88 Milbank, 'The Mystery of Reason', 77.
89 Burrell, *Freedom and Creation*, 3.
90 Sherman, 'No Werewolves In Theology?', 14; Milbank, *Theology and Social Theory*, 297.
91 Thomas Aquinas, *Summa Theologica*, I.46.2.
92 Milbank, *Being Reconciled*, 63; McCabe, *God Still Matters*, 11.
93 Burrell, *Freedom and Creation*, 21, 163.
94 Burrell, *Faith and Freedom*, 135; Burrell, *Freedom and Creation*, 5.
95 Sokolowski, *The God of Faith and Reason*, xi, 11, 15, 18, 31.
96 Burrell, *Faith and Freedom*, 131.
97 Sokolowski, *The God of Faith and Reason*, 19, 33.
98 Burrell, *Freedom and Creation*, 9; McCabe, *God Still Matters*, 6.
99 Desmond, *Being and the Between*, 231; Desmond, *Perplexity and Ultimacy*, 230, 235.
100 Sokolowski, *The God of Faith and Reason*, 116. McCabe writes: '"God", "Theos", "Deus" is of course a name borrowed from paganism'. This is fine as long as 'it does not mislead us into thinking that the God we worship (or don't) is a god' (McCabe, *God Still Matters*, 3).
101 Kierkegaard, *Philosophical Fragments*, 45–6; Kierkegaard, *Sickness Unto Death*, 99, 126; Burrell, *Faith and Freedom*, 116, 135; Burrell, *Knowing the Unknowable God*, 2.
102 Burrell, *Freedom and Creation*, 9; Sokolowski, *The God of Faith and Reason*, 1.

103 Kierkegaard, *Concluding Unscientific Postscript*, 119; Burrell, *Faith and Freedom*, xviii; Burrell, *Knowing the Unknowable God*, 35.
104 Burrell, *Knowing the Unknowable God*, 12–13, 15; Sokolowski, *The God of Faith and Reason*, 15, 18.
105 Burrell, *Freedom and Creation*, 62, 98.
106 Burrell, *Knowing the Unknowable God*, 3; Sokolowski, *The God of Faith and Reason*, 31, 33. This, McCabe notes, is due to the metaphysical gap between us and God – though, as he quips, 'of course being miserable sinners doesn't help' (McCabe, *God Matters*, 20).
107 McCabe, *God Still Matters*, 38; Burrell, *Knowing the Unknowable God*, 58.
108 Milbank, *Theology and Social Theory*, 306; Milbank, 'The Soul of Reciprocity (Part Two)', 505; Kaufman, 'Klossowski, Deleuze, and Orthodoxy,' 56.
109 Thomas Aquinas, *Summa Theologica*, I.21.4.
110 Kaufman, 'Klossowski, Deleuze, and Orthodoxy', 47; Pickstock, 'Theology and Post-modernity', 71.
111 Burrell, *Faith and Freedom*, 126; Aquinas, *Summa Theologica*, I.32.1ad3.
112 Milbank, *Theology and Social Theory*, 307.
113 Hart, *The Beauty of the Infinite*, 180.
114 Burrell, *Knowing the Unknowable God*, 14–15; Simpson, *Religion, Metaphysics, and the Postmodern*, 106.
115 McCabe, *God Matters*, 6–7. 'God is not an inhabitant of the universe; he is the reason why there is a universe at all. God is in everything holding it constantly in existence but he is not located anywhere' (McCabe, *God Still Matters*, 37).
116 Desmond, *Desire, Dialectic, Otherness*, 189, 192; Sokolowski, *The God of Faith and Reason*, 33; McCabe, *God Still Matters*, 43.
117 Desmond, *God and the Between*, 159, 163, 241, 304.
118 Sokolowski, *The God of Faith and Reason*, 19.
119 Hart, *The Beauty of the Infinite*, 130, 157, 159, 166.
120 Hart, *The Beauty of the Infinite*, 167.
121 Desmond, *God and the Between*, 161, 247, 291, 307.
122 Thomas Aquinas, *Summa Theologica*, I.46.1.
123 Burrell, *Freedom and Creation*, 8.
124 Hart, *The Beauty of the Infinite*, 251.
125 Hart, *The Beauty of the Infinite*, 130.
126 Burrell, *Freedom and Creation*, 166.
127 Pieper sees creation as the 'hidden key' to St Thomas's thought, noting Chesterton's proposed title: 'Thomas of the Creator' (Pieper, *The Silence of St. Thomas*, 32, 47ff.).

128 Thomas Aquinas, *Summa Theologica*, I.19.8, I.20.2, I.45.6; Burrell, *Freedom and Creation*, 3.
129 Thomas Aquinas, *Summa Theologica* I.20.1; McCabe, *Faith Within Reason*, 98–9.
130 Hart, *The Beauty of the Infinite*, 258.
131 McCabe, *God Matters*, 11.
132 Desmond, *God and the Between*, 161, 247, 291, 307.
133 McCabe, *God Still Matters*, 10–12.
134 Desmond, *Hegel's God*, 135–6; Desmond, *Being and the Between*, 166.
135 Desmond, *Perplexity and Ultimacy*, 133, 144, 196, 216–17; Desmond, *Ethics and the Between*, 505.
136 Desmond, *Being and the Between*, 257, 263–4; Desmond, *God and the Between*, 44.
137 Desmond, *God and the Between*, 289–90.
138 Hart, *The Beauty of the Infinite*, 183, 281.
139 Thomas Aquinas, *Summa Theologica*, I.32.1ad3.
140 Burrell, *Faith and Freedom*, 137.
141 Burrell, *Freedom and Creation*, 70.
142 Thomas Aquinas, *Summa Theologica*, I.8.1, I.45.5; Burrell, *Knowing the Unknowable God*, 95.
143 McCabe, *God Matters*, 10; Burrell, *Faith and Freedom*, 120.
144 Burrell, *Freedom and Creation*, 68.
145 Burrell, *Knowing the Unknowable God*, 95.
146 Kierkegaard, *Concluding Unscientific Postscript*, 332.
147 Thomas Aquinas, *Summa Theologica*, I.104.1, I.104.1ad4; Burrell, *Freedom and Creation*, 68; Burrell, *Knowing the Unknowable God*, 106; Milbank, *Theology and Social Theory*, 308.
148 Kierkegaard, *Sickness Unto Death*, 60; Kierkegaard, *Works of Love*, 8–10.
149 Burrell, *Faith and Freedom*, 135; Thomas Aquinas, *Summa Theologica*, I.8.1.
150 Sherman, 'No Werewolves In Theology?', 9; Pickstock, *After Writing*, 128.
151 Hart, *The Beauty of the Infinite*, 182.
152 Desmond, 'Wording the Between'; Teilhard, *The Divine Milieu*, 105. Cunningham writes 'the very relationship of immanence to transcendence, which cannot, on pain of invoking a third term, be set over and against each other. This intimacy, this noninvasive, divine concurrence, informs the world' (Cunningham, *Darwin's Pious Idea*, 411).
153 McCabe, *God Matters*, 46.
154 Thomas Aquinas, *Summa Theologica*, I.83.1ad3, III.20.1.

155 Teilhard, *The Divine Milieu*, 83–4.
156 Kierkegaard, *Concluding Unscientific Postscript*, 246; Kierkegaard, *Journals and Papers* 2:1237.
157 Burrell, *Knowing the Unknowable God*, 30; Burrell, *Freedom and Creation*, 61–2.
158 Thomas Aquinas, *Summa Theologica*, I.20.2, I.65.1ad2, I.65.2, I.91.3; Hart, *The Beauty of the Infinite*, 71; Desmond, *God and the Between*, 59, 167.
159 Sokolowski, *The God of Faith and Reason*, 128; Thomas Aquinas, *Summa Theologica*, I.22.3, I.23.8ad2.
160 Teilhard, *The Divine Milieu*, 90–1.
161 Kierkegaard, *Concluding Unscientific Postscript*, 86, 314.
162 Teilhard, *The Divine Milieu*, 24.
163 Milbank, 'Immanence and Life', 10. See Cunningham, *Darwin's Pious Idea*.
164 Hart, *The Beauty of the Infinite*, 286.
165 Desmond, 'Wording the Between'; Thomas Aquinas, *Summa Theologica*, I.18.2ad2, I.63.4ad2.
166 Milbank, 'Immanence and Life', 23; Thomas Aquinas, *Summa Theologica*, I.61.3, I.91.3, I.103.1.
167 Thomas Aquinas, *Summa Theologica*, I.47.1, II-II.183.3.
168 Hart, *The Beauty of the Infinite*, 275–6.
169 McCabe, *Faith Within Reason*, 47.
170 Desmond, *Philosophy and it Others*, 158; Sherman, 'No Werewolves In Theology?', 2.
171 McCabe, *Faith Within Reason*, 95.

Chapter 6

1 Deleuze, *Difference and Repetition*, 58; Deleuze, *The Logic of Sense*, 293–4; Deleuze and Guattari, *A Thousand Plateaus*, 252. 'More generally, the supposed identity of the I has no other guarantee than the unity of God himself' (Deleuze, *Difference and Repetition*, 86).
2 Deleuze and Guattari, *Anti-Oedipus*, 107; Deleuze, *The Logic of Sense*, 294.
3 Deleuze, *Difference and Repetition*, 58, 86–7; Deleuze, *The Logic of Sense*, 294.
4 Deleuze, *Difference and Repetition*, xix; Deleuze, *The Logic of Sense*, 294.
5 Deleuze, *Difference and Repetition*, 243.

NOTES

6   Deleuze, *Difference and Repetition*, 86–7.
7   Deleuze, *Pure Immanence*, 71; Deleuze, *Nietzsche and Philosophy*, 88–9; Deleuze, *Kant's Critical Philosophy*, 69; Deleuze, *The Logic of Sense*, 176.
8   Deleuze, *Difference and Repetition*, 87, 136; Deleuze, *The Logic of Sense*, 3, 176; Deleuze, *Abécédaire*.
9   May, 'Philosophy as a Spiritual Exercise', 228; Justaert, 'Liberation Theology', 156.
10 Goodchild, 'Theological Passion', 359.
11 A. Smith, 'Believing in this World', 104–5, 110; Goodchild, 'Philosophy as a Way of Life', 28.
12 Justaert, 'Liberation Theology', 154, 156, 160; Goodchild, 'Deleuze and Philosophy of Religion', 162.
13 O'Regan, *Gnostic Return*, 138.
14 Desmond, *God and the Between*, 221.
15 O'Regan, *Gnostic Return*, 138.
16 O'Regan, *Gnostic Return*, 133.
17 Shaviro, 'God,' 13.
18 Hallward, *Out of this World*, 92
19 Hallward, *Out of this World*, 55.
20 Hallward, *Out of this World*, 20, 62–3.
21 O'Regan, *Gnostic Return*, 151.
22 Hart, *The Beauty of the Infinite*, 113.
23 Kierkegaard, *Philosophical Fragments*, 47.
24 Sherman, 'No Werewolves In Theology?', 14.
25 Hart, *The Beauty of the Infinite*, 114.
26 Desmond, *God and the Between*, 191, 291.
27 Desmond, *God and the Between*, 191; Hart, *The Beauty of the Infinite*, 172.
28 Hart, *The Beauty of the Infinite*, 170–1; McCabe, *God Still Matters*, 49–52.
29 Kierkegaard, *Sickness Unto Death*, 14.
30 Hart, *The Beauty of the Infinite*, 286.
31 Kierekgaard, *Repetition*, 292, 307; Simpson, *The Truth is the Way*, 104.
32 Kierkegaard, *Concluding Unscientific Postscript*, 80, 180, 199, 314, 340; Simpson, *The Truth is the Way*, 61.
33 Sherman, 'No Werewolves In Theology?', 10.
34 Thomas Aquinas, *Summa Theologica*, I.60.3, I.60.5.
35 Pickstock, 'Theology and Post-modernity', 74; Burrell, *Faith and Freedom*, xx–xxi.
36 Hart, *The Beauty of the Infinite*, 115, 194.

37 Kierkegaard, *Concluding Unscientific Postscript*, 312, 411, 529–31.
38 Pickstock, *After Writing*, 129; Gregory of Nyssa, *Life of Moses*, II.Eternal Progress.
39 Burrell, *Faith and Freedom*, 135.
40 Teilhard, *The Divine Milieu*, 43.
41 Teilhard, *The Divine Milieu*, 34.
42 Thomas Aquinas, *Summa Theologica*, I.2.1ad1, I.12.1, I.13.7, III.1.3ad2.
43 Desmond, *God and the Between*, 40–3, 58.
44 Desmond, *God and the Between*, 33–4, 273.
45 Hart, *The Beauty of the Infinite*, 167, 190.
46 Hart, *The Beauty of the Infinite*, 255.
47 Hart, *The Beauty of the Infinite*, 194, 255.
48 Hart, *The Beauty of the Infinite*, 171.
49 Kierkegaard, *Concept of Anxiety*, 123–4.
50 Kierkegaard, *Sickness Unto Death*, 72–3; Kierkegaard, *Stages on Life's Way*, 197.
51 Thomas Aquinas, *Summa Theologica*, II-II.20.1ad1; Hart, *The Beauty of the Infinite*, 270; Kierkegaard, *Sickness Unto Death*, 52–3.
52 Hart, *The Beauty of the Infinite*, 196.

Chapter 7

1 Deleuze, *The Logic of Sense*, 294.
2 Deleuze, *The Logic of Sense*, 296; Deleuze and Guattari, *What is Philosophy?*, 92.
3 Deleuze, *Abécédaire*.
4 Faber, 'De-Ontologizing God', 216, 219; Hallward, *Out of this World*, 9–10, 90. Hallward writes that 'what "unifies" the field of being or creation in Spinoza isn't the idea of substance per se but the notion of God, i.e. the notion of an "infinity and perfection of essence". 52 Nowhere in his work does Deleuze put in question such infinity or perfection; on the contrary, his philosophy presupposes them at every turn' (Hallward, *Out of this World*, 156).
5 Hallward, *Out of this World*, 156; D. Smith, 'Univocity,' 175; Hardt, *Apprenticeship in Philosophy*, 69; Barber, 'Immanence and Re-expression,' 41; Beistegui, 'The Vertigo of Immanence'; Crockett, 'Post-Secular Spinoza', 6; Justaert, 'Transcendence'; Deleuze and Guattari, *Anti-Oedipus*, 326–7; Deleuze, *Negotiations*, 144; Deleuze, *Spinoza: Practical Philosophy*, passim; Deleuze, *Expressionism in Philosophy: Spinoza*, passim.

6 Deleuze, *Abécédaire*.
7 Justaert, 'Transcendence'.
8 Deleuze and Guattari, *What is Philosophy?*, 59–60; Sherman, 'No Werewolves In Theology?', 20.
9 Crockett, 'Post-Secular Spinoza', 3; Crockett, *Radical Political Theology*, 63.
10 Crockett, *Radical Political Theology*, 63.
11 Crockett, *Radical Political Theology*, 128–9, 144. This includes Deleuze as at least aspiring to be among 'the greatest philosophers' in Deleuze and Guattari's statement: 'Spinoza is the Christ of philosophers, and the greatest philosophers are hardly more than apostles who distance themselves from or draw near to this mystery' (Deleuze and Guattari, *What is Philosophy?*, 60).
12 Kerslake, 'Wronski,' 172.
13 O'Regan, *Gnostic Return*, 151.
14 O'Regan, *Gnostic Return*, 133.
15 Desmond, *God and the Between*, 221.
16 Hallward, *Out of this World*, 64, 90.
17 Hallward, *Out of this World*, 35–6.
18 McCabe, *God Still Matters*, 39; Milbank, *Being Reconciled*, 63.
19 Kierkegaard, *Practice in Christianity*, 61–2; Kierkegaard, *Philosophical Fragments*, 15; Desmond, *Hegel's God*, 194.
20 Hart, *The Beauty of the Infinite*, 257; McCabe, *God Matters*, 22.
21 Sokolowski, *The God of Faith and Reason*, 23, 26, 34; Burrell, *Knowing the Unknowable God*, 88–9; Burrell, *Freedom and Creation*, 60–1.
22 Pieper, *The Silence of St. Thomas*, 33; Sokolowski, *The God of Faith and Reason*, xi–xii.
23 Hart, *The Beauty of the Infinite*, 107
24 Justaert, 'Liberation Theology', 159–60.
25 Teilhard, *The Divine Milieu*, 119.
26 McCabe, *God Still Matters*, 7.

Chapter 8

1 Poxon, 'Embodied anti-theology', 45, 50.
2 Deleuze, *Difference and Repetition*, 37; Poxon, 'Embodied anti-theology', 42, 44.
3 Deleuze, *Difference and Repetition*, 86, 243; Deleuze, *The Logic of Sense*, 176; 'The death of God becomes effective only with the dissolution of the Self' (Deleuze, *Difference and Repetition*, 58).

NOTES

4 Deleuze, *The Logic of Sense*, 176; Deleuze, *Difference and Repetition*, 86–7.
5 Deleuze, *The Logic of Sense*, 3.
6 Deleuze, *Difference and Repetition*, 95.
7 Deleuze and Guattari, *A Thousand Plateaus*, 252.
8 Justaert, 'Transcendence'; Justaert, 'Évaluation Théologique', 532.
9 Ansell-Pearson, 'Pure Reserve', 141; Justaert, 'Transcendence'.
10 Sherman, 'No Werewolves In Theology?', 9.
11 Justaert, 'Transcendence'; Deleuze, *Abécédaire*. Speaking of the liberating withdrawal from constraints upon what one can do (in *Abécédaire*), Deleuze speaks of his illness as liberating him from the demands of society ('acquired all the rights accorded to a fragile state of health').
12 Deleuze, *Nietzsche and Philosophy*, 15.
13 Deleuze, *Spinoza: Practical Philosophy*, 23.
14 Deleuze, *Cinema 2*, 141; Deleuze and Guattari, *What is Philosophy?*, 74.
15 Marrati, 'Catholicism', 228.
16 Justaert, 'Transcendence'.
17 Crockett, *Radical Political Theology*, 75, 157; Crockett, 'Post-Secular Spinoza', 12.
18 Barber, 'Immanence and Re-expression', 44–5.
19 A. Smith, 'Believing in this World', 109.
20 Goodchild, 'Deleuze and Philosophy of Religion', 158, 163.
21 Goodchild, 'Deleuze and Philosophy of Religion', 147, 158, 161.
22 Barber, 'Immanence and Re-expression', 41, 42, 44.
23 Justaert, 'Évaluation Théologique', 532.
24 Justaert, 'Liberation Theology', 156; Justaert, 'Évaluation Théologique', 534; Justaert, 'Transcendence'.
25 Goodchild, 'Philosophy as a Way of Life', 27.
26 Goodchild, 'Philosophy as a Way of Life', 27–9.
27 Justaert, 'Évaluation Théologique', 534; Justaert, 'Transcendence'.
28 A. Smith, 'The Judgment of God and the Immeasurable', 79.
29 Keller, *Face of the Deep*, 24.
30 Crockett, *Radical Political Theology*, 68, 74–5; Crockett, 'Post-Secular Spinoza', 12.
31 Justaert, 'Liberation Theology', 156; Justaert, 'Évaluation Théologique', 534; Justaert, 'Transcendence'.
32 Crockett, 'Post-Secular Spinoza', 8; May, 'Philosophy as a Spiritual Exercise', 227–8.
33 Justaert, 'Liberation Theology', 162.
34 May, 'Philosophy as a Spiritual Exercise', 229.

35 Barber, 'Immanence and Creation', 136; A. Smith, 'Believing in this World', 108; A. Smith, 'The Judgment of God and the Immeasurable', 72.
36 A. Smith, 'Believing in this World', 108; Barber, 'Immanence and Creation', 131–2.
37 Goodchild, 'Philosophy as a Way of Life', 25; Goodchild, 'Deleuze and Philosophy of Religion', 163.
38 Justaert, 'Transcendence'; Justaert, 'Liberation Theology', 160.
39 Barber, 'Immanence and Re-expression', 44.
40 May, 'Philosophy as a Spiritual Exercise', 227; Goodchild, 'Theological Passion', 362.
41 Barber, 'Immanence and Creation', 131; Barber, 'Immanence and Re-expression', 45.
42 Barber, 'Immanence and Re-expression', 46–7.
43 Barber, 'Immanence and Re-expression', 45.
44 A. Smith, 'Believing in this World', 110.
45 A. Smith, 'The Judgment of God and the Immeasurable', 81.
46 Hallward, *Out of this World*, 3, 21, 44–5, 164.
47 Pearson, 'Pure Reserve', 141.
48 Hallward, *Out of this World*, 7, 20.
49 Desmond, *God and the Between*, 221.
50 O'Regan, *Gnostic Return*, 151.
51 O'Regan, *Gnostic Return*, 134, 138.
52 Hallward, *Out of this World*, 33–4, 50.
53 Hallward, *Out of this World*, 57, 67.
54 Desmond, *God and the Between*, 223.
55 Justaert, 'Évaluation Théologique', 543–4.
56 Hart, *The Beauty of the Infinite*, 70; Justaert, 'Évaluation Théologique', 536.
57 Hart, *The Beauty of the Infinite*, 70–1; Hallward, *Out of this World*, 6.
58 Hallward, *Out of this World*, 90.
59 Hallward, *Out of this World*, 20, 45.
60 Justaert, 'Transcendence'; Hallward, *Out of this World*, 80; Balthasar, *Cosmic Liturgy*, 45. Hallward is apparently undecided regarding whether Deleuze's philosophy can be described as ascetic or not (Hallward, *Out of this World*, 82, 86).
61 Justaert, 'Évaluation Théologique', 542–3.
62 Desmond, *God and the Between*, 210; Hallward, *Out of this World*, 1. As Hallward writes: 'All being is creative, we know, but it is unequally so. These material situations are governed by the lowest

form of creativity, in which almost nothing happens – in other words, they are situations in which what happens tends to conform to predictable patterns of causation' (Hallward, *Out of this World*, 41).
63 Quoted in Dosse, *Intersecting Lives*, 213.
64 Hallward, *Out of this World*, 3, 64, 80.
65 Justaert, 'Évaluation Théologique', 538–9; Hallward, *Out of this World*, 93.
66 Justaert, 'Transcendence'.
67 Hallward, *Out of this World*, 163; Piloiu, 'Anti-Juridical Utopia', 202; Milbank, 'Immanence and Life', 17.
68 Piloiu, 'Anti-Juridical Utopia', 224.
69 A. Smith, 'Believing in this World', 109.
70 Hallward sees Deleuze's as 'an account of the human and of the creatural more generally that both acknowledges its unreal or illusory status' (Hallward, *Out of this World*, 56).
71 A. Smith, 'The Judgment of God and the Immeasurable,' 81.
72 Pickstock, 'Theology and Post-modernity', 77–8.
73 Hallward, *Out of this World*, 153–4, 162; A. Smith, 'The Judgment of God and the Immeasurable', 72. 'By "relation" I mean a process that operates between two or more minimally discernible terms, in such a way as to condition or inflect (but not fully to generate) the individuality of each term. A relation is only a relation in this sense if its terms retain some limited autonomy with respect to each other. A relation is only a relation if it is between terms that can be meaningfully discerned, even if the means of this discernment proceed at the very limit of indiscernment' (Hallward, *Out of this World*, 152).
74 Pickstock, 'Theology and Post-modernity', 81.
75 Hart, *The Beauty of the Infinite*, 281.
76 Justaert, 'Évaluation Théologique,' 532.
77 Desmond, *God and the Between*, 219; O'Regan, *Gnostic Return*, 45.
78 Hart, *The Beauty of the Infinite*, 92.
79 Deleuze and Guattari, *A Thousand Plateaus*, 35.
80 Deleuze and Guattari, *Anti-Oedipus*, 366.
81 Desmond, *Being and the Between*, 260–1; Desmond, *Perplexity and Ultimacy*, 211–15.
82 Thomas Aquinas, *Summa Theologica*, I.20.1ad3, I.20.2ad3.
83 Hart, *The Beauty of the Infinite*, 255.
84 Desmond, *God and Between*, 164, 167–8, 252, 320.
85 Thomas Aquinas, *Summa Theologica*, I-II.25.2, I-II.27.4, II-II.23.8, II-II.23.8ad3, II-II.184.1.

86 Burrell, *Freedom and Creation*, 88; McCabe, *God Still Matters*, 4.
87 Hart, *The Beauty of the Infinite*, 107; Desmond, 'Wording the Between'.
88 Teilhard, *The Divine Milieu*, 30.
89 Teilhard, *The Divine Milieu*, 90–1
90 Sherman, 'No Werewolves In Theology?', 2.
91 Desmond, *God and the Between*, 4, 134–40.
92 Hart, *The Beauty of the Infinite*, 255; Sokolowski, *The God of Faith and Reason*, 113.
93 Pieper, *The Silence of St. Thomas*, 29; Thomas Aquinas, *Summa Theologica*, I.20.2, I.65.1ad2, I.65.2, I.91.3; Burrell, *Knowing the Unknowable God*, 29.
94 Deleuze, *Empiricism and Subjectivity*, 44; Deleuze, *Nietzsche and Philosophy*, 133.
95 Milbank comments on Ravaisson: 'Rather, the more habit grows active and intellectual, the more it becomes second nature, the more it acquires continuity and consistency within time as a process of non-identical repetition which combines both the ecstatic fusion of past, present and future and the sequential unfolding of ordinary clock-time' (Milbank, 'The Habit of Reason', 28).
96 Hart, *The Beauty of the Infinite*, 172; Desmond, *God and the Between*, 36, 110–12, 275.
97 Teilhard, *The Divine Milieu*, 29.
98 Teilhard, *The Divine Milieu*, 34; Pickstock, 'Theology and Postmodernity', 74.
99 Sherman, 'No Werewolves In Theology?', 10.
100 Kierkegaard, *Fear and Trembling*, 88. Thomas Aquinas, *Summa Theologica*, II-II.24.4, III.15.10resp.
101 Teilhard, *The Divine Milieu*, 77.
102 Sherman, 'No Werewolves In Theology?', 6.
103 Teilhard, *The Divine Milieu*, 36, 55.
104 Teilhard, *The Divine Milieu*, 66. Thus Teilhard writes that, 'the Christian . . . is at once the most attached and the most detached of men' (Teilhard, *The Divine Milieu*, 37).
105 Hart, *The Beauty of the Infinite*, 196.
106 Hart, *The Beauty of the Infinite*, 115, 194; Maximus the Confessor, *On the Cosmic Mystery of Christ*, 41–2.
107 Sherman, 'No Werewolves In Theology?', 12.
108 Teilhard, *The Divine Milieu*, 105–14; McCabe, *God Still Matters*, 50, 53; McCabe, *God Still Matters*, 24.
109 Sherman, 'No Werewolves In Theology?', 11.

110 Desmond, 'Wording the Between'; Desmond, *God and the Between*, 151.
111 Desmond, *God and the Between*, 153.
112 Deleuze, *Dialogues II*, 52.
113 Justaert, 'Liberation Theology', 159–60.
114 Deleuze, *Dialogues II*, 38.
115 Deleuze and Guattari, *A Thousand Plateaus*, 33–4.
116 Desmond, 'Wording the Between'.
117 Hart, *The Beauty of the Infinite*, 179.
118 Hart, *The Beauty of the Infinite*, 107.
119 Raschke, *GloboChrist*, 121; 'Micropolitics', Justaert writes, 'is a politics that takes place on the "molecular" level, before all forms of centralization (the macro- or molar level). It doesn't consist of decisions that need to be implemented, but of lines of desire, of intensities, of flows' (Justaert, 'Liberation Theology', 162).
120 . . . even if such pincers should wear churchly lobster-gloves.

BIBLIOGRAPHY

Works by Gilles Deleuze

Bergsonism. Translated by Barbara Habberjam and Hugh Tomlinson. Brooklyn: Zone Books, 1990. (Originally published as *Le Bergsonisme*. Paris: Presses Universtaires de France, 1966.)

Cinema 1: The Movement-Image. Translated by Barbara Habberjam and Hugh Tomlinson. Minneapolis: University of Minnesota Press, 1986. (Originally published as *Cinéma, tome 1. L'Image-mouvement*. Paris: Éditions de Minuit, 1983.)

Cinema 2: The Time-Image. Translated by Hugh Tomlinson and Robert Galeta. Minneapolis: University of Minnesota Press, 1989. (Originally published as *Cinéma, tome 2. L'Image-temps*. Paris: Éditions de Minuit, 1985.)

David Hume, sa vie, son oeuvre. Paris: Presses Universtaires de France, 1952.

Desert Islands and Other Texts, 1953–74. Translated by Mike Taormina. Los Angeles: Semiotext(e), 2004. (Originally published as *L'île déserte et autres textes*. Paris: Éditions de Minuit, 2002.)

(with Claire Parnet). *Dialogues II*. Translated by Hugh Tomlinson, Barbara Habberjam and Eliot Ross Albert. London: Continuum, 2006. (Originally published as *Dialogues*. Paris: Flammarion, 1977.)

Difference and Repetition. Translated by Paul Patton. New York: Columbia University Press, 1995. (Originally published as *Différence et répétition*. Paris: Presses Universitaires de France, 1968.)

Empiricism and Subjectivity. Translated by Constantin V. Boundas. New York: Columbia University Press, 2001. (Originally published as *Empirisme et subjectivité*. Paris: Presses Universitaires de France, 1953.)

Essays Critical and Clinical. Translated by Daniel W. Smith and Michael A. Greco. Minneapolis: University of Minnesota Press, 1997. (Originally published as *Critique et clinique*. Paris: Éditions de Minuit, 1993.)

Expressionism in Philosophy: Spinoza. Translated by Martin Joughin. Brooklyn: Zone Books, 1992. (Originally published as *Spinoza et le problème de l'expression*. Paris: Éditions de Minuit, 1968.)

The Fold: Leibniz and the Baroque. Translated by T. Conley. Minneapolis: University of Minnesota Press, 1993. (Originally published *Le pli: Leibniz et le baroque*. Paris: Éditions de Minuit, 1988.)

Foucault. Translated by S. Hand. Minneapolis: University of Minnesota Press, 1988. (Originally published *Foucault*. Paris: Éditions de Minuit, 1986.)

Francis Bacon: The Logic of Sensation. Translated by Daniel W. Smith. Minneapolis: University of Minnesota Press, 2005. (Originally published as *Francis Bacon: Logique de la sensation*. Paris: Éditions de la Difference, 1981.)

Kant's Critical Philosophy: The Doctrine of the Faculties. Translated by Hugh Tomlinson and Barbara Habberjam. Minneapolis: University of Minnesota Press, 1985. (Originally published as *La philosophie critique de Kant*. Paris: Presses Universitaires de France Vendôme, 1963.)

(with Claire Parnet). *L'Abécédaire de Gilles Deleuze*. 3 DVDs. Montparnesse: Arte Video, 1997. English overview by Charles J. Stivale at <http://www.langlab.wayne.edu/CStivale/D-G/ABC1.html> (accessed 13 September 2011).

(with Leopold von Sacher-Masoch) *Masochism: Coldness and Cruelty* and *Venus in Furs*. Translated by Jean McNeil. New York: Zone Books, 1989. (Originally published as *Présentation de Sacher-Masoch*. Paris: Éditions de Minuit, 1967.)

Negotiations 1972–90. Translated by Martin Joughin. New York: Columbia University Press, 1997. (Originally published as *Pourparlers*. Paris: Éditions de Minuit, 1990.)

Nietzsche and Philosophy. Translated by Hugh Tomlinson. New York: Columbia University Press, 1983. (Originally published as *Nietzsche et la philosophie*. Paris: Presses Universitaires de France, 1962.)

Nietzsche: sa vie, son oeuvre, avec un exposé de sa philosophie. Paris: Presses Universtaires de France, 1965.

Périclès et Verdi: La philosophie de François Châtelet. Paris: Éditions de Minuit, 1988.

Proust and Signs. Translated by Richard Howard. Minneapolis: University of Minnesota Press, 2000. (Originally published as *Proust et les signes*. Paris: Presses Universitaires de France, 1964.)

Pure Immanence: Essays on A Life. Translated by Anne Boyman. Brooklyn: Zone Books, 2001. (Containing essays originally published in French in 1965, 1972 and 1995.)

'Responses to a Series of Questions' In *Collapse III*. Edited by Robert Mackay. Falmouth: Urbanomic, 2007: 39–43.

Spinoza: Practical Philosophy. Translated by Robert Hurley. San Francisco: City Lights Publishers, 2001. (Originally published as *Spinoza – Philosophie pratique*. Paris: Éditions de Minuit, 1981.)

Spinoza textes choisis. Collection Philosophes. Paris: Presses Universitaires de France, 1970.
The Logic of Sense. Edited by Constantin V. Boundas. Translated by Mark Lester and Charles Stivale. New York: Columbia University Press, 1990. (Originally published as *Logique du sens.* Paris: Éditions de Minuit, 1969.)

Works by Gilles Deleuze and Félix Guattari

Anti-Oedipus: Capitalism and Schizophrenia. Translated by Robert Hurley and Mark Seem. New York: Penguin Classics, 2009. (Originally published as *L'Anti-Oedipe: Capitalisme et Schizophrenie.* Paris: Éditions de Minuit, 1972.)
Kafka: Toward a Minor Literature. Translated by Dana Polan. Minneapolis: University of Minnesota Press, 1986. (Originally published as *Kafka: Pour une Littérature Mineure.* Paris: Éditions de Minuit, 1975.)
A Thousand Plateaus: Capitalism and Schizophrenia. Translated by Brian Massumi. Minneapolis: University of Minnesota Press, 1987. (Originally published as *Capitalisme et Schizophrénie, tome 2: Mille Plateaux.* Paris: Éditions de Minuit, 1980.)
What is Philosophy? Translated by Janis Tomlinson and Graham Burchell III. New York: Columbia University Press, 1996. (Originally published as *Qu'est-ce que la philosophie?* Paris: Éditions de Minuit, 1991.)
For a near-exhaustive bibliography of Deleuze's writings, see Timothy S. Murphy's bibliography on Web Deleuze:
<http://www.webdeleuze.com/php/texte.php?cle=187&groupe=Bibliographie%20et%20mondes%20in%E9dits&langue=2>

Other works

Albert, Eliot. 'Deleuze's Impersonal, Hylozoic Cosmology: The Expulsion of Theology'. In *Deleuze and Religion.* Edited by Mary Bryden. London: Routledge, 2001.
Alliez, Eric. *The Signature of the World, Or, What is Deleuze and Guattari's Philosophy?* Translated by Eliot Ross Albert and Alberto Toscano. London: Continuum, 2004.
Altizer, Thomas Jonathan Jackson and William Hamilton. *Radical Theology and the Death of God.* Indianapolis: Bobbs-Merrill, 1966.

Ansell-Pearson, Keith. 'Pure Reserve: Deleuze, Philosophy, and Immanence'. In *Deleuze and Religion*. Edited by Mary Bryden. London: Routledge, 2001.
Aquinas, Thomas. *Summa theologica*. Translated by the Fathers of the English Dominican Province. Christian Classics, 1981.
— *Compendium of Theology*. Translated by Richard J. Regan. Oxford: Oxford University Press, 2009.
von Balthasar, Han Urs. *Cosmic Liturgy: The Universe According to Maximus the Confessor*. Translated by Brian E. Daley. San Francisco: Ignatius, 2003.
Barber, Daniel Colucciello. 'Immanence and Creation', *Political Theology* 10:1 (2009): 131–41.
— 'Immanence and the Re-expression of the World', *SubStance* 39:1 (2010): 38–48.
— 'Secularism, Immanence, and the Philosophy of Religion'. In *After the Postsecular and the Postmodern: New Essays in Continental Philosophy of Religion*. Edited by Anthony Paul Smith and Daniel Whistler. Newcastle upon Tyne: Cambridge Scholars Publishing, 2010.
Baugh, Bruce. "Georg Wilhelm Friedrich Hegel." In *Deleuze's Philosophical Lineage*. Edited by Graham Jones and Jon Roffe. Edinburgh: Edinburgh University Press, 2009: 130–46.
de Beistegui, Miguel. 'The Vertigo of Immanence: Deleuze's Spinozism'. *Research in Phenomenology* 35:1 (2005): 77–100.
Betcher, Sharon V. 'Take My Yoga upon You', In *Polydoxy: Theology of Multiplicity and Relation*. Edited by Catherine Keller and Laurel C. Schneider. London: Routledge, 2011: 57–80.
Bogue, Ronald. *Deleuze and Guattari*. London: Routledge, 1989.
Bonta, Mark. 'Rhizome of Boehme and Deleuze: Esoteric Precursors of the God of Complexity'. *SubStance* 39:1 (2010): 62–75.
Burrell, David. *Faith and Freedom*. London: Blackwell, 2004.
— *Freedom and Creation in Three Traditions*. South Bend: University of Notre Dame Press, 1993.
— *Knowing the Unknowable God: Ibn-Sina, Maimonides, Aquinas*. South Bend: University of Notre Dame Press, 1986.
Caputo, John D. 'Open Theology – Or What Comes after Secularism?' In *Council of Societies for the Study of Religion Bulletin* 37:2 (April 2008): 45–9.
Clark, Tim. 'A Whiteheadian Chaosmos: Process Philosophy from a Deleuzean Perspective'. *Process Studies* 28:3–4 (1999): 179–94.
Colebrook, Claire. *Gilles Deleuze*. London: Routledge, 2001.
Crockett, Clayton. *A Theology of the Sublime*. London: Routledge, 2001.
— 'Gilles Deleuze and the Sublime Fold of Religion'. In *Rethinking Philosophy of Religion: Approaches from Continental Philosophy*. Edited by Philip Goodchild. New York: Fordham, 2002.

—*Interstices of the Sublime: Theology and Psychoanalytic Theory*. New York: Fordham University Press, 2007.
— 'Post-Secular Spinoza: Deleuze, Negri and Radical Political Theology'. *Analecta Hermeneutica* 2 (2010)
— *Radical Political Theology: Religion and Politics After Liberalism*. New York: Columbia University Press, 2011.
'Secular Theology and the Academic Study of Religion'. In *Council of Societies for the Study of Religion Bulletin* 37:2 (April 2008): 37–40.
Cunningham, Conor. *Darwin's Pious Idea: Why the Ultra-Darwinists and Creationists Both Get It Wrong*. Grand Rapids: Eerdmans, 2010.
Dale, Catherine. 'Knowing One's Enemy: Deleuze, Artaud, and the Problem of Judgment'. In *Deleuze and Religion*. Edited by Mary Bryden. London: Routledge, 2001.
Gasché, Rodolphe. *The Tain of the Mirror: Derrida and the Philosophy of Reflection*. Cambridge: Harvard University Press, 1988.
Davies, Oliver. 'Thinking Difference: A Comparative Study of Gilles Deleuze, Plotinus and Meister Eckhart'. In *Deleuze and Religion*. Edited by Mary Bryden. London: Routledge, 2001.
DeLanda, Manuel. *Intensive Science and Virtual Philosophy*. London: Continuum, 2002.
Desmond, William. *Art, Origins, Otherness: Between Philosophy and Art*. Albany: SUNY Press, 2003.
— *Being and the Between*. Albany: SUNY Press, 1995.
— *Desire, Dialectic, and Otherness*. New Haven: Yale University Press, 1987.
— *Ethics and the Between*. Albany: SUNY Press, 2001.
— 'From Under the Ground of the Cave: Schopenhauer and the Philosophy of the Dark Origin'. In *A Companion to Schopenhauer (Blackwell Companions to Philosophy)*. Edited by Bart Vandenabeele. Oxford: Wiley-Blackwell, 2012 (forthcoming).
— *God and the Between*. Oxford: Blackwell, 2008.
— *Hegel's God: A Counterfeit Double?* Aldershot: Ashgate, 2003.
— *Perplexity and Ultimacy*. Albany: SUNY Press, 1995.
— 'Schopenhauer, Art and the Dark Origin'. In *Schopenhauer: New Essays in Honor of his 200th Birthday*. Edited by Eric Luft. Lewiston, NY: E. Mellon Press, 1988: 101–22.
— 'Wording the Between'. In *The William Desmond Reader*. Edited by Christopher Ben Simpson. Albany: SUNY Press, 2012 (forthcoming).
Dosse, François. *Gilles Deleuze & Félix Guattari: Intersecting Lives*. Translated by Deborah Glassman. New York: Columbia University Press, 2010.
Faber, Roland. 'De-Ontologizing God: Levinas, Deleuze, and Whitehead'. In *Process and Difference*. Edited by Catherine Keller and Anne Daniell. Albany: SUNY Press, 2002.

Gasché, Rodolphe. *The Tain of the Mirror*. Cambridge: Harvard University Press, 1988.
Gilkey, Langdon. *Naming the Whirlwind: The Renewal of God-Language*. Indianapolis: Bobbs-Merrill, 1969.
Goodchild, Philip. 'A Theological Passion for Deleuze'. *Theology* 99:791 (1996): 357–65.
— *Deleuze and Guattari: An Introduction to the Politics of Desire*. London: SAGE, 1996.
— 'Deleuze and Philosophy of Religion'. In *Continental Philosophy and Philosophy of Religion*. Edited by Morny Joy. *Handbook of Contemporary Philosophy of Religion*. Vol. 4. Dordrecht: Springer, 2011: 139–64.
— 'Meaningless Suffering . . . despite the fine-tuning of the cosmos'. Krakow 2011 (unpublished paper).
— 'Philosophy as a Way of Life: Deleuze on Thinking and Money'. *SubStance* 39:1 (2010): 24–37.
— 'Why is Philosophy So Compromised with God?' In *Deleuze and Religion*. Edited by Mary Bryden. London: Routledge, 2001.
Gregory of Nyssa. *The Life of Moses*. Translated by Abraham J. Malherbe and Everett Ferguson. New York: HarperCollins, 2006.
Gutting, Gary. *Thinking the Impossible: French Philosophy Since 1960*. Oxford: Oxford University Press, 2011.
Hallward, Peter. *Out of this World: Deleuze and the Philosophy of Creation*. London: Verso, 2006.
Hadot, Pierre. *Philosophy as a Way of Life: Spiritual Exercises from Socrates to Foucault*. Edited by Arnold Davidson. Oxford: Wiley-Blackwell, 1995.
Hardt, Michael. *Gilles Deleuze: An Apprenticeship in Philosophy*. Minneapolis: University of Minnesota Press, 1993.
Hart, David Bentley. *The Beauty of the Infinite: The Aesthetics of Christian Truth*. Grand Rapids: Eerdmans, 2003.
Justaert, Kristien. '"*Ereignis*" (Heidegger) or "*La Clameur de l'etre*" (Deleuze): Topologies for a Theology Beyond Representation?' *Philosophy & Theology* 19:1–2 (2007): 241–56.
— 'Gilles Deleuze and the Transcendence of the Immanent'. Unpublished essay (2011).
— 'Gilles Deleuze: Évaluation Théologique'. *Laval Théologique et Philosophique* 65:3 (October 2009): 531–44.
— 'Liberation Theology: Deleuze and Althaus-Reid'. *SubStance* 39:1 (2010): 154–64.
Kaufman, Eleanor. 'Klossowski, Deleuze, and Orthodoxy'. *Diacritics* 35:1 (Spring 2005): 47–59.
Keller, Catherine. *Face of the Deep: A Theology of Becoming*. London: Routledge, 2003.

Kerslake, Christian. 'Hoëne Wronski and Francis Warrain'. In *Deleuze's Philosophical Lineage*. Edited by Graham Jones and Jon Roffe. Edinburgh: Edinburgh University Press, 2009: 167–89.

— 'The Somnambulist and the Hermaphrodite: Deleuze and Johann de Montereggio and Occultism'. Culture Machine, InterZone. <http://www.culturemachine.net/index.php/cm/article/viewArticle/243/225> (accessed 11 August 2011).

Kierkegaard, Søren. *The Concept of Anxiety*. Edited and translated by Reidar Thomte and Albert B. Anderson. Princeton: Princeton University Press, 1998.

— *Concluding Unscientific Postscript to* Philosophical Fragments. Edited and translated by Howard V. Hong and Edna H. Hong. Princeton: Princeton University Press, 1992.

— *Søren Kierkegaard's Journals and Papers*. Edited by Howard V. Hong and Edna H. Hong, assisted by Gregor Malantschuk. 7 vols Bloomington: Indiana University Press, 1967–78.

— *The Moment and Late Writings*. Edited and translated by Howard V. Hong and Edna H. Hong. Princeton: Princeton University Press, 1998.

— *Repetition* (published with *Fear and Trembling*). Edited and translated by Howard V. Hong and Edna H. Hong. Princeton: Princeton University Press, 1983.

— *The Sickness Unto Death: A Christian Psychological Exposition For Upbuilding And Awakening*. Edited and translated by Howard V. Hong and Edna H. Hong. Princeton: Princeton University Press, 1983.

— *Stages on Life's Way*. Edited and translated by Howard V. Hong and Edna H. Hong. Princeton: Princeton University Press, 1988.

— *Upbuilding Discourses in Various Spirits*. Edited and translated by Howard V. Hong and Edna H. Hong. Princeton: Princeton University Press, 2005.

Marrati, Paolo. '"The Catholicism of Cinema": Gilles Deleuze on Image and Belief'. In *Religion and Media*. Edited by Hent de Vries and Samuel Weber. Stanford University Press, 2002: 227–40.

May, Todd. 'Philosophy as a Spiritual Exercise in Foucault and Deleuze'. *Angelaki* 5:2 (August 2000): 223–9.

Maximus the Confessor. *On the Cosmic Mystery of Christ*. Edited and translated by Paul M. Blowers and Robert Louis Wilken. Crestwood, NY: St. Vladimir's Seminary Press, 2003.

McCabe, Herbert. *Faith Within Reason*. London: Continuum, 2007.

— *God Matters*. London: Continuum, 1987.

— *God Still Matters*. London: Continuum, 2002.

Milbank, John. *Being Reconciled: Ontology and Pardon*. London: Routledge, 2003.

— 'Immanence and Life'. Stanton Lectures at Cambridge University (26 January 2011).
— 'The Habit of Reason'. Stanton Lectures at Cambridge University (23 February 2011).
— 'The Mystery of Reason'. In *The Grandeur of Reason: Religion, Tradition and Universalism*. Edited by Peter M. Candler Jr. and Conor Cunningham. London: SCM Press, 2010.
— 'The Soul of Reciprocity (Part Two)'. *Modern Theology* 17:4 (October 2001): 485–507.
— *Theology and Social Theory*. Second edition. Oxford: Blackwell, 2006.
O'Regan, Cyril. *Gnostic Return in Modernity*. Albany: SUNY Press, 2001.
Palmer, Martin. *The Jesus Sutras: Rediscovering the Lost Scrolls of Taoist Christianity*. New York: Wellspring/Ballantine, 2001.
Pickstock, Catherine. *After Writing: On the Liturgical Consummation of Philosophy*. Oxford: Blackwell, 1998.
— 'Messiaen and Deleuze: The Musico-Theological Critique of Modernism and Postmodernism'. *Theory, Culture & Society* 25:7–8 (December 2008): 173–99.
— 'Theology and Post-modernity: An Exploration of the Origins of a New Alliance'. In *New Directions In Philosophical Theology: Essays In Honour Of Don Cupitt*. Edited by Gavin Hyman. Aldershot: Ashgate, 2004.
Pieper, Josef. *The Silence of St. Thomas*. Translated by John Murray, S. J., and Daniel O'Connor. South Bend: St. Augustine Press, 1957.
Piloiu, Rares. 'Gilles Deleuze's Concept of "Immanence" as Anti-Juridical Utopia'. *Soundings* 87:1–2 (Spring 2004): 201–29.
Poxon, Judith. 'Embodied Anti-Theology: The Body without Organs and the Judgement of God'. In *Deleuze and Religion*. Edited by Mary Bryden. London: Routledge, 2001.
Protevi, John. 'The Organism as the Judgement of God: Aristotle, Kant and Deleuze on Nature (that is, on biology, theology and politics)'. In *Deleuze and Religion*. Edited by Mary Bryden. London: Routledge, 2001.
Raschke, Carl. *GloboChrist: The Great Commission Takes a Postmodern Turn*. Grand Rapids: Baker Academic, 2008.
Robbins, Jeffery W. 'Theses on Secular Theology'. In *Council of Societies for the Study of Religion Bulletin* 37:2 (April 2008): 31–6.
Shaviro, Steven. 'God, or the Body without Organs'. <http://www.shaviro.com/Othertexts/God.pdf> (accessed 10 August 2011).
Sherman, Jacob Holsinger. 'No Werewolves In Theology? Transcendence, Immanence, and Becoming-Divine In Gilles Deleuze'. *Modern Theology* 25:1 (Jan 2009): 1–20.

Simpson, Christopher Ben. *Religion, Metaphysics and the Postmodern: William Desmond and John D. Caputo*. Bloomington: Indiana University Press, 2009.
— *The Truth is the Way: Kierkegaard's Theologia Viatorum*. London: SCM Press, 2010; Eugene, OR: Cascade Press, 2011.
Smith, Anthony Paul. 'Believing in this World for this Making of Gods: Ecology of the Virtual and the Actual'. *SubStance* 39:1 (2010): 103–14.
— 'The Judgment of God and the Immeasurable: Political Theology and Organizations of Power'. *Political Theology* 12:1 (2011): 69–86.
Smith, Anthony Paul and Daniel Whistler. 'Editors' Introduction: What is Continental Philosophy of Religion Now?' In *After the Postsecular and the Postmodern: New Essays in Continental Philosophy of Religion*. Edited by Anthony Paul Smith and Daniel Whistler. Newcastle upon Tyne: Cambridge Scholars Publishing, 2010.
Smith, Daniel W. 'The Doctrine of Univocity: Deleuze's Ontology of Immanence'. In *Deleuze and Religion*. Edited by Mary Bryden. London: Routledge, 2001.
Sokolowski, Robert. *The God of Faith and Reason*. South Bend: University of Notre Dame Press, 1982.
Teilhard de Chardin, Pierre. *The Divine Milieu*. New York: HarperCollins, 1960.
Teschke, Henning. 'What is the Difference? Deleuze and Saint Thomas'. *Verbum* VI:2 (2004): 413–22.
Tracy, David. *Blessed Rage for Order: The New Pluralism in Theology*. Reprinted with a new preface. Chicago: University Of Chicago Press, 1996.
— *Plurality and Ambiguity: Hermeneutics, Religion, Hope*. Chicago: University Of Chicago Press, 1994.
Westphal, Merold. *Overcoming Onto-Theology: Toward a Postmodern Christian Faith*. New York: Fordham University Press, 2001.
Williams, James. *Gilles Deleuze's Difference and Repetition: A Critical Introduction and Guide*. Edinburgh: Edinburgh University Press, 2004.

INDEX

absence 23, 85, 106
absolute 15, 25, 39, 43, 63–4,
    67–70, 73, 78, 84, 108
    erotic 79
actual(ity) 20–2, 25–6, 28–30,
    32–40, 56, 66–7, 78–80,
    91–2, 96, 98, 101–5,
    122n. 179
actualization 13–14, 21, 25, 30,
    33–7, 40, 80, 132n. 430
    see also differenciation
affirmation 7–8, 12–13, 15, 19,
    36, 43–6, 59, 65, 82,
    97–100, 103, 105
    ideal 105
    original 13
    pure 13
    subterranean 17
Agapeic being 106, 108
Aion 28–30
Albert, Eliot 116n. 56, 142n. 61,
    144nn. 24, 30, 145nn. 43,
    51, 54, 59, 149n. 2, 164,
    166
aleatory point 24, 31, 144n. 20
Alliez, Eric 11, 25, 30, 113n. 7,
    114n. 14, 115nn. 42,
    46, 116n. 51, 119n. 110,
    120n. 148, 121nn. 166,
    168, 122n. 172,
    124nn. 223–4, 125n. 262,
    127n. 307, 128n. 323,
    129n. 348, 130nn. 374,
    396–7, 131nn. 406, 409,
    419, 132nn. 440, 444,
    135n. 517, 166
Altizer, Thomas J. J. 52,
    140nn. 24, 26, 166
analogy 14, 16, 18, 72, 76, 80–1,
    83–5, 152n. 78
Ansell-Pearson, Keith 149n. 1,
    159n. 9, 167
Antichrist 64, 94, 98
    system of 94
apatheia 73, 84, 93
appropriation 1, 19, 42, 50–1,
    53, 59–60, 62, 88–9
Aquinas, St. Thomas 54, 59,
    71–2, 76, 85–7, 97,
    107, 143nn. 82–3,
    148nn. 121, 133, 135,
    138–9, 152nn. 78, 91,
    153nn. 109, 111, 122,
    127, 154nn. 128–9, 139,
    142, 147, 149, 154,
    155nn. 158–9, 165–7,
    156nn. 34, 157nn. 42, 51,
    161nn. 82, 85, 162nn. 93,
    100, 167, 171–2
Archimedean point 50
Artaud, Antonin 17, 23, 168
assemblage 23, 39–40, 89, 97,
    100, 109
    Christ 97, 109
asymmetry 25
    hyperbolic 85

INDEX

atheism 49, 74, 94
atonement 58, 95
   mystery of 95
autonomy 41, 146n. 88,
   161n. 73

Bacon, Francis 9
Badiou, Alain 9, 95
von Balthasar, Hans Urs
   142n. 75, 147nn. 95, 104,
   160n. 60, 167
Baphomet 64, 78
Barber, Daniel Colucciello 49,
   52, 66, 100–1, 139n. 5,
   140nn. 28, 31, 144n. 37,
   145nn. 52, 64,
   150nn. 35–6, 41,
   46, 51–3, 157n. 5,
   159n. 18, 159n. 22,
   160nn. 35–6, 41–3, 167
Baugh, Bruce 64, 112n. 21,
   144n. 10, 167
beatitude 99, 107–8
becoming 1, 7, 13–17, 19–20,
   22–3, 26, 29–30, 35,
   38–9, 41–6, 58, 64, 66–9,
   74, 78–9, 87, 91–2, 95,
   99–102, 105–9
   eternal 60, 69
   inhuman 41–2, 92, 98, 108
   nonhuman 99
   process of 14, 64, 78, 91
Beethoven, Ludwig van 141
being-between 87, 91
de Beistegui, Miguel 157n. 5,
   167
Bergson, Henri 6–8, 14–15,
   21–2, 27–8, 35, 65, 67,
   111n. 12, 122n. 179
Betcher, Sharon V. 140n. 35, 167
between, the 24, 61, 71, 81,
   83–7, 91, 96–7, 101,
   106–7, 109

Blondel, Maurice 55
body 21–3, 26, 28–30, 35,
   37–8, 40, 42–3, 45, 98,
   101, 109
   of Christ 97, 109
   mystical 97
   perverse 98
body-as-organism 75
body without organs (BwO) 23,
   25–6, 33, 39–40, 42–3,
   57, 75
   see also virtual
Boehme, Jakob 56–7, 68, 80,
   142n. 58
Bogue, Ronald 114n. 15,
   116n. 58, 120n. 144,
   121nn. 155, 166,
   122nn. 170, 179–80, 186,
   123nn. 189, 204,
   124n. 208, 125nn. 238,
   254, 127n. 297,
   128n. 321, 129n. 366,
   130n. 373, 131nn. 409,
   416, 418–19, 132n. 448,
   135n. 503, 138nn. 585,
   598, 606, 167
Bonta, Mark 57, 140n. 32,
   141n. 47, 142n. 59,
   144n. 34, 145nn. 45, 50,
   146nn. 80, 89, 147n. 101,
   151n. 71, 167
Burrell, David 59, 82–3, 85,
   87, 142nn. 76–7,
   143nn. 80, 87, 91,
   147n. 106, 148nn. 133–4,
   151nn. 56–7, 152nn. 89,
   93–4, 96, 98, 101–2,
   153nn. 103–7, 111, 114,
   123, 126, 154nn. 128,
   140–5, 147, 149,
   155n. 157, 156n. 35,
   157n. 39, 158n. 21,
   162nn. 86, 93, 167

INDEX

calculus 56, 114n. 14
transcendental 69,
  147n. 100
Calvin, John 151n. 57
Caputo, John D. 57,
  139n. 11, 167
Carnot High School 5
Caumaüer, Odette 5
causa sui 16
Cave, the 69
chance 13, 19, 24, 44, 64
chaos 19–20, 43, 65–6, 69
chaosmos 20, 63, 144
Châtelet, François 10
Chenu, M. D. 55
Chesterton, G. K. 153n. 127
Christ, Jesus 1, 58, 71, 82,
  94–7, 109
Christianity 54–5, 58, 60,
  70–1, 99, 109,
  143n. 86
  dominological 65
Christology 96
Chronos 28, 37
church, the 52, 108–10
Clark, Tim 65, 143nn. 1, 3,
  144nn. 19–20, 41,
  145nn. 42–4, 146n. 84,
  147n. 101, 167
Colebrook, Claire 14, 20, 41,
  115n. 44, 116nn. 54–5,
  59–60, 117n. 71,
  119n. 126, 120nn. 135,
  151, 121nn. 152–3, 159,
  122n. 169, 129nn. 355,
  364, 130nn. 380, 394,
  131n. 403, 135nn. 520–1,
  136n. 546, 137nn. 554,
  562–3, 138n. 602,
  148n. 137, 167
communion 84, 86, 91, 96–7,
  107, 109
  metaxological 96

community 60–1, 71–3, 85–6,
  91, 107–9
  agapeic 72, 83, 106, 109
  metaxological 71, 87, 106
complication 31, 81, 83
conatus essendi 92
concept 7–8, 11–13, 16,
  18–19, 21, 32–3, 52, 54,
  59–61, 68, 85, 92, 94–5,
  100, 103
consciousness 7, 20, 24, 28,
  33, 40, 42, 103–4,
  122n. 179
  a-subjective 42
  devaluation of 42
  illusion of 103
consistency 20, 32, 77, 162n. 95
  plane of 23, 25–6, 39, 41, 43,
    118n. 104
contemplation 26–7, 31, 34, 42,
  45–6
contraction 8, 22, 26–8, 34
creation 1, 11, 13–14, 34, 37,
  42, 44–5, 52, 55–6,
  58–9, 61–2, 64, 66–7, 73,
  82–7, 90, 96–7, 101–2,
  104, 106–8, 153n. 127,
  157n. 4
ex nihilo 84–5
  free 82
  passive 26
creativity 13, 45, 52, 64–5, 69,
  75, 100, 102, 161n. 62
Cresson, André 6
Crockett, Clayton 51–3,
  65–6, 95, 100–1,
  139nn. 11–13,
  140nn. 15, 17–20, 22,
  25, 27, 30, 38, 141n. 45,
  144n. 40, 145nn. 61–2,
  150nn. 37, 41, 44, 47,
  157n. 5, 158nn. 9–11,
  159nn. 17, 30, 32, 167

INDEX

crowned anarchy 17, 96
Cthulhu 69, 99
Cunningham, Conor 154n. 154, 155n. 163, 168, 171

Dale, Catherine 144n. 14, 149n. 11, 168
dark precursor 24, 64, 123, 144n. 20
Davies, Oliver 82, 146n. 82, 146n. 92, 147n. 115, 152n. 87, 168
death 1, 6, 10, 50, 52, 69, 74, 69, 93–5, 97–8, 108, 152n. 78, 158n. 3
  anthropomorphic 90, 101
  the great 13
DeLanda, Manuel 25, 39, 116n. 59, 118n. 105, 121nn. 153, 166, 122n. 169, 123nn. 196, 202, 124nn. 212, 214, 126nn. 267–8, 131nn. 410, 416–17, 132nn. 440, 448, 134nn. 484, 488, 499, 135nn. 501, 503, 168
Deleuze, Georges 5
Deleuze, Gilles
  'The Actual and the Virtual' 10, 113n. 59
  Anti-Oedipus: Capitalism and Schizophrenia 9, 32, 38, 40, 103, 113n. 43, 114nn. 16, 26, 115n. 27, 116nn. 52–3, 57–8, 60, 62, 117nn. 74–5, 90, 119n. 110, 121n. 159, 123nn. 189, 193, 196–8, 200, 124nn. 226, 229, 129nn. 356–61, 363–4, 366–71, 130n. 372, 133n. 473, 134nn. 478, 492–3, 495–7, 135nn. 511, 524, 136nn. 525, 528–31, 535, 544–5, 548, 550–1, 137nn. 552–3, 138nn. 598–600, 602–5, 149n. 8, 155n. 2, 157n. 5, 161n. 80, 166
  Bergsonism 7–8, 112nn. 19, 29, 114n. 15, 115n. 32, 116nn. 53–5, 60, 117n. 70, 122nn. 171, 175–6, 178–9, 124n. 224, 125nn. 235, 245, 259–63, 130nn. 396, 398, 132nn. 431, 443–4, 146n. 79, 164
  Cinema 1: The Movement-Image 10, 113nn. 4–5, 49, 116nn. 57–8, 117nn. 69, 72, 74, 118n. 108, 120nn. 135, 142, 122nn. 175–6, 125n. 262, 126n. 278, 130n. 378, 131n. 400, 133nn. 450–2, 137n. 557, 138n. 595, 164
  Cinema 2: The Time-Image 10, 28, 113n. 50, 114n. 26, 115n. 48, 116nn. 54–7, 59–60, 63, 117nn. 67, 69–71, 119nn. 114–15, 121nn. 160, 122nn. 178–9, 125nn. 257–8, 261, 126nn. 267–8, 133n. 449, 135nn. 501–2, 137nn. 580, 582, 138nn. 590, 139nn. 607–14, 148n. 137, 149nn. 13, 19, 159n. 14, 164

INDEX

David Hume, sa vie, son oeuvre 111n. 7, 164
Desert Islands and Other Texts, 1953-74 112nn. 27-8, 113nn. 1-2, 114n. 25, 115n. 39, 116n. 65, 118n. 96, 120n. 140, 122nn. 172, 174, 177, 123n. 207, 124nn. 222, 231, 125n. 236, 126nn. 277, 280, 284, 127nn. 308-10, 128nn. 319, 340, 342-3, 129nn. 344, 357-8, 360, 365, 369, 371, 130nn. 372, 375, 382-3, 387, 131nn. 412, 415, 132nn. 424-7, 430, 437-8, 443, 134n. 480, 135n. 524, 138n. 589, 139n. 616, 164
Dialogues II 113n. 59, 114n. 24, 115nn. 30, 42, 44, 116n. 55, 117nn. 67-8, 89-90, 118n. 93, 119n. 109, 120n. 150, 121nn. 160, 166, 122nn. 171, 175, 179, 124nn. 216, 234, 125nn. 260-1, 126nn. 265, 268, 130n. 389, 131n. 417, 132n. 423, 133nn. 450, 456-7, 463-4, 134nn. 477, 490, 135n. 515, 137n. 569, 138n. 589, 163nn. 112, 114, 164
Difference and Repetition 8, 11, 21, 23, 27, 31, 56, 81, 111n. 3, 112n. 38, 113nn. 1-3, 6, 47, 114nn. 11, 15, 18-19, 21-2, 115nn. 32-6, 38, 40-1, 45-6, 48-9, 116nn. 59, 61, 117nn. 75-7, 80, 82-5, 88, 90, 118nn. 92, 94-6, 98-102, 119nn. 114-28, 120nn. 129-31, 133-4, 136-41, 143, 146-7, 121nn. 153-6, 159-61, 164-6, 122nn. 169-74, 177-9, 123nn. 201, 203-4, 207, 124nn. 222-3, 228, 231-4, 125nn. 235-9, 241-8, 250-6, 126n. 283, 127nn. 290-1, 293, 299-301, 305-6, 308-9, 310-17, 128nn. 318-19, 321-39, 341-3, 129nn. 344-8, 359, 130nn. 374, 377, 379-80, 383-4, 388, 390-3, 131nn. 401, 403-5, 407-9, 411-13, 415-16, 419-21, 132nn. 423, 425-6, 428-40, 446, 133nn. 469, 474, 134nn. 476, 480, 489, 135nn. 507, 518-19, 522, 524, 136nn. 527, 532-3, 539-43, 549, 137nn. 564, 580-1, 138nn. 591-2, 594-7, 139n. 610, 144n. 30, 149nn. 7, 14, 150n. 31, 152n. 79, 155nn. 1, 3-5, 156nn. 6, 8, 158nn. 2-3, 159nn. 4, 6, 164
Empiricism and Subjectivity 6-7, 111n. 8, 115n. 30, 120n. 150, 125nn. 242,

248–9, 128n. 336,
 135n. 523, 136n. 541,
 162n. 94, 164
Ensembles and
 Multiplicities 10
Essays Critical and
 Clinical 144n. 17,
 149n. 23, 164
Expressionism in Philosophy:
 Spinoza 6, 8, 112nn. 30,
 32, 39, 114nn. 19–20,
 115nn. 29, 31, 118nn. 97,
 99, 102, 106, 119nn. 113,
 116, 127nn. 305, 314,
 130n. 391, 139n. 615–16,
 620, 150nn. 28, 32,
 157n. 5, 164
The Fold 10, 113n. 52, 165
Foucault 113n. 51, 165
Francis Bacon: The Logic of
 Sensation 113n. 47, 165
'Immanence, A Life" 10,
 113n. 58
Kafka: Toward a Minor
 Literature 113n. 45, 166
Kant's Critical Philosophy:
 The Doctrine of the
 Faculties 7, 111n. 15,
 120n. 149, 149n. 9,
 156n. 7, 165
L' Abécédaire de Gilles
 Deleuze 139n. 8,
 141n. 46, 144n. 20,
 149nn. 4, 11, 156n. 8,
 157n. 3, 158n. 6,
 159n. 11, 165
The Logic of Sense 9, 21–3,
 28, 30, 50, 112n. 41,
 115nn. 37, 40–1, 45, 49,
 116nn. 61, 65, 117nn. 75,
 85, 118nn. 95–6, 99,
 120nn. 131–2, 139, 141,
 145, 147, 121nn. 162–3,
 166, 122nn. 177,
 180–7, 123nn. 188, 191,
 201–7, 124nn. 208–10,
 125n. 236, 126nn. 264–6,
 269–80, 282–6, 288,
 127nn. 290, 292–305,
 315, 128nn. 318,
 320, 322, 325–6, 335,
 129n. 359, 130nn. 373–4,
 379, 381–2, 385,
 399, 131nn. 400–4,
 132nn. 422, 447–8,
 133nn. 450–3, 469, 474,
 134n. 480, 135nn. 506–7,
 524, 136nn. 527, 532–3,
 536, 543, 138nn. 591,
 593, 144nn. 25, 27, 29,
 149nn. 6, 12–13, 15–17,
 150n. 27, 155nn. 1–4,
 156nn. 7–8, 157nn. 1–2,
 158n. 3, 159nn. 4–5, 166
Masochism: Coldness and
 Cruelty & Venus in
 Furs 7, 112n. 20, 165
Negotiations 1972–90
 112n. 30, 113nn. 3–4,
 115nn. 31, 33, 37, 43,
 116nn. 51, 56, 62–3,
 65–6, 117nn. 67, 69,
 71–2, 74, 86, 118n. 104,
 119nn. 109, 112, 126,
 122n. 171, 124n. 221,
 126nn. 281, 285, 289,
 129nn. 350, 357–8,
 364, 130nn. 372, 379,
 131n. 414, 133nn. 462,
 466, 468, 136nn. 526–7,
 137nn. 569, 572,
 138n. 606, 139n. 607,
 157n. 5, 165
Nietzsche and Philosophy 6–7,
 111n. 14, 112nn. 23,
 25, 114nn. 15–19, 22,

INDEX

25–6, 115nn. 27, 29–30, 39, 116nn. 53, 60, 63, 117nn. 87–8, 119n. 127, 120nn. 129, 132, 134, 137, 150, 125nn. 239, 249, 126n. 282, 136n. 537, 138nn. 586–8, 591–2, 606, 139n. 620, 144n. 13, 149n. 22, 156n. 7, 159n. 12, 162n. 94, 165

Nietzsche: sa vie, son oeuvre, avec un exposé de sa philosophie 112nn. 18, 24, 165

Périclès et Verdi: La philosophie de François Châtelet 113n. 53, 165

Proust and Signs 7, 111n. 16, 165

"Responses to a Series of Questions" 114n. 23, 118n. 108, 165

Spinoza: Practical Philosophy 8–9, 94, 112nn. 34–5, 114nn. 23, 25–6, 115nn. 27–8, 116nn. 55, 66, 118nn. 104–5, 107, 119n. 109, 123n. 195, 130n. 385, 131n. 417, 135n. 502, 136nn. 537–8, 137nn. 578–9, 138nn. 583, 585, 587, 589, 139nn. 615–16, 620, 149n. 10, 157n. 5, 159n. 13, 165

A Thousand Plateaus 9, 17, 25–6, 32, 35, 38, 63, 74, 113n. 44, 115nn. 34, 43, 116nn. 52, 56, 63–4, 66, 117nn. 67–8, 72, 88, 91, 118nn. 92–3, 99, 104–5, 107, 119n. 111, 120nn. 141, 143, 145, 122n. 182, 123nn. 189, 193–6, 198–200, 124nn. 213–18, 220–1, 225–6, 229–30, 126nn. 267, 269, 271, 281–2, 129nn. 357, 362, 130n. 386, 131nn. 414, 417, 132nn. 441, 448, 133nn. 454–65, 467–72, 474, 134nn. 475–9, 481–3, 485–9, 491, 493–500, 135nn. 502–4, 508–9, 512–16, 518–19, 136nn. 525, 534, 541, 545–7, 137nn. 555–8, 561, 565–74, 576–7, 580, 138nn. 598, 600–3, 139n. 618, 143n. 2, 149nn. 5–6, 14, 155n. 1, 159n. 7, 161n. 79, 163n. 115, 166

What is Philosophy? 10–11, 95, 112nn. 30, 35, 113n. 54, 115nn. 31, 35, 40, 46, 116n. 59, 117n. 73, 118nn. 104–5, 119nn. 109, 111–12, 120nn. 142, 144, 146, 121nn. 152–3, 156, 162–3, 166, 168, 122nn. 171, 182, 124n. 222, 125nn. 239–40, 247, 126nn. 278–9, 281, 287, 129nn. 349–55, 130n. 397, 131n. 400, 132n. 442, 133nn. 450, 452, 134n. 496, 136nn. 527, 541, 139n. 613, 149nn. 13, 18–19, 157n. 2, 158nn. 8, 11, 159n. 14, 166

Deleuze, Louis 5
Demiurge 75, 80
depth 16, 21–2, 25–6, 38, 52–3,
    65–6, 145n. 50
Dionysian 19
Derrida, Jacques 6, 57,
    124n. 211, 146n. 85
desire 33, 42, 45–6, 70, 72–3, 76,
    79, 84, 89, 92–3, 100–1,
    106, 121, 163n. 119
  positive 45
  pure 90
desiring-machine 33, 42
Desmond, William 2, 54, 61,
    67–9, 71–3, 78–9, 81,
    83–7, 90–2, 102–3,
    106–7, 109, 142n. 71,
    143nn. 93–5, 146nn. 72,
    76–7, 90–3, 147nn. 94,
    97, 148nn. 118–20,
    130, 138, 143,
    149n. 145, 151nn. 55,
    62, 65–7, 69, 71,
    73, 152n. 99,
    153nn. 116–17, 121,
    154nn. 132, 134–7,
    152, 155nn. 158, 165,
    170, 156nn. 14, 26–7,
    157n. 43–4, 158nn. 15,
    19, 160nn. 49, 54, 62,
    161nn. 77, 81, 84,
    162nn. 87, 91, 96,
    163nn. 110–11, 116, 168
desubjectification 42–3
detachment 108
  gnostic 57
determination 30, 34, 36–7, 40,
    43, 64
  reciprocal 25, 30
deterritorialization 25, 39–43,
    102–3, 108
Deus 60, 66, 77, 152n. 100
dialectic 61, 81–3

difference 1, 7–8, 12–22, 24–7,
    31–2, 34–7, 41–4, 46,
    53, 56, 60–1, 63–4, 66,
    68–73, 76, 81–4, 86–7,
    91, 93, 96, 101, 105, 107,
    123n. 207, 145n. 50,
    146nn. 85, 88
  absolute 15, 63
  affirmative 13, 15, 44, 64
  Christian 70
  depth of 26
  divine 63–4, 70, 73
  Hegelian understanding of 7
  intensive 26–7
  (infinite) qualitative 44, 83, 96
  internal 18, 30–1
  non-relational 68, 104
  ontological 31
  ontology of 9, 63,
  pure 17, 31–2, 81, 105, 108
  togetherness of 61
  virtual 69, 104
  see also intensity
differenciation 30, 35–7,
    132n. 430
  double 37
  see also actualization
differentiation 14, 25, 29–32,
    35–7, 44, 56, 67, 69–72,
    76–7
  divine 70
  infinite 72
  self 67, 77
Dionysius the Areopagite 142n. 58
Dionysus 15, 44, 64, 68, 95
disembodiment 102–3
distinction 21, 23, 28, 30, 38–9,
    56, 59, 71, 83–4, 86, 96,
    121n. 159
distribution 18, 26, 30, 32, 34, 98
  divine 98
  nomadic 38–9
  sedentary 38–9

INDEX

Divine Schizophrenic, the 65
divinity 65–6, 69, 79–80, 90
  deficient 90
Dosse, François 111nn. 1–2,
    5–6, 9–10, 12–13, 17,
    112nn. 22, 26, 31,
    34, 37, 40, 113nn. 7,
    42, 46, 48, 55–7,
    114nn. 12–13,
    116nn. 50–1, 117n. 76,
    139nn. 2–4, 143n. 96,
    144nn. 11, 21,
    161n. 63, 168
dramatization 30, 35–7
Dualism 7, 17, 38, 61, 68, 76,
    78–9, 86
  Gnostic 79
  hierarchical 82
Duns Scotus, John 17
duration 15, 27–8
Dynamism 15, 35–6, 72–3, 84
  eternal 73, 84
  original 72–3
  pure 67, 100
  spatio-temporal 35–7

ego 41–2, 91, 99
element 2, 11, 15, 22–4,
    27–8, 30, 32, 34, 55,
    65, 69, 78–9, 83, 90,
    141n. 56, 144n. 20,
    147n. 101
embodiment 80
empiricism 20–1
  transcendental 20–1
energy 15, 24, 26, 30, 33–4,
    36, 64–5, 67–8, 93,
    101, 106
  divine 67, 78
equivocal/equivocity 17, 55,
    57, 63, 76, 81, 105,
    142n. 68, 152n. 78
  affirmative 61

escape 12, 17, 24–5, 38, 40–4,
    77, 79–81, 89–90, 92,
    97–8, 100–4, 105,
    107–8, 111n. 12
eternal return 19–20, 44,
    72–3, 89
eternity 15, 60, 67, 72
  univocal 78
evaluation 44, 80, 99, 103
  ethical 99
  immanent 76
Event, the 24, 29
event 20–4, 29–33, 38–9, 44, 67,
    95, 99, 109
  virtual 29, 32, 35, 38
evil 44, 52, 58, 93

Faber, Roland 77, 145n. 54,
    150n. 42, 157n. 4, 168
faith 53, 59, 73, 91, 99–100
  Christian 106
  Deluzian 99–101
Father 70, 72, 84, 97
field 1, 23, 26, 30, 33–4, 36–7,
    39, 45, 118n. 104,
    121n. 159, 157n. 4
  of individuation 33–6
  transcendental 33–4, 41, 65
force 14–15, 19, 21, 26–7,
    29, 57, 63–5, 67,
    69, 72, 74, 80, 90,
    98–101, 106,
    147n. 100
  unconscious 24, 65, 89–90
Foucault, Michel 6–7, 9–10
France 5–9, 54
  Paris 5–6, 10
freedom 85, 87
French Resistance 5
French Society for Nietzsche
    Studies 7
friendship 6, 72, 106, 109
future 28, 44, 109, 162

INDEX

game 19, 44, 64, 67–8, 75
Gasché, Rodolphe 124n. 211, 168–9
generality 19
generation 13–15, 18, 25, 28, 66, 69, 78, 80, 84, 101
Genesis 20, 35
Gilkey, Langdon 140n. 24, 169
gift 72, 82, 84–5, 87, 93
  true 85
Girard, René 103
gnosis 96
Gnosticism 54–5, 58–9, 69, 75, 80, 90, 103, 105, 142
  modern 68
God 1, 18–19, 40, 44, 49–54, 57–8, 60–1, 63–6, 68–101, 106–9, 144n. 14, 151n. 57, 152n. 100, 153nn. 106, 115, 155n. 1, 157n. 4
  of Abraham, Isaac and Jacob 95
  Alien 151n. 67
  becoming 66, 92, 102, 105, 108
  changelessness of 73–4
  creator 58, 80, 82, 85, 96
  death of 50, 52, 89, 98, 158n. 3
  dynamic 72–3
  as *esse* 86
  of Genesis 80
  Gnostic 79–80
  guarantor 75, 89
  image of 90–1
  immanent 66, 77–9
  as lobster 53, 74, 80, 110
  -Man 96
  Old Testament 80
  Spinoza's 66, 94–5
  transcendent 66, 74–6, 78, 83, 91, 94–5, 101

Triune/Trinitarian 71–3, 84, 88, 91, 96, 106, 108–9
the Unknown 81
voluntarist 75, 80
good 14, 44–5, 52, 69, 78–9, 82, 85, 87, 92–3, 96–7, 99, 105–7
  Deluzian 99
goodness 44–5, 77, 84–5, 87
  divine 86
Goodchild, Philip 49, 53, 65, 100, 114n. 13, 119n. 114, 121nn. 152, 168, 123nn. 190, 192, 194, 196, 126n. 281, 129n. 350, 133n. 471, 135nn. 503–5, 508, 510, 137nn. 557, 559, 561, 579, 138nn. 584–5, 590, 598, 600, 602, 139nn. 1, 6, 9, 140nn. 29, 33–4, 36–7, 144nn. 31–2, 37, 39, 145nn. 53, 66–9, 150nn. 33–4, 37, 40, 44, 47, 53, 156nn. 10–12, 159nn. 20–1, 25–6, 160nn. 37, 40, 167, 169
Grandjouan, Denise Paul 'Fanny' 6
Gregory of Nyssa 92, 157n. 38, 169
Griffon d'Or 56
ground 14–15, 21, 27–8, 31, 33, 40, 53, 56, 69, 72, 81–2, 86, 106
  ungrounding 24
Guattari, Felix 9–11, 14, 16, 23, 25–6, 28–9, 32–3, 35, 38–43, 45, 52, 74, 95, 102, 104
Gutting, Gary 111nn. 4, 11–12, 112nn. 21, 30, 169

INDEX

habit   27–8, 42, 87, 107, 162n. 95
Hadot, Pierre   53, 140n. 34, 169
haecceity   23, 29, 34–5, 39
Hallward, Peter   55, 67–8, 76, 79, 96, 102–4, 141n. 44, 142n. 68, 143n. 8, 145n. 70, 146nn. 74–5, 78–9, 87–8, 92, 147nn. 102–3, 150n. 24, 151nn. 58, 60–1, 63, 72–4, 76, 156nn. 18–20, 157nn. 4–5, 158nn. 16–17, 160nn. 46, 48, 52–3, 57–60, 62, 161nn. 64–5, 67, 70, 73, 169
Hamilton, William   140nn. 24, 26, 166
Hardt, Michael   25, 114nn. 14, 19, 22, 116nn. 52, 54, 60, 117nn. 78–9, 90, 118n. 108, 119nn. 110, 112–13, 121nn. 158, 167–8, 127n. 314, 130n. 396, 132n. 445, 138n. 586, 139nn. 615–17, 157n. 5, 169
Hart, David Bentley   54–5, 57, 59, 61, 68, 70–3, 79–81, 84–7, 91, 93, 103, 105–9, 141n. 43, 142nn. 63, 65, 74, 143nn. 89, 92, 144n. 16, 146n. 83, 147nn. 95–6, 109–14, 148nn. 116, 123–4, 126, 128–32, 136, 138, 140–1, 149n. 146, 151n. 57, 152nn. 78, 83, 153nn. 113, 119–20, 124–5, 154nn. 130, 138, 151, 155nn. 158, 164, 168, 156nn. 22, 25, 27–8, 30, 36, 157nn. 45–8, 51–2, 158nn. 20, 23, 160nn. 56–7, 161nn. 75, 78, 83, 162nn. 87, 92, 96, 105–6, 163nn. 117–18, 169
Hegel, G. W. F.   6, 61, 111n. 12,
Heidegger, Martin   6, 8, 146n. 85
Henry IV   5
heterodoxy   59
heterogeneity   43
  pure   63
hierarchy   17–19, 38, 44, 78–9, 81, 99, 101
Holy Spirit   70, 72, 84, 97
Hume, David   6
humanism   6, 41–2, 100
Husserl, Edmund   6

idea   7, 17–18, 21–2, 25–6, 29–37, 39, 44, 50, 56, 64, 79, 85, 128n. 336, 157n. 4
  Absolute   64
  Deleuze's   16, 32
  see also problems
idealism   14, 17
  German   114n. 14
identity   14–16, 18–20, 24, 26, 29–30, 37, 41, 43, 66, 75, 80–1, 83, 89–90, 98, 100, 102, 155n. 1
  fixed   99–100
illusion   16, 42, 76, 90, 96, 102–4
image   14–16, 28, 33–4, 42–3, 59, 90–1, 109
  of thought   13–14, 16, 42–3
imago Dei   1, 91
imitation   15

INDEX

immanence 1, 13, 18, 34, 52, 55, 60–2, 64–6, 71, 74–87, 94, 96, 100, 104, 107, 154n. 152
  affirmation of 8, 100
  creative 94
  metaphysics of 9
  non-human 102
  plane of 17–19, 23, 33, 52, 77, 94–6, 99, 118n. 104, 119nn. 109–10
  pure 14, 17
  rebirth of 76
implication 21, 34–7, 77
incarnation 30, 33–7, 55, 61, 91, 96–7, 106, 108, 110
indeterminacy 24, 66
indi-different/citation 30
individualization 34
individuation 23, 30, 33–7, 41
impersonal 41
infinite regress 30
infinite reserve 73
infinity 36, 61, 66, 84, 86
  Trinitarian 85
inhuman 41–2, 60, 67, 90, 92–3, 96, 98, 102
integrity 69, 87
intensity 17, 22–3, 26–7, 31–7, 39, 41, 46, 99–101, 123n. 207, 163n. 119
  matrix of 26
  see also difference
inter-esse 87, 92
intermediation 61, 71, 91, 107
intimacy 72, 81, 86, 92, 97, 109, 154n. 152
  infinite 78
Irenaeus 54

Janaway, Christohper 146n. 90
John, Gospel of 70
joy 46, 64, 106, 109
Joyce, James 20
judg(e)ment 18, 74, 78, 103–5
  of God 40, 44, 64, 74–5, 79–80, 90, 98
  system of 37, 40, 44, 75
  transcendent 75
Justaert, Kristien 54, 66, 77, 94, 97, 99–101, 103–5, 140n. 39, 143nn. 5–6, 144n. 28, 145nn. 58, 60, 149nn. 2, 17, 20, 150nn. 24–5, 34, 38–40, 151n. 61, 156n. 9, 12, 157n. 5, 158nn. 7, 24, 159nn. 8–9, 11, 16, 23–4, 27, 31, 33, 160nn. 38, 55–6, 60–1, 161nn. 65–6, 76, 163nn. 113, 119, 169

Kafka, Franz 9
Kaufman, Eleanor 150nn. 26, 28–30, 152nn. 78, 82, 86, 153nn. 108, 110, 169
Keller, Catherine 65–6, 78, 101, 140n. 21, 144n. 35, 145nn. 46–50, 55–7, 63, 150nn. 47–50, 159n. 29, 167–9
Kerslake, Christian 55–6, 114n. 14, 141nn. 47–51, 142nn. 58–9, 62, 146nn. 73, 80, 147nn. 100–1, 151n. 58, 158n. 12, 170
Kierkegaard, Søren 54, 71–3, 83, 86–7, 91–3, 96, 143n. 84, 148nn. 127, 142, 152n. 101, 153n. 103, 154nn. 146, 148, 155nn. 156, 161,

156nn. 23, 29, 31–2,
157nn. 37, 49–51,
158n. 19, 162n. 100, 170
  as Johannes Climacus   86, 91
Klossowski, Pierre   94
knowledge   20, 33, 56, 58, 70–1,
77, 86, 90, 92, 95

La Borde   9
Leibniz, Gottfried   10, 50
Levinas, Emmanuel   57
LeviNietzscheanism   57
liberation   13, 40, 42, 45, 50, 52,
54, 93, 95, 98–100, 103,
108, 159n. 11
life   1, 7–10, 12–15, 29, 33,
42–6, 52–3, 55, 61,
64–7, 69–73, 75–6, 78,
80, 85–6, 89–92, 95–7,
99–102, 105, 107–9,
147n. 100
  divine   61–2, 65, 67,
69–73, 84, 96–7, 99,
101, 107–9
  goodness of   44–5, 97
  immanent   33, 46, 65, 76, 83
  interpersonal   70
  non-individual   43
  non-organic   15, 29, 56,
64, 72
logic   17, 38, 45, 61, 63–4
  Christian   61
love   71–3, 85, 88, 91–2, 97,
105–6, 108
  agapeic   71
  divine   73
  eternal   73
  revolutionary   105
  Trinitarian   84, 106
Lovecraft, H. P.   53, 65, 69
Louis Le Grande High School   5
de Lubac, Henri   55
Lyotard, Jean-François   9

Malfatti de Montereggio,
Johann   5, 56–7,
114n. 14, 141nn. 48, 56,
142n. 58
Martinism   56–7, 141n. 48
Marrati, Paolo   99,
159n. 15, 170
Marxism   9
materialism   12, 17, 55
  atheistic   55
  speculative   12, 34
  theological   54, 100
May, Todd   114n. 10, 156n. 9,
159nn. 32, 34,
160n. 40, 170
Maximus the Confessor   162n. 106,
170
McCabe, Herbert   70–1,
84–6, 88, 96–7, 108,
142n. 77, 143n. 88,
147nn. 105, 107,
148nn. 121, 135, 138,
149n. 147, 151nn. 56,
77, 152nn. 92, 98, 100,
153nn. 106–7, 115–16,
154nn. 129, 131, 133,
143, 153, 155nn. 169,
171, 156n. 28,
158nn. 18, 20, 26,
162nn. 86, 108, 170
mediation   16, 51, 54, 71, 78, 82
memory   10, 22, 25, 27–8, 40
Merleau-Ponty, Maurice   6, 8,
112n. 28
metamorphosis   45, 66, 99
metaphysics   7–8, 11–12, 15, 71,
86, 147n. 101
  Deleuze's   9, 12, 49
  new   12
  positive   1
metaxu/metaxological   6,
83, 107
micropolitics   101, 104

INDEX

Milbank, John 54, 68, 70–1, 81–2, 84, 143nn. 3, 5, 8, 144nn. 15, 22, 26, 71, 146n. 85, 147nn. 96, 104, 108, 110, 113, 148nn. 117, 120, 122, 125, 130, 132, 144, 150nn. 24, 31, 151nn. 59, 61–2, 152nn. 80–1, 84, 88, 90, 92, 153nn. 108, 112, 154n. 147, 155nn. 163, 166, 158n. 18, 161n. 67, 162n. 95, 170
milieu 19–20, 39, 75
divine 86–7, 106, 109
modernity 54, 56–7
monism 17, 61, 68, 79, 82
dialectical 67
hyperbolic 79
pluralist 63
morality 7, 44, 75
Morgoth 144n. 14
movement 8, 15, 18–19, 21, 25, 29–30, 34, 36, 39, 44, 67, 72–3, 80–1, 93, 100, 105, 108
eternal 72, 85, 93
virtual 69
multiplicity 13, 15–17, 23, 26, 31–3, 36–8, 41–4, 66, 68, 97, 105–6, 109, 119n. 109
arborescent 38
actual 26
implicated 34
material 71
rhizomatic 26, 39
virtual 21–2, 26, 28, 30–1, 33
mysticism 104
cabbalist 56
Hindu 57
Indian 142n. 58
Jewish 147n. 101

nature 15–17, 42, 59, 65–7, 77–8, 80, 83, 88–90, 94–5, 101
negation 13, 16, 26, 107
nondialectical 13
negativity 1, 64
neo-Kantianism 55
neo-orthodoxy 52
Neo-Platonism 142n. 58
Nietzsche, Friedrich 6–8, 12–13, 19, 50, 53, 64, 67–8, 95, 111n. 12
Nietzschean-Spinozist ethic 99
nihilism 61
Christian 99
nomadic space 38–9, 41
nonsense 24, 30, 35
noology 14

occult 5, 56–7, 114n. 14, 142n. 58
One, the 16, 38, 59–61, 65, 69–71, 73, 86
ontology 8–9, 22, 63, 70, 77, 146n. 85
affirmative 12
flat 17
pure 28, 75
onto-theology 61
Open, the 15
opposition 13–14, 38, 51–2, 64, 73–4, 76, 106
order 15–16, 18–22, 26, 30–1, 33–7, 41, 64, 66, 69, 74–6, 78, 80, 87, 93–4, 98, 101, 106–8
alternative 66
good 93
hierarchical 57, 74, 78
O'Regan, Cyril 55, 58, 69, 79–80, 95, 142nn. 60, 66–7, 69–73, 146nn. 81, 86, 147nn. 98–9,

151nn. 64, 68, 75, 77,
    152n. 85, 156nn. 13,
    15–16, 21, 158nn. 13–14,
    160nn. 50–1, 161n. 77, 171
organism   23, 37, 40, 43, 75,
    123n. 198
organization   11, 13, 23, 33, 37,
    39–40, 43, 45, 66–7,
    74–6, 89, 101, 104–5
  plane of   39–40
origin(al)   31, 57–8, 64, 68, 70,
    83–5, 102, 106
  agapeic   85
  dark   68–9, 79, 151n. 67
  Dionysian   79
  erotic   67
original   14–15, 19, 30
orthodox(y)   14, 59, 76, 96, 101,
    152n. 78
otherness   61, 70, 72, 84

paganism   55, 152n. 100
Palmer, Martin   143n. 86, 171
paradox   14, 27, 61, 71, 81
  Christological   96
paradoxical instance   24, 27,
    29–31, 144n. 20
participation   14, 44, 62, 67, 69,
    81, 86, 109
de Pasqually, Martinès   141n. 48
passio essendi   93
perfection   58, 85, 157n. 4
  divine   58, 68, 79–80, 102
perichoresis   70, 72, 87, 91, 93, 96
phenomenology   20
philosophy   1, 5–7, 11–14, 18,
    32, 44, 49–54, 56, 60–1,
    68, 77, 82, 87, 94–6, 102,
    104, 116n. 51, 142n. 58,
    147n. 101, 157n. 4,
    160n. 60
  Buddhist   60
  continental   1

end of   8
Greek   60
history of   6, 111n. 12
modern   1
non-humanist   41
pagan   54
process   66
secular   50
speculative   13
spiritual   53
Taoist   60
Pickstock, Catherine   84,
    86, 104, 145n. 71,
    151n. 62, 153n. 110,
    154n. 150, 156n. 35,
    157n. 38, 161nn. 72, 74,
    162n. 98, 171
Pieper, Josef   97, 107, 153n. 127,
    158n. 22, 162n. 93, 171
Piloiu, Rares   161nn. 67–8, 171
Plato   11–12, 31
Platonism   14
  overturned   14, 31–2
  reversed   14, 59, 69, 79
plenitude   85
pleroma   67, 69, 80–1, 90, 151n. 67
pluralism   16–17
plurality   20, 69–71, 87, 89, 107
politics   12, 18, 40, 54, 101, 105,
    163n. 119
  spiritual   53
porosity   72, 86, 107
possibile/possibility   13, 22, 25,
    38, 45, 59, 61, 63, 65–6,
    76–8, 99–101
postestas   66, 101
potentia(l)   66–8, 99
  virtual   66, 78, 101
power   14–15, 29, 39, 42, 45–6,
    64–9, 75–8, 85–6,
    99–100, 104–6, 110
  autonomous   67
  creative   46, 64, 66, 68, 85

generative 65
immanent 14, 65–6
virtual 66–7, 80
will to 45, 64, 69
Poxon, Judith 98, 144n. 15, 149nn. 6–7, 15, 150n. 43, 158nn. 1–2, 171
presence 6, 55, 81, 83, 106
present 22, 27–9, 35, 37, 78, 162n. 95
problems 14, 22, 26, 29, 31–2, 34–5, 37, 39, 43
see also Ideas
Proclus 142n. 58
Protevi, John 74, 76, 149nn. 2–3, 21, 171
Proust, Marcel 22
psychoanalysis 18, 33

question 31–2, 34, 39

Raschke, Carl 110, 163n. 119, 171
rationalism 14
Ravaisson-Mollien, Félix 162n. 95
real(ity) 11, 15, 20–2, 24, 28, 32, 42–3, 53, 68, 79, 86, 89, 97, 102–3, 105, 107, 109, 121n. 159, 147n. 100
reason 16, 20–1, 26, 30, 35–6, 59, 79, 153n. 115
recollection 28
  pure 22, 28
redemption 82, 96, 104
relation 1, 11, 14–15, 17–18, 21–9, 31–2, 34–6, 38, 40, 44, 49, 51, 53, 56, 59, 61–2, 66, 70–2, 82–4, 87, 91–3, 95, 99–101, 103–4, 107–9, 146nn. 79, 88, 161n. 73
  difference-in- 66, 71, 81

differential 22, 26, 30–2, 34–7
social 71, 91
religion 49–53, 56, 65, 77, 95, 100, 142n. 58
  Spinozist 95
repentance 107–8
repetition 7, 18–19, 27, 31, 44–5, 67, 70, 73, 87, 91, 100, 107, 162n. 95
  non-identical 61, 73
  second 19
  true 72–3
  virtual 30
representation 14, 16–17, 40, 50, 68–9, 79, 103
  quadripartite yoke of 16, 18
resemblance 16, 19, 22, 30
resurrection 55, 106
reterritorilization 39–40, 102
revelation 59–60, 70, 82, 84, 96
  Christian 59, 83
rhizome 2, 35, 38, 41
Ricouer, Paul 49
Robbins, Jeffrey W. 140n. 20, 171

von Sacher-Masoch, Leopold 7, 112n. 20, 165
Saint-Martin, Louis Claude 141n. 48, 142n. 58
salvation 2, 58, 77, 93, 98, 100, 102–3, 107–8
  Gnostic 102
Same, the 16
sameness 19, 76, 81–2
Sartre, Jean-Paul 6
schizoanalysis 33, 42, 45
schizophrenia 42
Schopenhauer, Arthur 67–8
self 16, 18–19, 34, 41–2, 68, 89, 91–3, 98–9, 104, 106–9, 158n. 3
  autonomous 68, 79
  fluid 107

fractured 1
identical 33
modern 91
post-theological 89
self-identical 105
-understanding 1, 12
sense 21–5, 27–32, 35, 38
  common 14, 18
  good 18
  para- 30
sensibility 26–7
  Christian 82
Shaviro, Steven 149n. 1, 150n. 43, 156n. 17, 171
Sherman, Jacob Holsinger 54, 92, 107–8, 140n. 42, 141n. 44, 144nn. 12, 22–3, 147n. 96, 152n. 90, 154n. 150, 155n. 170, 156nn. 24, 33, 158n. 8, 159n. 10, 162nn. 90, 99, 102, 107, 109, 171
signification 40, 43
simulacra 14, 19, 22, 29–30
sin 93, 107–8
singularity 22, 29, 31–7, 42, 107, 109
  pre-individual 34–5, 39, 41
Smith, Anthony Paul 65, 67, 80, 100–1, 104, 139n. 14, 140nn. 16–17, 23, 33, 40–1, 144nn. 36, 38, 145n. 65, 151nn. 54, 70, 156n. 11, 159nn. 19, 28, 160nn. 35–6, 44 5, 161nn. 69, 71, 73, 167, 172
Smith, Daniel 16, 63, 113n. 8, 114n. 9, 117n. 81, 118nn. 98, 103, 141n. 47, 143nn. 4, 7, 9, 144n. 19, 149n. 18, 150nn. 44–5, 157n. 5, 164–5, 172

Socrates 91
Sokolowski, Robert 82–4, 142n. 78, 143nn. 79–80, 152nn. 95, 97, 100, 102, 153nn. 103, 106, 116, 118, 155n. 159, 158n. 21–2, 162n. 92, 172
Son 70, 72, 84, 97
Sorbonne, the 5–6, 8
Spinoza, Baruch 6, 8–9, 13, 17, 43, 45, 50, 66–7, 77, 94–6, 103–4, 111n. 12, 137n. 575, 157n. 4, 158n. 11
  as 'Christ of philosophers' 95–6, 158n. 11
Spinozism 16, 63
spirituality 100–1, 105
strata 23, 39–41, 43, 75, 78, 87, 90, 96, 102, 108, 110n. 503
structuralism 24
subject 16, 23, 29, 33–4, 39, 40–3, 98, 103–4
  schizoid 42
subjectification 40–3
subjectivity 40–3, 97
sublime 65, 68, 103
substance 16, 63, 72–5, 81, 83, 103, 157n. 4
symmetry 102
synthesis 27–8, 32, 34, 36, 40, 44, 65, 69
  passive 27, 35, 40, 42
  second 27–8
system 11–12, 16, 20, 22, 30–1, 33, 36–40, 43–4, 68, 74–5, 94, 147n. 101
  anti 68
  closed 11
  Deleuze's 11
  open 11

teleology 75, 101
Tertullian 50
Teschke, Henning 172
theism 50
theologia viatorum 107
theology
  anemic 54, 91
  anti 50, 78, 98
  confessional (Christian) 1, 50–1, 53–5, 60–2, 70–1, 82, 87, 91, 107–8
  creation 82
  Deleuzian 1, 51, 77–8, 100–1
  immanent 52, 77
  liberation 54, 66, 78, 98, 100–1
  process 66, 78
  radical 52–3, 100
  secular 50–3, 55, 95
  tehomic 65
theosis 2, 108–9
Thomism 55
Teilhard de Chardin, Pierre 54–5, 86, 92, 97, 106–8, 154n. 152, 155nn. 155, 160, 162, 157nn. 40–1, 158n. 25, 162nn. 88–9, 97–8, 101, 103–4, 108, 172
territorialization 39–40
Tillich, Paul 52–3, 140n. 19, 142n. 67
Time magazine 53
time 15–16, 26–8, 36–7, 44, 78, 91, 97, 162n. 95
Tolkien, J. R. R. 144n. 14
totality 11, 22, 28, 30
Tracy, David 60, 143n. 90, 172
transcendence 8, 17–19, 34, 41, 52, 55, 60–3, 73–87, 94–6, 100, 154n. 152
  divine 83
  self 67

transcendentalism 64
Trinity 61, 66, 68, 70–3, 83–5, 87, 91, 106, 108–9, 145n. 50
Typhon 91

unconscious 21–2, 24, 27–9, 31–3, 36, 41, 64–5, 89–90, 103
  cosmic 64
Ungrund 21, 66
unity 11, 13, 16, 19, 42, 60–1, 64, 68–71, 76, 86, 98, 106–7, 155n. 1
  dialectical 7
  divine 70
  self-mediating 107
  static 107
  transcendental 71
University of Lyon 7–8
University of Paris-VIII, Vincennes 9
univocal/univocity 13, 17, 29, 61, 63, 76–7, 80–1, 152n. 78
  of being 17, 63, 76, 78, 80
  transcendental 81

Valentinian narrative grammar 57–9, 69, 80–1, 95
Villani, Arnaud 7, 61
virtual(ity) 13, 20–41, 43, 56, 64, 66–7, 69, 78–80, 96, 100–3, 105, 118n. 104, 119n. 109, 122nn. 171, 179, 145n. 70
virtualization 25
vitalism 56, 65
vitality 50, 64
voluntarism 67

INDEX

Warrain, Francis 5, 56–7, 69, 95, 111n. 3, 114n. 14, 147nn. 100–1
Westphal, Merold 60, 143nn. 85, 89, 172
Whistler, Daniel 139n. 14, 140nn. 16–17, 23, 40, 167, 172
whole 7, 12, 15–17, 19, 22, 28, 61, 71, 84, 109
  fragmentary 32
  God beyond the 84
  monstrous 19
will 14, 44–5, 64, 67–9, 76, 93
  blind 68, 79
Williams, James 21, 25, 41, 115n. 47, 116n. 59, 117n. 78, 118n. 101, 121nn. 153, 156–9, 164, 168, 122n. 169, 124nn. 219, 227, 128nn. 323, 331, 334, 342, 130n. 379, 131nn. 403, 406, 409–10, 419, 421, 132n. 445, 135n. 517, 136n. 541, 137n. 563, 138n. 583, 172
Word, the 70
world 1–2, 6–7, 9–10, 12–22, 26, 33–4, 38, 43, 45, 50, 52, 54–5, 57–60, 64–6, 68–70, 72, 74, 76–9, 82–90, 93, 95–109, 144n. 14, 154n. 152
  acentered 19
  actual 34, 39–40, 67, 102–3
  becoming 87
  created 82, 87
  Deleuze's 53
  Dionysian 12, 15, 46
  extrapleromatic 95
  human 90
  living 15
  material 88
  modern 18
  pre-modern 18
  supra-sensible 7, 76
World War II 7, 55–6
Wronski, Hoëne 5, 56–7, 67, 69, 111n. 3, 114n. 14, 141n. 48, 147n. 101